REAL RABBITS:

CHASING AN

AUTHENTIC LIFE

Dear Don—
Best of l
succeed!

COREY A. CIOCCHETTI

For additional copies of *Real Rabbits* or for more information about AUTHENTIC SUCCESS, please contact:

Corey Ciocchetti, Corey Speaks, LLC
cciocche@du.edu
(303) 522-7110
www.coreyspeaks.com

Cover Design: Andrea Tilliss

TO JILLIAN - MY LIFE

TABLE OF CONTENTS

ON CHASING RABBITS

A woman sat on her porch one summer evening and talked with her prized possession – a world-renowned racing greyhound named Cash. When he raced, Cash ran with all his might and won and won and won. After each victory, his owner happily deposited the large paychecks into her retirement fund. The two often spent hours on the porch recounting these victories and pondering future races.

This evening was different, however. After decades of success and millions of dollars in winnings, the greyhound told his owner that he was hanging it up. Cash had run his final race. Upon hearing the news, the shocked owner asked:

"Just be honest. Are you getting too old to keep up this pace?"

Cash answered, "No, no, I still have a lot of race left in me."

Moving on, the owner pried, "So, are you injured?"

"No." Cash replied, "Actually, I've never felt better!"

"Well," inquired the woman, becoming increasingly frustrated, "do I mistreat you in any way?"

"Come on," came the response, "you know you always treat me kindly."

"Then why? Why won't you race? I must know. You are so good at what you do and you've worked for years to get to this point – the pinnacle of your career. If you retire, we will miss out on even larger paydays, worldwide fame and a chance to go down as the most successful owner-greyhound combo in history!"

To that Cash replied:

"I do not want to race anymore because, after all of that running and running and running, I finally discovered that the rabbits I have been chasing all my life aren't even real."[1]

---

[1] This wonderful tale was adapted from a version of the story related to me by John Bogle (founder of the Vanguard Group) during a presentation to the University of Denver's Daniels College of Business on November 1, 2006. Bogle stated that the story was passed on to him by Reverend Fred Craddock (Professor Emeritus at Emory University's Candler School of Theology).

INTRODUCTION:
LIFE IS TOUGH

> "Life is tough. It takes a lot of your time, all your weekends. . . ."
> --- JACK KORNFIELD
>
> "Don't go around saying the world owes you a living. The world owes you nothing. It was here first."
> --- MARK TWAIN
>
> "Life is tough, but it's tougher when you're stupid."
> --- JOHN WAYNE

Life is tough. Just ask one of the billions of people across the globe living on less than one dollar per day. Then, talk to anyone suffering from terminal cancer, someone paralyzed from the neck down, any resident of Manhattan on September 11, 2001 or of the Gulf Coast during Hurricane Katrina. Although your life may never be this tough, you can count on encountering many uphill battles during your eighty or so years on Earth. Fortunately, each battle you face presents you with an opportunity to make several key decisions which can influence the outcome. Whether these choices revolve around your attitude, a family relationship or friendship, a spiritual or moral dilemma, peer pressure, your career or education, each decision places you front and center at a pivotal crossroads. Here, you can choose wisely and succeed or choose poorly and struggle. This book exists to help you choose wisely.

A wise choice here and there interrupted by a slew of poor choices will provide you with bits of happiness eclipsed by bouts of struggles. A bunch of wise choices strung together is better, but leaves you vulnerable to failures you could have prevented. The ability to consistently make wise choices, however, punches your ticket to an authentically successful life. Authentic success is not the kind of success much of the world appreciates such as wealth, fame and adoration. These things represent the fake rabbits Cash the greyhound used to chase. Authentic success is the kind of success that makes a person genuinely happy. As opposed to worldly success, think of authentic success as encompassing basic contentment, a wonderful family, bona fide friendships, a rewarding career and the ability to grow personally, professionally and spiritually. These things represent the real rabbits worth chasing.

Each person's definition of authentic success may vary but invariably revolves around the idea of basic contentment. Basic contentment is a concept that is tough to define but is obvious when you sense it in others or when you possess it yourself.[2] You are truly content with your life when you can wake up most mornings happy to be alive, progress through most days with a hopeful heart and a desire to improve yourself and the world around you and sleep well at night knowing you have actually helped rather than harmed. Authentically successful people still struggle to get out of bed on some mornings and to motivate themselves for certain tasks like everyone else; the major difference is that authentically successful people spend the vast majority of their time experiencing contentment and happiness rather than anxiety, depression or unhappiness.

---

[2] United States Supreme Court Justice Potter Stewart used a similar concept in trying to define obscenity in the case of Jacobellis v. Ohio, 378 U.S. 184 (1964): "I shall not today attempt further to define the kinds of material I understand to be embraced within that shorthand description [of obscenity]; and perhaps I could never succeed in intelligibly doing so. **But I know it when I see it,** and the motion picture involved in this case is not that." The point is that basic contentment is tough to define in a precise manner. The concept is something that is best understood by observing contentment in another person or by experiencing contentment yourself.

Fortunately, membership in the authentic success club is non-exclusive, non-discriminatory and open to people of all ages and abilities. You must understand, however, that the club requires you to commit to three obligations before your membership becomes valid: (1) the development of a solid foundation from which you can base your efforts, (2) effective preparation to handle life's challenges successfully and (3) the ability to do a few important things very well and very consistently as you experience the world in real time.

If you are interested in achieving this type of success, you are in the right place. *Real Rabbits* is a compilation of the hard lessons I have learned thus far in my life as a kid with a tough past, college student, law student, corporate lawyer, small business owner, business law and ethics professor, author, boyfriend, fiancée, husband, friend and sincerely religious person. Organized into three parts – *On Your Mark, Get Set,* and *Go* – the next fifteen chapters will introduce you to many of the important roadblocks you must hurdle on the road to authentic success.

Part I develops the idea that authentic success requires a solid foundation made up of a strong work ethic, a virtuous character, a clear set of priorities and the proper perspective on life. Like a long-distance runner, you must find your mark on the track of life and ground yourself there before you can begin the journey to the finish line. Having properly grounded yourself, you will begin to see that authentic success does not depend on luck and that you are able to determine your own destiny if you can incorporate certain foundational attributes into your daily routine.

After finding your mark, you must get set for the journey ahead. Part II elaborates on the idea that getting set requires effective preparation and the honing of life skills necessary for authentic success – skills such as professionalism, learning to think and managing your time effectively. You must also develop the ability to consistently persevere over long periods of time and throughout the moments of despair you will certainly encounter – a skill I refer to as consistent persistence. You must strive to recession-proof your life by finding a way to become more flexible, develop a plethora of different skills and make yourself as irreplaceable as possible.

Finally, after grounding yourself and properly preparing for success, you are ready to go – ready to live your life successfully as it happens (or, as the twenty-first century, technologically-sophisticated world might label it, in real time). Part III encourages you to develop meaningful relationships, make excellent decisions, take personal responsibility for your actions and learn from your failures each and every day. The final few chapters will teach you how to rid your life of less meaningful stressors and to hustle, fight, listen and laugh (even at yourself).

By the end of this journey, you will be well on your way to achieving authentic success. Dedicate yourself to this process and you will finally find a place where the vast majority of your days will be full of contentment and genuine happiness. Even in the midst of a life that is tough, you will shine. And, you will shine in a way that makes others wonder, and maybe even ask, what makes you so happy – not that it should matter to you, remember. After telling your story to these inquirers, they may desire to feel the same contentment and strive to incorporate these principles into their lives. Either way, this book is designed to open up your mind to the idea that life is tough, but that authentic success rests only a few uphill battles away. So fight on and, in this endeavor, I wish you good luck. Just kidding, instead, I wish you the . . .

Best of Success,

Professor C.

Corey A. Ciocchetti

Westminster, Colorado
February 27, 2007

PART I:
ON YOUR MARK!

DEVELOPING A SOLID FOUNDATION FOR YOUR CAREER AND LIFE

"Success is not the result of spontaneous combustion; you must set yourself on fire first."
--- **REGGIE LEACH**

"There are no shortcuts to anywhere worth going."
--- **BEVERLY SILLS**

"I have learned this at least by my experiment: that if one advances confidently in the direction of his dreams and endeavors to live the life he has imagined, he will meet with success unexpected in common hours."
--- **HENRY DAVID THOREAU**

"Never leave 'till tomorrow that which you can do today."
--- **BENJAMIN FRANKLIN**

CHAPTER 1:
GO SCREW YOURSELF
. . . DOWN

"Life's tragedy is that we get old too soon and wise too late."
--- **BENJAMIN FRANKLIN**

"There are no shortcuts in life – only those that we imagine."
--- **FRANK LEAHY**

"If you haven't the strength to impose your own terms upon life, you must accept the terms it offers you."
--- **T.S. ELIOT**

"The greatest quest in life is to reach one's potential."
--- **MICHAEL WYNN**

"As you climb the ladder of success, check occasionally to make sure it is leaning against the right wall."
--- **UNKNOWN**

Take my advice and go screw yourself. Do it right now. Okay, hold on, wait a second! I realize that it is possible, and maybe even likely, for you to interpret this statement the wrong way. However, before you counsel me likewise, please understand the context of my advice. The type of screwing I refer to is of the positive variety and can change your life.

I believe that authentic success requires each of your decisions and actions to be based off of a firmly-constructed foundation. This foundation is not something that you are born with or something that you coincidentally pick up as you grow older. Instead, you must create it in your own life from scratch. Then, you must screw yourself down to this foundation before you begin to build an authentically successful life. Think of an analogy to the most basic construction project. When a physical object is screwed into a solid base, both pieces are forced to work in tandem with each other as the base provides the strength and stability. The same is true of your life. You cannot afford to neglect your foundation or develop a base that you only consult periodically. Success is too important and too elusive to grasp without first creating a solid foundation and then allowing it to continually provide you with strength and support. So, with your future and your foundation in mind, I encourage you to go screw yourself . . . down. No offense taken I hope.

Picture your foundation as an internal GPS device, continually guiding you closer and closer to the wisest choice each and every time you face a decision. This navigational system is fueled by personal qualities such as your work ethic, character, priorities and perspective – qualities I refer to as your four foundational attributes. Your GPS is only accurate and effective when these attributes are well-developed. Therefore, you must carefully hone and improve each one of them before even thinking about embarking upon a successful career or living a happy life. The next four chapters discuss each attribute in detail and are designed to help you get started on your journey to authentic success.

Unfortunately, improvement can be a long and tedious process. This is especially true if the subject of the improvement is weak to begin with. To properly build your foundation, however, you must take the time to determine the strength of your four foundational attributes, develop them and then incorporate each one into your life. Spending precious time on something that will not produce immediate results is a bitter pill to swallow. It is especially bitter in the twenty-first century, where we are accustomed to a hustle-bustle, constant-motion world with little time to spare.

Unfortunately, something as fundamental as your foundation is the last place you should cut corners in order to save time.

You have undoubtedly witnessed that physical structures built on solid foundations continually withstand the harshest conditions nature tosses in their direction. Structures with poorly-constructed foundations, on the other hand, often crumble under similar circumstances. Building upon a solid foundation is the cardinal rule in any physical construction project and is also the only way to begin the life reconstruction project you are about to undertake. Therefore, develop a solid foundation and build away. Neglect this foundation and duck for cover.

OLD TOO SOON, WISE TOO LATE

The reason why Benjamin Franklin's perceptive declaration that "we get old too soon and wise too late" rings true in many people's lives is because they neglect this first and crucial step. Operating above a poorly-developed foundation, people make decisions daily without any consistent philosophy guiding their actions. They merely act and react. They wing it. By the time these people recognize the importance of developing a solid foundation, a significant portion of their life has come and gone.

We have all suffered the consequences stemming from this type of poor internal guidance. Lacking a well-developed foundation, we have all winged it at some point or another and made poor decisions we later regret. Instead of listening intently, studying hard and bolstering our ability to think in school, we rely on luck or connections when it comes to landing our first job. After a tough week at work, we complain that we have spent too little time with our loved ones, yet we continue to put in long hours chasing a promotion and a bulging bank account. When something trivial goes wrong in our lives, we get angry, sulk or otherwise overact when we should shrug it off and press onward. At some point, and well down the road of our lives, we begin to understand what we have been doing wrong and attempt to radically change course. Wisdom descends upon us like manna from heaven and we lament the fact that we neglected to take advantage of a solid foundation much earlier.

Fortunately, this predicament is not predestined to occur in your life. In fact, wisdom is not reserved only for people who are advanced in age. And, come to think of it, neither is happiness or contentment. However, you must keep in mind that being young, wise and content is not something that you just stumble upon by accident. Instead, you must dedicate yourself to the development of your foundation, then thoroughly understand how to effectively build upon it and, finally, sharpen the skills necessary to thrive while conducting your life in real-time. This entire process starts with an understanding of your internal GPS and the attributes that fuel it.

YOUR INTERNAL GPS

Global Positioning Systems are designed to locate someone's exact location on a map and provide guidance to a desired destination. As briefly mentioned above, each of us possesses something similar to an internal GPS, even though we may not recognize it or utilize it effectively. Our system is programmed to guide us towards making excellent decisions in our lives by using our: (1) work ethic, (2) character, (3) priorities and (4) perspective as inputs. The major drawback of our GPS is that, in order to navigate effectively, each of these four attributes must be well-developed. They are the fuel running its engine.

Because humans do not inherently posses solid foundations, your GPS operates as a "garbage in, garbage out" type of system. If you have a poor work ethic, a shaky character, a disorganized priority structure and the wrong perspective, your GPS will provide you with really bad information. If both your work ethic and character are average, your priorities are somewhat clear and your perspective is semi-appropriate, then your guidance will be a bit more accurate. It will lead to a better decision, but not the type of excellent decision you need to make consistently in order to summon success. The bottom line is that the better developed your foundational attributes are, the better your internal GPS performs.

Hopefully, my encouragement to screw yourself down has provided you with the itch to enhance each of the four foundational attributes in your life. Tackle them in order and proceed cautiously to ensure that you build a foundation worthy of authentic success. Now that you understand what your internal guidance system is all about, there are two prerequisites to foundation-building that require your immediate attention. Because they are prerequisites, you need to adopt these two key concepts into your mindset before you attempt to incorporate work ethic, character, priorities and perspective into your life. The first prerequisite relates to the idea that the "same-old, same-old" is no longer good enough if you desire to be authentically successful. The second revolves around the idea that there are no shortcuts to anyplace you need to go on this journey. The remainder of this chapter discusses these two prerequisites and concludes with a brief summary of the four chapters that begin your transformation process.

PREREQUISITE ONE: THE SAME-OLD, SAME-OLD

Albert Einstein defined insanity as "doing the same thing over and over and expecting different results." We grasp the idea that this statement hits the nail right on the head and yet we go about our daily lives as if it were untrue or as if we really don't care. It is ridiculously ironic that we desire to be more successful, but continue to fill each of our days with the same-old, same-old. Nothing changes unless and until something drastic happens that motivates us to alter our course. It is as if we place our life on autopilot and then fall asleep at the wheel. Think about how many of your run-of the-mill days have been completely unmemorable. How often do you make the same mistake over and over again without seriously trying to determine why? How many New Year's resolutions have you broken within a week or so? What about within the next day or so? If your responses to such questions cause anxiety, you have become accustomed to the wrong type of mentality dominating your life. Welcome to the Same-Old, Same-Old Club (SO-SO Club); an iconic institution that is jam-packed full of lifetime members.

Each member of the SO-SO Club falls into one of two categories. Group One is made up of the people who have no idea about what is required to improve their lives or do not care about life improvement in the first place. Their days are full of the same-old, same-old and will remain that way forever or until a major life event forces them to change. These people need more than this book to rescue them from their predicament. Group Two, which is much larger in scope, is made up of people who know they need to change some things in their lives to be more successful, but for whatever reason, fail to do so. The majority of the people in the second group find themselves there because they merely roll through each day doing the same things over and over again and expecting different results. They desire to change, but their lack of consistent motivation prevents them from moving forward. They are basically expecting their life to improve via osmosis. Unfortunately, your life never gets much better without you initially taking some action to improve it and then following the process through to its conclusion. Hoping for a transformation via osmosis is a silly and unproductive way to journey through your life.

You cannot move forward until you adopt the mindset that the same-old, same-old is no longer good enough. You have to make a 180 degree turn and adopt a "different-new, different-new" approach in order to break this bad habit. Once you see the positive results stemming from your new approach, you will find the success addicting. Before you know it, you will eliminate practices in your life that consistently bring you down and understand the inability of the same-old, same-old approach to produce authentic success. With this out of the way, you can take your SO-SO Club membership card and shred it.

IN WHICH GROUP DO YOU BELONG?

Are you having trouble classifying yourself into one of the two SO-SO Club groups? I do not anticipate that people in Group One are likely to even get this far in a book like this. I am more concerned with people who are already in Group Two, but cannot admit it or do not realize it yet. The following example is a tool you can use to determine if you are indeed a Group Two member.

Our topic: gossip. How often do you gossip about other people? How many times have you made a commitment to avoid gossiping about someone else and then broken it? Once, twice, twenty times? My guess is that you have made this type of resolution quite often, kept it for a while and then reverted to your old gossipy self. I hate to admit it, but I have been there time and time again in the past; I have resolved to stop gossiping and failed.

If you are hesitant to answer until I properly define the term, here is my definition of the word gossip: to gossip is to say something about somebody behind his or her back — even if you feel like you are trying to be helpful by doing so. We gossip about our family members, our friends and people we do not know (and for some reason excessively about Hollywood celebrities). We are a gossipy society. Gossiping is generally considered immoral and yet it happens all of the time. Talking behind someone's back injures feelings, devastates relationships and is usually done out of spite and/or jealousy. Although a small number of people find nothing morally wrong with the fact that they gossip, the vast majority of people understand the motivations behind gossiping and its consequences and they desire to quit. They resolve to stop talking bad about other people, but invariably fail miserably and revert back to their same-old, same-old gossip routine.

The reason people fail to stop gossiping is that they cannot shake their same-old, same-old mentality. Resolutions to stop gossiping will get you nowhere unless you are mentally ready to change your daily routine. In fact, ceasing to gossip is something that is difficult to execute and takes a good-hearted character, a big-picture perspective and a solid foundation. We have not arrived at these topics yet. Instead of making a resolution to stop gossiping right away, scratch this first prerequisite off of your "to-do" list by making a resolution to adopt a different-new, different-new approach and start from there.

PREREQUISITE TWO: THERE ARE NO SHORTCUTS TO ANYWHERE WORTH GOING

The famous American opera singer Beverly Sills once said "there are no shortcuts to anywhere worth going." This piece of advice encapsulates the second prerequisite you must master before moving on to develop a solid foundation. You surely recognize that the road leading to such a foundation is clearly a place worth going. Getting there, however, presents a major dilemma: although there are no shortcuts to developing a solid foundation, we have been skillfully trained throughout our lives to utilize shortcuts in order to reach our destinations. In fact, we inherently look to take a shortcut even when one is unnecessary. Just look around at the different forms of shortcuts people attempt – athletes take steroids, young people starve themselves to "look thinner and more attractive" and students race to enroll in the "easy" classes. We are conditioned from childhood to look for shortcuts. We see it in our parents, on the news, in school and at work. We have become a shortcut-crazed society.

The reason that we take shortcuts is that we imagine that they will be less painful. Unfortunately, the long-term implications stemming from our shortcuts generally cause us more pain. Have you ever noticed that when you exit the highway to avoid traffic, the side streets are just as packed and that your shortcut generally takes much longer to get you to your destination? In the end, the less painful choice ends up being the highway and not the shortcut. In the same vein, but on more important topics, it is clear that steroids ruin your body, forced starvation often leads to anorexia and other health problems, and taking easy classes leaves you ill-equipped to function in your personal and professional life. The short-term gains these shortcuts provide are dwarfed by their more painful long-term consequences.

The primary problem with a shortcut is that it causes you to bypass some of the steps required to complete an endeavor successfully. Shortcuts are undertaken to save time, money, effort or mental agony. A shortcut may pay off if you skip only the most trivial steps and have the experience necessary to successfully complete the endeavor. However, people who begin to skip the small steps eventually get cocky and soon find themselves skipping as many steps as possible or putting in the minimal effort necessary to get the job done. This sloppy process almost always leads to unacceptable work product, mistakes and inaccuracies. It breeds bad habits and rarely creates the satisfaction of a job well done. At the end of the day, although a shortcut may get you by, you will be unimpressed with the long-term results you obtain by cutting corners.

The reason why this discussion about shortcuts is included at the very beginning of this book is because the advice is especially true when it comes to developing your foundation. If you cut corners at this early and important stage in the process, the rest of your journey will be a waste. Instead, you have to dedicate yourself to toughing through the long and arduous trek towards success. Make sure that you avoid shortcuts and take extreme care when going through the examples and strategies located within the following four chapters.

Dedicate yourself to improving your work ethic and, at the same time, dumping your reliance on luck. Take the time to carefully practice key virtues and abide by the Golden Rule to develop a strong character. Focus your energies on your priorities and goals and then try to stick with them when times get tough. Finally, every time you stress-out about a trivial failure in your life, take a step back and a few deep breaths and keep your big-picture perspective in mind.

PART ONE: ON YOUR MARK

The first section of this book is entitled *On Your Mark* for a reason. You likely recognize this terminology from the sport of track. Before beginning a track event, athletes are assigned to individual lanes and must find their particular mark at the starting line before the event begins. Their mark is their foundation – everything begins at this point. Runners do not just jump on the track and immediately head in the general direction of the finish line. Can you imagine the reaction if this were to happen? The runners would have a hard time determining where to go and everyone in the crowd would assume they were crazy.

Bewilderingly, people wander about their lives in this reckless manner all of the time; they find themselves on the track of life aimlessly meandering onward without first identifying their mark. They are at the mercy of fate – faced with a crossroads moment in their lives and only able to cross their fingers, wing it and hope for the best. Although they may be aware of the general direction of their destination, they are ill-equipped to successfully complete the journey. Their GPS system spits out poor guidance due to the poor inputs they provide.

I am convinced that you must find your mark before you prepare to live an authentically successful life or even attempt to thrive in your daily endeavors. Remember, your mark is your foundation. It is the place where you go when you are ready to run and the place where you retreat to when you are lost or unsure about how to proceed; your foundation is your starting line as well as your safe and steady shelter from the storm of life. From here, you can base each of your decisions on a carefully crafted set of principles and then act accordingly. This strategy will lead to more consistent and positive results over time. You will be young and wise, happy and content – you will be on your mark and ready to get set and go!

Chapter 2:
The Role of Luck

> "Luck is what you have left over after you give 100 percent."
> --- **Langston Coleman**
>
> "The winds and waves are always on the side of the ablest navigators."
> --- **Edward Gibbon**
>
> "I'm a great believer in luck and I find the harder I work, the more I have of it."
> --- **Thomas Jefferson**
>
> "Depend on the rabbit's foot if you will, but remember it didn't work for the rabbit."
> --- **R.E. Shay**
>
> "I never knew an early-rising, hard-working, prudent man, careful of his earnings, and strictly honest who complained of bad luck."
> --- **Henry Ward Beecher**

One "Lucky" Kid

Some may say that Jason McElwain is one lucky kid. I disagree. I think Jason would disagree as well. He recently completed his season as the team manager for the Greece Athena High School men's basketball team near Rochester, New York. Although he wasn't officially on the varsity squad, he handed out water and towels at practice and during games. After every missed basket or bad pass, Jason was there encouraging his teammates. He also loved playing basketball and consistently worked on his jump shot. Because of his amazing work ethic and dedication to the team, Jason's coach allowed him to suit-up for the final regular season game – a home game hosted in Greece Athena's gym. That being said, nobody truly thought Jason would get into the game. However, with four minutes left, and Greece Athena holding a big lead, the coach motioned for McElwain to head to the scorer's table.

Seeing Jason rise off the bench made the crowd go wild. And, by wild, I mean really wild. In the bleachers, people began to stand – some of them jumped up and down – cheering for Jason. During the first few possessions, Jason got the ball and promptly airballed a jump shot and then missed a lay-up. His coach admitted that he started to get anxious and second-guessed his decision to put Jason in the game. But Jason's teammates kept passing him the ball.

Finally, something amazing happened. Jason made a three pointer – shooting the ball a good twenty feet from the hoop. The crowd cheered as loud as they had all evening. Now everyone in the gym was standing. This one shot alone would have been enough to cement this story into Greece Athena basketball lore. Jason, however, wasn't finished. He subsequently made another three pointer, and then another, and another, and another, and another. Jason sank six three-point baskets in all and later claimed that he was "hotter than a pistol." Somewhere in this madness, Jason managed to score a two-point basket as well. The crowd erupted, and I mean really erupted, and rushed the court in Jason's direction looking to carry him out of the gym on their shoulders. After the game, his coach said, "If I wasn't there to witness it, I wouldn't have believed it!" Greece Athena won the game but no one seemed to care much about that fact. There was a different buzz in the air.

Jason McElwain scored 20 points in four minutes. You're probably thinking, "Well that's exciting but not THAT exciting." What if I told you that Jason is autistic? In case you are unsure about what this means, let me briefly explain the disorder. Autism is a developmental disability affecting a person's social interaction and communication abilities. The disorder affects one out of every 166 births and its symptoms often (1) hinder a person's ability to make friends, (2) stimulate a fear of touching and (3) impair the ability to communicate effectively with peers and adults. Studies show that only twenty-five percent of people suffering from autism experience a significant improvement in their condition over time – and this percentage assumes the implementation of proper treatment. Currently, there is no cure for autism. Now you can begin to see why everyone was so emotional that evening.

Jason says, "I'm not really that different. I don't really care about this autistic situation, really. It's just the way I am. The advice I'd give to autistic people is just keep working, just keep dreaming, you'll get your chance and you'll do it." Jason's mother stated that this basketball game was the first time that she recalled Jason being proud of himself. Ever since his hard work and dedication paid off, Jason has met with the President of the United States and Columbia Pictures has signed on to make a movie based on his life. One of his teachers remarked that this "couldn't happen to a nicer kid." And, by the way, millions of people were inspired by Jason's performance when a home video taken of the game was posted on the Internet and viewed across the world.[3] Inspired may be too insignificant a word for what I experienced as I watched the video for the first time. In fact, I've seen this performance at least twenty times and I have shed more than a few tears. Additionally, I show the video in every course I teach for its emotional value and the life lessons it portrays. By the end, there are few dry eyes in the room. This is inspirational stuff.

---

[3] The home video of Jason's game on the Internet is something that you must watch. To locate the story online just open a search engine and enter the name Jason McElwain into the search box. The video quality is below average but, trust me, the underlying message is crystal clear.

As you can probably tell by now, Jason's positive results in the basketball game that changed his life and inspired millions of others had much more to do with his hard work and preparation than it had to do with luck. In fact, I'm not sure luck had anything to do with it at all. Had he not honed his jump shot for countless hours and been such a dedicated member of the team, it wouldn't have mattered how long he would have been on the court during Greece Athena's final home game. He certainly wouldn't have scored twenty points in four minutes. In fact, I would be willing to wager that the average varsity college basketball player – even with a large portion of luck on his or her side – would struggle to make six out of seven three point shots within a four minute period.[4]   Jason's story is inspirational because of his hard work and his dedication to overcome the odds and not because he got lucky.

I BELIEVE IN LUCK

I believe in luck. I believe that luck can change your life for the better and for the worse. I believe that people get lucky and win the lottery, get lucky and edge someone out for a job or a spot in graduate school or get lucky and meet someone special via a chance encounter. I believe that luck can push you over the edge and towards a successful outcome if you are in the right place at the right time. However, I know for a fact that luck alone can neither get you to the right place at the right time nor provide you with the proper tools and character necessary to take advantage of lucky situations when they occur. For example, what good is winning the lottery if you do not have the sense to save or to spend the money you win wisely? The news media is full of stories covering people who win the lottery and find themselves broke within a few years.[5]

---

[4] In any given game, the average male or female varsity college basketball player averages well below 50% on his or her three point attempts. This is nowhere close to Jason's 86% shooting percentage.

[5] Consider the stories of Evelyn Adams and William Post. Adams remarkably won the New Jersey lottery two years in a row! Today,

Each of the people involved in these riches to rags stories got very lucky and won the lottery, but their luck did not pay off in the long run. Even more ironic is the fact that these former lottery winners often lament their tremendous good fortune.

These types of stories cause me to ponder an important piece of wisdom from Louis Pasteur who said that "chance favors the prepared mind." Luck may exist, but people who have a solid work ethic are able to accumulate crucial experience, skills and wisdom which allow them to open up the doors of opportunity much more consistently. These opportunities include, but are not limited to, caring relationships, successful educational endeavors, competitiveness in job situations and better chances to experience authentic success. In the end, a prepared mind and a solid work ethic create something for success to cling to. Positive outcomes in these cases are the result of hard work itself and anything that luck adds is merely a fringe benefit. This is in dramatic opposition to the living of a lackadaisical life filled with minimal effort. This type of effort offers nothing for success to cling to. Success in these cases only occurs if you happen to get lucky. A person exhibiting this type of effort is better off buying a lottery ticket than she is expecting authentic success to come her way without having to work for it.

Speaking of gambling, I believe that the only places where you can rely solely on luck to bring about successful outcomes are coin tosses, lottery tickets and maybe a fantasy football draft. No amount of hard work will allow you to alter the outcome of a coin toss. The same goes for a lottery ticket and pulling fantasy football numbers out of a hat. None of us feels that confident when we encounter any of these situations – we just cross our fingers and hope for the best.

---

however, her winnings of $5.4 million are all but gone - most of it lost gambling. Post won over $16 million in the Pennsylvania lottery in 1998. Today, he lives off of social security and food stamps. His money was lost by bad investment decisions and unfaithful family members. If this is luck, I don't want any of it and I certainly won't rely on it.

The results are entirely out of our control. Thankfully, the vast majority of our endeavors present the opportunity to alter the outcome via our own hard work. Therefore, instead of relying on luck, I encourage you to develop a solid work ethic and increase your chances for success. You can still cross your fingers if it makes you feel better – but you won't need to.

DEVELOP A SOLID WORK ETHIC IN LIEU OF LUCK

Because luck is inherently unreliable, it is a very good idea to stop relying on it as even a small part of your overall success calculation. In lieu of luck, authentic success requires you to develop a solid work ethic comprised of: (1) dedication to a task, (2) the ability to give a good faith effort and (3) the persistence to follow something through to successful completion. If you get lucky, a solid work ethic will allow you to take advantage of your good luck. If you are unlucky, you can use your work ethic to get yourself to the same place. Recall that a solid work ethic is one of the four key principles necessary to properly develop your foundation. Fortunately, the idea of a work ethic is an easy concept to grasp; unfortunately, the effort required to develop one proves much more difficult.

As you begin to develop a solid work ethic and dump your reliance on luck, keep in mind the following three reasons why you are taking such great pains to make the shift. First, you must understand that the harder you work, the luckier you will get. Second, you have to deal with the fact that luck can change your life for better or for worse and that you will have no idea when, where, how, or to what extent this will happen. Third, you need to realize that being the authentically successful person you desire to be cannot be accomplished via luck alone. The next three sections of this chapter will discuss these principles in order beginning with a story of someone who took advantage of good luck and changed the world. This story shows that the harder you work, the luckier you get.

THE HARDER YOU WORK, THE LUCKIER YOU GET

Luck is not irrelevant in your life. As we discussed earlier, there are plenty of situations where luck (in the form of a chance encounter, discovery, or occurrence) can play a role in altering the outcome of a situation. Over time, however, the harder you work at something, the luckier you will get. What this means is that you will be able to take advantage of most of the good luck and dodge many of the consequences stemming from the bad luck that comes your way. This idea was on display when Dr. Alexander Fleming discovered penicillin in 1928.

THE "LUCKY" DISCOVERY OF PENICILLIN

Most stories about the discovery of penicillin omit the early parts of Alexander Fleming's life and pre-laboratory days and only detail the discovery itself. But, in order to look more closely at the relationship between hard work and luck, Fleming's early days prove very informative. As a young man, Alexander had no desire to become a doctor; he was far more concerned with playing water polo and practicing as a rifleman. After serving in the Boer War of 1900 between the United Kingdom and its colonies in southern Africa, Fleming was encouraged by his brother to take the medical school entrance examination. He did, achieved one of the top scores and was accepted into three prestigious medical schools.

Fleming chose St. Mary's Hospital in London primarily because he had played water polo against its team in the past. As it would turn out, this was a lucky choice for the human population. In 1906, Fleming graduated from St. Mary's with merit and chose to stay at the hospital to study bacteriology instead of becoming a surgeon and moving to a different hospital. The main reason why he stayed at St. Mary's was to join its rifle team and this proved to be another chance occurrence.

Fleming grew bacteria in Petri dishes in his lab at St. Mary's – an office that was continuously in a state of disorder and disarray. During one weekend in 1928, the doctor went on a vacation and stacked a pile of bacteria-laden Petri dishes in the sink to be cleaned when his vacation was over. Upon his return, Fleming noticed one of the dishes in the sink looked rather odd – there was mold growing on it. But, more importantly for Fleming's purposes, the bacteria around the mold were beginning to dissolve. This was a highly unusual occurrence. Why were the bacteria dissolving?

A sample from the mold showed that it was a rare penicillin-producing strain. This mold was clearly affecting the bacteria but Fleming was not sure why. However, his extensive medical and scientific training prodded him to investigate further while someone without such training might just have cleaned the dish. How did the mold get on the dish in the first place? Some speculate that it floated in through an open window, others that it came from a different lab. Either way, this was surely a chance happening – a closed window or even a different weather pattern might have stopped the mold from entering Fleming's lab and landing on his dirty dish.

After Fleming's discovery, other scientists were able to piece more of the picture together as to why the penicillin from this mold in particular was so important. They discovered that this rare strain could fight disease-causing bacteria inside of the human body. This discovery increased human survival rates and gave hope to dying patients. Before its discovery, patients suffering from bacterial infections were subject to a "wait and hope" treatment plan and the chances of recovery were usually bleak. Fleming's discovery saved countless millions of lives and changed the history of modern medicine forever.

HARD WORK LEADS TO LUCK

Although Alexander Fleming's discovery of penicillin can be partially attributed to luck, it is doubtful that any live-saving medicine would have been discovered without the doctor's strong work ethic throughout his entire medical career. There are at least four instances where Fleming's hard work led to the discovery of penicillin:

1. Fleming obtained a top score on the medical school entrance examination which gained him admission to a prestigious medical school;

2. Fleming worked exceptionally hard in medical school and graduated with merit which earned him a job at St. Mary's Hospital;

3. Fleming's extensive training in medicine and, more particularly, in the field of bacteriology allowed him to observe that the interaction between the mold and the bacteria was out of the ordinary. A less intelligent, less dedicated person would have just cleaned the dish; and

4. Fleming's ability to understand that the dissolving mold was medically significant allowed him to aid greatly in the discovery of penicillin.

As you can see, Alexander Fleming was a hard worker and a dedicated scientist. Without all of his hard work, he would not have been in the right place at the right time and he would have been unable to take advantage of the lucky mold that floated his way. Because he worked so hard, Fleming was able to use the following lucky circumstances to his advantage:

1. The fact that Fleming chose water polo as his sport of choice and that this sport constituted the primary reason he picked St. Mary's for medical school;

2. The fact that Fleming decided to stay at St. Mary's as a doctor primarily because of its rifle team;

3. The chance occurrence that the right kind of mold found its way onto the proper location on the right kind of dish in Fleming's laboratory; and

4. The fact that this particular dish happened to be in the sink in a position where it would be noticed by the scientist before being cleaned.

The following chart summarizes this discussion and the places where hard work and where luck played an especially important role in the discovery of penicillin. The bottom two lucky occurrences were directly correlated to Fleming's hard work.[6]

ATTRIBUTABLE TO HARD WORK	ATTRIBUTABLE TO LUCK
Dedication to athletic activities	The fact that water polo sparked Fleming's interest and that St. Mary's had a team
High medical examination score	Deciding to work at St. Mary's Hospital
Earning a medical degree with merit	Occurrence of rare mold on Petri Dish
Training in Bacteriology	Chance discovery of rare mold

[6] It should be noted at this point that the story of Alexander Fleming's discovery has recently come full circle in a rather amusing way. The actual dish with the miracle mold recently sold at an auction at Christie's auction house to an American bidder for 8,050 pounds. The dish contained an inscription - written one year before Fleming's death - on its bottom reading, "the mold that makes penicillin, Alexander Fleming, 1954."

From a luck standpoint, imagine if Fleming had cleaned the dish before he left on vacation or even shut his laboratory window for the evening. At some point in the future, someone surely would have discovered the miracle of penicillin. In the meantime, a great many people would have lost their lives. But Fleming did not clean the dish and he did not shut his window and the bottom line is that Alexander Fleming's dedication to his training and to his field allowed him to notice and analyze the lucky set of circumstances that led to the discovery of penicillin.

LUCK CAN MAKE YOUR LIFE BETTER AND WORSE

Another interesting characteristic of luck is that it can change your life for the better (good luck) or for the worse (bad luck) at any time. Luck does not phone ahead to let you know it is coming. It can strike without your consent and regardless of your plans and desires. Luck can impact your life in a small way or a gigantic way no matter how prepared you are to encounter it. Additionally, the positive and the negative consequences stemming from luck are completely unpredictable and you cannot avoid them. In other words, good luck can help you (and help you a great deal) while bad luck can harm you (and harm you a great deal). Since you cannot control the influence of luck in your life, you need to live as if luck is not a factor at all. Any time you spend worrying about bad luck or hoping for good luck is merely wasted time. A better strategy is to forget about luck completely and develop a solid work ethic instead. This work ethic will allow you to both take advantage of your good luck and minimize the negative effects of your bad luck.

GOOD LUCK

Good luck is wasted on people who rely on it as the only way they can improve their lives. On the other hand, good luck can really help you after you have developed a solid work ethic and thoroughly prepared a game plan for your life. Recall the lottery "winners" mentioned earlier. It appears that they were unprepared to handle the good luck they encountered. The good luck helped them by providing them with money – a lot of money. But, the money ended up disappearing and their lives became worse instead of better. These people needed a more solid foundation underneath them before they won the lottery – they needed something that could have provided better guidance for their decisions and allowed them to better handle their good luck.

BAD LUCK

Bad luck will hurt you much more if your work ethic is poor. An undeveloped work ethic will leave you ill-equipped to deal with the negative consequences accompanying bad luck. When bad luck strikes, it is human nature to pout, doubt your ability to fully recover and lose the motivation to strive for success. The problem is that this normal reaction is prolonged in someone not expecting or unable to deal with bad luck. Fortunately, the negative effects of bad luck can be minimized if your work ethic is strong enough. If you are prepared to shake off the bad luck and strive to get back on your feet, you can generally get to the place you were heading before the bad luck struck. The following example shows how I overcame a string of bad luck in my life.

I began my legal career working at a prominent law firm serving clients involved in the emerging technology industry. The firm was consistently on the cutting edge of business strategy and began taking stock in lieu of cash as payment for legal services. I liked this rather risky approach. Additionally, the people were friendly and encouraging, the work was interesting and I was planning for the future. This would be the place where I would retire. Unfortunately, a string of really bad luck struck the country and the aftershocks brought some negative consequences into my world. The terrorist attack of September 11, 2001 was shocking. The country's economy, which was already struggling, tanked. As the United

States entered a recession and businesses struggled, the stock my law firm held became far less valuable. This drop in market capitalization caused the firm to dig into its reserve bank accounts to pay expenses and salaries. Soon after the recession started, the partners voted to dissolve the partnership. Just like that, one of the most prominent law firms in the country imploded and over 1,000 lawyers lost their jobs in an instant. These jobs were not lost because of bad lawyering or hostile competition. Although the stock in lieu of cash strategy proved to be a bad idea in hindsight, it was becoming popular and made sense at the time. In my opinion, the downfall of the firm was caused primarily by some really bad luck.

At this point in time, bad luck was trying its best to make my life much worse. Fortunately, my work ethic was strong and I was diligent in my approach to finding another job. Because of these two things, this string of extremely bad luck impacted me only at the margins. I was without a job along with hundreds of other people, but because I worked extremely hard in school, learned how to think and solve problems, cultivated key relationships and was passionate about my career, I had an advantage and was able to get back on my feet relatively quickly. When a new position opened up, I was ready to apply and I received an offer. Without this type of preparation, professionalism and experience, however, this string of bad luck would have had a much longer and much more negative impact on my life.

LUCK AND THE REALLY IMPORTANT THINGS IN LIFE

The third reason why you should never rely solely on luck is the most obvious of them all. Adopting such a practice will stop you from achieving any of the really important things in your life. For instance, you cannot become a doting father, a caring mother, a supportive spouse or a sincere friend by getting lucky. You will not come out of college with the knowledge you need to succeed in the real world by lucking out. You will never find yourself in good physical shape based solely on the fact that you were lucky enough to inherit good genes. These are likely some of your highest priorities and satisfying them will require great effort rather than luck. In other words, to be really good at the really important things in your life, you must strive every day to care for your family, your significant other and your friends. You must learn how to think while you are in school and then utilize this knowledge to solve problems and complete projects effectively and efficiently throughout your career. You must exercise consistently in order to find yourself healthy and in good physical shape (this takes more and more effort as you get older, trust me). I did not pick these examples by mistake. Rather, I deliberately chose them to illustrate that you cannot leave the most important things in your life to chance. What you need to do is develop a solid work ethic and leave luck on the sidelines. The results stemming from this change in mindset help create a contentment that makes the entire effort worthwhile.

CHAPTER 3:
YOUR CHARACTER COUNTS

"Your net worth to the world is usually determined by what remains after your bad habits are subtracted from your good ones."
--- **BENJAMIN FRANKLIN**

"Character is doing the right thing when nobody is looking."
--- **J.C. WATTS**

"Sometimes the hardest decision to make is the right thing to do."
--- **NATASHAH YANNY**

"The time is always ripe to do what is right."
--- **MARTIN LUTHER KING, JR.**

A MONUMENTAL COLLAPSE OF CHARACTER

The scent of money permeated the rarefied air of Enron's Houston headquarters in December of 2000. It was one of the first winters of the twenty-first century but the company, which began as a small natural gas distribution and pipeline company, was on fire. By the turn of the century, Enron was one of the largest and most respected organizations in the United States and had been recently honored as America's Most Innovative Company for the fifth year in a row and as one of the 100 Best Companies to Work for in America. Revenues were up, the company was profitable and Enron had agreed to pay $100 million to name a professional baseball stadium in the Houston area as Enron Field.

Enron made the vast majority of its money acting as the middleman by trading natural gas and electricity (i.e.., energy) and energy-related derivatives. The company would make a profit if it could sell its energy to a utility at a higher price than it purchased it for from a producer. The company claimed in its public filings that it was very good at executing this business strategy – so good, in fact, that at its height during the dawn of the twenty-first century, the company employed over 21,000 people and generated over $110 billion in revenues.

Enron's innovative business model and rapid growth eventually became its downfall. As the company's stock price rose, Wall Street demanded continued upticks in earnings and profitability. To meet these ever-increasing demands, Enron was forced to come up with new business strategies because energy trading in and of itself was not profitable enough. A decision was made to enter into new business lines and purchase non-energy-related assets that could be traded in the same way as the company traded energy. Enron was no longer all about energy trading – now the company traded everything from paper to bandwidth to future weather patterns. The company would enter into forward-looking contracts with other parties looking to hedge their risks of huge price increases in the future. Even if Enron made money in the deal, the purchaser would be assured of a fixed price for the commodity it needed.

This new business strategy cost money and Enron took on a great deal of debt to finance the transactions. Enron did not want its balance sheet to show that it was continually increasing its debt for fear of a lower credit rating, higher borrowing rates in future transactions as well as potential downgrades in its stock valuation. With this in mind, the company began to hide its liabilities from its purchases in secret, non-Enron-related partnerships. The partnerships would take on the liabilities while Enron's financial statements made the company appear more profitable than it really was. Investors saw the ever-increasing profits and growth and continued to drive the stock price higher and higher – upwards of $90 a share at one point.

Recent investigations proved that Enron began secretly transferring debt off of its books and simultaneously overstating profits beginning in 1997. Public attention was drawn to these problems in 2001 when the company filed a report claiming that it lost $618 million dollars in the third quarter of that year. From that point forward, Enron found itself immersed in a major investigation by the United States Securities and Exchange Commission looking into questionable partnership transactions where Enron executives allegedly enriched themselves while at the same time allowing the company to hide its debt on the books of the secret partnerships. The negative press surrounding these events caused the company to experience a $1.2 billion reduction in shareholder equity in a very short period of time. On November 28, 2001, Enron's stock was worth less than $1 a share, down from its all-time high of $90.56 in August 2000. On December 2, 2001, Enron filed what would turn out to be the second largest corporate bankruptcy in history – writing off over $63 billion in liabilities. Congressional and criminal investigations, mass layoffs, document destruction and one suicide soon followed.[7] In the end, evidence arose demonstrating that the people involved in bringing Enron down suffered from their own form of bankruptcy – moral bankruptcy.

The awful circumstances that took down one of America's biggest companies were the direct result of a monumental collapse of character. In fact, it seems that character was completely missing from the "win at all costs and consider the implications later"

---

[7] For example, Andrew Fastow, Enron's former Chief Financial Officer, was indicted on 98 counts of fraud and conspiracy including securities fraud, wire fraud, mail fraud and money laundering. Fastow eventually pleaded guilty to two counts of conspiracy to avoid a trial on the 98 counts and was sentenced to ten years in prison. Even more horrible was the suicide of Cliff Baxter - a former Enron vice president - who was found dead from a self-inflicted gunshot wound in January 2002.

corporate culture in place inside of Enron. Aside from a few courageous whistleblowers, many of Enron's key executives spent their time mired in greed, manipulation, self-dealing and a major conspiracy to cover up their tracks. Ironically, at the same time these conspiracies and cover ups were afoot, the same executives were breaking their fiduciary duties to their shareholders – the people who ended up with virtually nothing upon the company's bankruptcy.

A fiduciary duty is an unwritten obligation to act in someone else's best interests; fiduciary duties are required of professionals and other key employees in positions of trust. Enron's key executives and directors owed a fiduciary duty to their shareholders and were legally required to act in their best interest. Instead, the company's CEO, Ken Lay, talked up the company's future while selling his shares at the same time. Lay was quoted as telling employees that Enron was "fundamentally sound" and that "the third quarter is looking great." He went on to add that the company was "well positioned for a very strong fourth quarter." This conversation took place on September 26, one month before Enron restated its earnings and less than two months before its bankruptcy. Enron's Board of Directors waived its Code of Ethics to allow the shady partnership deals that were responsible for hiding hundreds of millions of dollars in Enron debt from the market. The same Board was notoriously lax in its oversight duties and let Enron management run amok on its watch. Employees enrolled in Enron's retirement program collected Enron stock but were not allowed to sell their shares. This policy, which caused many employees to lose the vast majority of their retirement funds upon the bankruptcy, did not apply to the company's top executives who sold millions of shares as Enron's problems intensified under the cover of darkness.

And it wasn't just the Enron executives who exhibited shoddy character. The company's chief accountants, outside lawyers, as well as prominent Wall Street analysts all played a role in the pre- and post-investigation cover-up. Arthur Andersen, one of the top accounting firms in the world at the time, failed to dig deep enough into the financial statements that they had a duty to scrutinize. Instead, Andersen poured its efforts into its consulting role with Enron and helped the company create the partnerships that it then audited. These dual roles earned Andersen major consulting and auditing fees as well as a major conflict of interest. The auditors were also accused of shredding Enron-related documents (i.e., evidence in the criminal investigation). After having once billed Enron accounting fees of over $52 million in one year, Andersen is now a shell of the $9.2 billion behemoth it once was. The former Big-Five firm now employs around 200 employees, down from 28,000 at the height of its success, and this skeleton crew is basically employed to handle the remaining work stemming from the Enron lawsuits.[8] In addition to the company's accountants, Enron's outside lawyers failed to ask the right questions during an early investigation of improprieties and gave the legal stamp of approval to the fraudulent partnerships. All of this occurred while the lawyers were billing Enron between $27 million and $30 million in legal fees a year. Finally, many financial analysts strengthened the credibility of Enron's misleading earnings outlooks by issuing "buy" ratings on the company's stock without digging deeply enough into what was really occurring. These ratings caused more investors to trust in Enron's misleading statements and purchase Enron stock. Recently, a jury convicted several former Merrill Lynch and Co. executives of conspiracy and fraud stemming from their roles in the debacle.

All in all, Enron represented a collapse of character on a colossal scale. The bad actors involved were dishonest, disrespectful, disloyal, uncompassionate and entirely self-interested. There was no

---

[8] A glance at the company's current bare-bones, one-page website paints an interesting and rather sad picture. Arthur Andersen Homepage, *available at* http://www.arthurandersen.com (last visited January 12, 2007).

evidence that these people consulted their character in any substantial manner during the five-year period when Enron was engaging in these illegal and immoral activities. This type of character collapse does not just happen overnight. It is not as if the top Enron executives woke up one morning in the year 2000, lost their minds for one day and said to themselves, "I think I am going to commit a billion dollar accounting fraud today, lie to my shareholders and make myself filthy rich in the process." Rather, it is my opinion that their characters were deficient long beforehand.

Think about how a lifetime of seemingly minor bad decisions and unethical actions can lead a person towards a total character collapse. For instance, assume that a young person begins to tell small lies which go unpunished; this young person grows up to be a young businessman who ignores the tug of his conscience, begins to sense the luxuries that come with wealth and misleads clients to get his deals done; this young businessman is eventually promoted to a young executive and caves into his urge to self-deal and his desire to get rich. Finally, a head-hunter phones to ask if the executive is interested in joining an up-and-coming company called Enron. The character flaws that allowed this executive to take these unethical actions in the first place are bad in and of themselves. However, these flaws can be devastating when strung together and combined with a diseased corporate culture. This type of environment can cripple someone's already weakened character to the point where hiding debt and falsifying financial statements even enters the realm of possibility. I can guarantee you that if each of Enron's top executives had developed a more solid foundation bolstered by a stronger character, the entire Enron tragedy could have been averted. Someone's conscience would have been consulted at some point and changes in business practices would have been made or the whistle would haven been blown earlier. This chapter will help to explain why.

THE CONTENT OF YOUR CHARACTER

Your character counts. It helps guide your decisions every hour, every day. Your character allows you to differentiate right from wrong and then prods you to act morally. It also dictates your reactions to life's happy moments and your responses to anger, hurt and disappointment. Other people determine what you are made of by looking at your character. Ultimately, your character serves as your moral compass and is the most important of the four attributes that comprise your foundation. Therefore, you must make certain that it is structurally sound. People with solid characters are able to accomplish two things very well: (1) they successfully incorporate character-enhancing virtues into each of their endeavors, decisions and reactions and (2) they consistently abide by some form of the Ethic of Reciprocity (i.e., the Golden Rule).

Remember when your parents or other authority figures in your life urged you to "do the right thing." If you were anything like me, this advice tended to get annoying and repetitive. You wanted to do what you wanted to do and the "right thing" never seemed to be as rewarding. In fact, doing the right thing often caused you to have less fun, admit you were wrong, and sometimes, swallow your pride. Deep down inside, however, you inherently knew that this advice was good and that doing the right thing was the best decision you could make in any given situation.

Aside from others urging you to do the right thing, you have an internal voice specifically designed to let you know when you stumble upon shaky moral ground. This voice represents your conscience. Just as you disobey other people's advice on how to act morally, you do not always follow the advice your conscience provides. Although you may struggle to obey it, you cannot stop your conscience from making its viewpoint known. When your character is strong, your conscience speaks with a resonating voice and drastically influences your decisions. On the contrary, when your character is weak, the voice of your conscience is muzzled and more easily ignored. This chapter will help you resuscitate your conscience by building up your character.

Character building is a detailed, time consuming process that must constantly garner your attention. You should always strive to do the right thing regardless of whether you are amongst family, friends, colleagues, superiors, strangers or even all alone. The comment by Martin Luther King, Jr. that "the time is always ripe to do what is right" captures the essence of this concept. Ironically, however, we only act morally some of the time and in certain situations.

For instance, it is relatively easy for us to do the right thing all of the time in front of our parents, our professors and our bosses. There is simply too much at stake in these situations to let our bad character traits shine through. Therefore, we often act morally merely for the sake of appearances. On the other hand, it is much easier to act immorally with our friends or when we are all alone and free from scrutiny. With our friends, we are subject to peer pressure and the desire to be respected and fit in. This causes us to disobey our conscience when we should heed its advice instead. When we are by ourselves, nobody is around to judge or punish us for our actions and we do not have anyone to hold us accountable, to impress or to depend upon. These situations provide a reduced chance of injuring ourselves and our reputations and it is much easier to allow our character to collapse. Unfortunately, the actions we take both with our friends and by ourselves paint the most accurate picture of our true character. A solid character is forged when you consistently make excellent decisions in both of these instances.

Character building requires you to practice doing the right thing when you are all alone. Although you are the only person available to correct your mistakes when you are by yourself, this setting provides you with a chance to practice your morality without others holding you responsible, judging your mistakes or pressuring you into making more of them. For example, the next time you mistreat or lose someone else's property without their knowledge, go ahead and own up to your mistake. Although it is easy to pretend you are not responsible because there were no witnesses, deceiving someone else will hinder your character growth.

After you are comfortable building your character when you are by yourself, make the harder change and attempt to do the right thing all of the time when you are with your friends. The peer pressure and desire to fit in will make this process harder than it was when you were alone. For example, the next time your friends decide to drink and subsequently make bad decisions, you need to make sure you counsel them against these decisions and then walk away. This type of action will cost you some social capital and maybe a few relationships, but you will be doing the right thing in a tough situation. Your character will grow.

Unfortunately, character-building is tough because most of us cannot consistently do the right thing for more than a few brief moments at a time, let alone all of the time. We resolve to act morally more often and then life gets in the way and we crash. For instance, we treat people with respect and stop overreacting for a few days and then someone says something rude to us and our character collapses. We then respond inappropriately and likely immorally and we have to start all over. We drive to work patiently and peacefully until we get cut off in traffic and nearly rear-end the offending vehicle. In these situations, we invariably make a bad decision to swear at the other person, honk our horn and heaven knows what else. We know that we should treat others the way that we want to be treated, yet we walk into our workplace day after day and treat our colleagues as if their relationships with us are all but meaningless.

We realize that each and every one of these actions is wrong, yet we seem to forget about doing the right thing in the heat of the moment.

We need a stronger character in order to withstand the events that cause us to act immorally.

It is important to consult your conscience in order to avoid character collapses when responding to trivial problems such as a rude comment directed your way or a driver who cuts you off in traffic. Unfortunately, merely consulting your conscience by itself is not enough to lead you to moral decisions in life's more difficult ethical dilemmas. To solve these dilemmas, you must be able to hear your conscience, interpret the reasons for its advice and then utilize this advice to make moral decisions. These more specific abilities require you to: (1) habitualize life's most precious virtues and (2) abide by the Golden Rule. These two practices, working in tandem, will strengthen your character to the point where you can handle even the toughest moral dilemmas. The remainder of this chapter is dedicated to demonstrating how you can begin to strengthen your character. At the end of the day, you will be able to finally thank your parents and your conscience for advising you to do the right thing all of the time.

HONE VIRTUES TO DEVELOP YOUR CHARACTER

A virtue is a moral quality that human beings generally consider to be good. Many high-profile virtues, such as compassion, courage, honesty, integrity, loyalty and patience, are easily identified as such. When you read these words, you tend to think of good overcoming evil and of qualities you wish you possessed in greater quantities. In addition to these popular virtues, there are also many lesser known virtues such as forgiveness, industry, modesty, pride and temperance.

Unfortunately, virtues are not something that people are born with or innately develop without practice. When you are born, you are not honest or dishonest, compassionate or uncompassionate, patient or impatient. You may be a bit self-interested but otherwise you are morally neutral. Your moral character develops over time and depends upon two things: (1) your ability to practice the various virtues until they become a habit in your life and (2) your ability to surround yourself with as many positive influences and relationships as possible. These two character-building principles are derived from Aristotle and his ethical framework of Virtue Ethics.

ARISTOTLE AND VIRTUE ETHICS

Aristotle is still one of the world's foremost philosophers and yet he lived over two thousand years ago. Aristotle spent his time pondering the innermost workings of biology, logic, poetry, physics and political philosophy. He was also very interested in ethics, virtues and the living of a virtuous or happy life. Aristotle believed that people would never be truly happy if they only thought about being ethical or thought about being happy; rather, he understood that they must practice the virtues that lead to happiness in order to actually be happy. Additionally, Aristotle understood that human beings are the only creatures that possess the ability to reason and believed that this rationality must be utilized effectively in order for humanity to prosper. At the end of the day, Aristotle's theory holds that a rational person should desire to adhere to certain virtues and this adherence will lead to a happy life.

Aristotle formulated his approach into an ethical framework commonly referred to as Virtue Ethics. Today, Virtue Ethics is experiencing a resurgence throughout various academic and business communities. An Aristotelian analysis differs from other prominent ethical frameworks that require people to look to various duties or to the consequences of their actions in determining whether an action is moral. Under Virtue Ethics, virtues are the primary factor you must consider to determine if an action is moral or immoral. The framework is built around two key principles: (1) you must habitualize virtues in order to effectively incorporate them into your life and (2) you need to strive for the Golden Mean of each virtue instead of acting near its extremes.

HABITUALIZING VIRTUES

Habitualizing anything is a difficult task – just ask anyone who has ever made a New Year's resolution. A habit is an activity that you undertake almost instinctively and find a way to accomplish even during the times when you would rather avoid it. Exercise, etiquette and promptness are typical examples of good habits while overeating, oversleeping and swearing are typical examples of bad habits. Acquiring a good habit in your life takes dedication, time and practice while acquiring a bad habit quickly happens all on its own.

Virtue Ethics claims that virtues themselves require habitualization in order to be effectively incorporated into a person's life. Unfortunately, habitualizing virtues is much harder than forming other more trivial habits such as eating less or waking up earlier. According to Virtue Ethics, you cannot be a truly honest person without continually striving to be honest and by associating yourself as much as possible with honest people.

This idea tends to make intuitive sense when you look at the idea through the lens of an example. Most of us find it relatively easy to tell a small lie. In fact, I would bet that even the most honest person you know tells a white lie every once in a while. The problem occurs when we get away with the white lie. Bolstered by the success of our previous lies, we tend to lie again and often tell a bigger lie in place of the smaller lie we told before. Then, we witness our family, friends, colleagues and bosses lying and these lies make us feel that lying is somewhat socially acceptable. Before we know it, lying becomes second nature and a big, bad habit in our lives. We become liars and potentially chronic liars over time. We contract *Enronitis* and run the risk of a major character collapse.

The only way to reverse course and become more honest is to practice being more honest and start hanging around people who are honest. This process is a lot like learning how to ride a bicycle – tiring, frustrating and repetitive, but worth it when you get it down pat.

THE GOLDEN MEAN

The second major principle of Virtue Ethics is that each virtue lies directly between its two extremes in a place referred to as the Golden Mean.[9]   One extreme defines someone who exhibits too much of the particular virtue and the other extreme defines someone who exhibits too little of the particular virtue. For instance, a person who is too honest is considered blunt while a person who is not honest at all is considered a liar. The Golden Mean – the exact center between these two extremes – is the embodiment of the virtue itself and the place where you want to be in order to properly develop your character. Get close to the Golden Mean and you will understand what it takes to act morally in relation to that particular virtue; get close to the Golden Mean of all the virtues and you will understand what it takes to act morally in any ethical dilemma you face. This is the place where you can live a life filled with authentic success.

For example, take the virtue of honesty and a hypothetical person who is too honest all of the time. People would refer to someone like this as being blunt. Someone who is blunt is at one extreme of the virtue spectrum of honesty and needs to become less blunt to reach the Golden Mean. Such a person must still be honest, however, as moving away from the extreme of bluntness does not require more lying to even things out. In fact, it is unhelpful to think

---

[9] The Golden Mean is more accurately placed between the extreme and the deficiency of any given virtue but for ease of reading I will refer to both of these points as "extremes."

of reaching the Golden Mean as a mathematical type of formula. Rather, in order to be more honest, you still need to be honest, just less blunt. For example, if your significant other asks you if he or she looks fat in an outfit, someone who is blunt may say "yes, indeed you do." Someone who is honest knows that bluntness hurts feelings and will say something different like "you look beautiful." This is not a lie and you avoid the hurt feelings that come with the blunt answer. You are moving closer to the Golden Mean. The following virtue spectrum helps explain this concept for the virtue of honesty.

EXTREME – not honest	HONESTY (GOLDEN MEAN)	EXTREME – too honest
LIAR		BLUNT

As you can see, reaching the Golden Mean for any particular virtue is a daunting task. This task is made even more difficult because Aristotle would have you head toward the Golden Mean of every virtue you can think of in order to understand how to act morally in any situation. The following spectra contain a few additional virtues and their extremes. Keep in mind that this is not an exclusive list and that my classifications of the extremes are not set in stone. For instance, I use the word "doormat" to describe someone who is excessively loyal or excessively generous. If you are not fond of my description, feel free to choose a synonym to describe the same attribute.

What I would like you to do right now is to chart out your life and place a mark on each virtue spectrum below where you feel that you currently fall. Do not forget to mark your position on the honesty chart above as well. Be honest and thoughtful when conducting this exercise. Also, be careful because your exact placement on each spectrum is important as it tells you how close you are to the Golden

Mean or how far you need to go to get there, depending upon how you look at it.

EXTREME – not courageous

COURAGE

EXTREME – too courageous

COWARD		**FOOLHARDY**

EXTREME – not loyal

LOYALTY

EXTREME – too loyal

TRAITOR		**DOORMAT**

EXTREME – not generous

GENEROSITY

EXTREME – too generous

STINGY		**DOORMAT**

EXTREME – not humble

HUMILITY

EXTREME – too humble

ARROGANT		**MEEK**

EXTREME – not industrious

INDUSTRY

EXTREME – too industrious

LAZY		**OVER-AMBITIOUS**

It is my feeling that this final spectrum below – detailing the virtue of integrity – is especially important. In fact, the Golden Mean of integrity is best encompassed by the Golden Mean of every possible virtue combined. Please take the average placement of all of your left-side marks above and place a mark on that spot on the left side of the integrity spectrum. Then, take the average placement of all your right-side marks above and place a mark on that spot on the right side of the integrity spectrum. These two marks provide a snapshot of how solid your overall character is at this point in time.

EXTREME   EXTREME

INTEGRITY

AVERAGE	**AVERAGE**
PLACEMENT OF	**PLACEMENT OF**
EXTREMES LISTED	**ETREMES LISTED**
ABOVE	**ABOVE**

YOUR CHARACTER AND THE GOLDEN RULE[10]

> "We have committed the Golden Rule to memory; let us now commit it to life."
> --- **EDWIN MARKHAM**

I hope I have convinced you that habitualizing virtues and associating with good people and institutions allows you to make more ethical decisions easily and more often. Golden Means are important to your moral guidance as they instruct you on how to act when you are faced with an ethical dilemma – just head in their

---

[10] Much of this section is taken from an article I wrote for the ENCYCLOPEDIA OF BUSINESS ETHICS AND SOCIETY (Sage Publishing, 2007) about the Golden Rule.

general direction. Your habitualized virtues encourage you to tell the truth, be loyal and stop getting walked all over. They urge you to be courageous, modest and industrious. Most importantly, your virtues make it clear that a moral life is a life filled with integrity. You are well on your way to developing your character. You should supplement your search for Golden Means with an effort to abide by the Golden Rule and by using the Rule as a second opinion, especially if you find that two or more virtues conflict in a given situation.

As an example, assume that you are trying to reach the Golden Mean of loyalty; you are not a very loyal person and fall somewhere on the untrustworthy end of the spectrum. Assume also that you are working on being a more honest person. You are a bit of a liar and are striving towards the Golden Mean of honesty. How are you supposed to act if your best friend asks you to take her side in a major fight with her roommate where you feel that your friend has acted unethically?

Assume that your best friend's roommate accused your best friend of stealing $300 from her purse. You were not around when the theft allegedly happened and your friend swears that she did not do anything wrong. You know that your friend is always hard up for cash and has stolen small amounts of money from your purse in the past. Coincidentally, you witnessed your friend buying an expensive new outfit last evening at the mall while two days earlier she was complaining about needing a second job to pay her bills. Your gut feeling is that your friend took the money but you cannot be sure.

Your friend has been consistently telling you that she treasures your friendship and appreciates your loyalty; she also claims that she wants to be as loyal to you as you are to her. On the other hand, the roommate states that she was saving the $300 to pay the final bit of her tuition to allow her to stay in school and asks you if you suspect that your friend took the money. If you provide your honest opinion that the evidence points in your friend's direction, you may be disloyal to your friend. Disloyalty is something you have been trying to avoid. If you remain loyal to your friend, your response to the roommate will not be an entirely honest one. This dilemma presents a major conflict of two virtues and relying on Virtue Ethics alone apparently leaves you stuck. What should someone who is striving to develop a solid character do in this situation in order to act morally?

Here, you must use the Golden Rule to obtain a second opinion and as a tool to supplement your decision-making process. Otherwise, you will be stuck every time that your virtues conflict and you will quickly begin winging your decisions as you used to do in the past. In order to more fully develop your character, you need something else to guide you alongside your virtues. The remainder of this section fully describes the Golden Rule, its benefits and its criticisms.

THE GOLDEN RULE

"Do unto others as you would have others do unto you." Often referred to as the Golden Rule or the Ethic of Reciprocity, this ecumenical moral principle implores adherents to contemplate the feelings and preferences of fellow human beings before acting. Although the rule finds its prominence in Christian theology through the teachings of Jesus, its origin can be traced back to the Hindu tradition and a pronouncement circa 3,000 BC: "This is the sum of duty. Do not unto others that which would cause you pain if done to you."

The Golden Rule is contained within the ethical systems of many of the world's most prominent religions such as Buddhism, Christianity, Confucianism, Hinduism, Islam, Jainism, Judaism, Sikhism, Taoism and Zoroastrianism. Alongside these world religions, many prominent thinkers also incorporate the Golden Rule into their philosophies. Plato, for instance, stated: "May I do to others as I would that they should do unto me" while Socrates urged, "Do not do to others that which would anger you if others did it to you." The philosopher Immanuel Kant's categorical imperative disallows personal exceptions unless the same exception can be made for all others in similar situations without an irrational result. Similar to the Golden Rule, this Kantian categorical imperative requires people to think of others as ends instead of as means to an end and also about the consequences stemming from actions.

Why is the Golden Rule compelling as a moral principle? The morality or immorality underlying a proposed action is not always apparent and such unanalyzed uncertainty often leads people to act without moral clarity. The Golden Rule is compelling as a moral principle because it requires a person contemplating an action to undertake a comprehensive ethical analysis before acting. First, the actor must analyze the potential consequences of the contemplated action on the primary recipient and then assess how the actor would feel if the roles of actor and recipient were reversed. Second, the actor must look beyond the immediate recipient to others who may be remotely affected and assess how the actor would feel if the roles were again reversed. Because the Golden Rule is a moral principle and not a comprehensive ethical system this sequential thought process will not result in a determination as to whether any particular action is moral or immoral. Such contemplation of consequences will, however, allow people to monitor their actions to determine whether they are acting in a manner consistent with their morals and, theoretically, lead them towards taking moral actions. The application of the Rule also allows adherents to more clearly see the commonalities between themselves and others.

The Golden Rule has two common formulations – a positive formulation and a negative formulation. The positive formulation requires people to "Do unto others as you would have others do unto you." In other words, this formulation tells people what they should do. The negative formulation of the Rule – often referred to as the Silver Rule – is formulated "Do not do unto others as you would not have them do unto you." In other words, this formulation tells people what they should not do. While certain adherents claim that each formulation captures a different moral principle other adherents claim that the Golden and Silver Rules encompass the same moral principle and need not be bifurcated.

THE GOLDEN RULE AND ITS CRITICS

The Golden Rule – despite its broad theological, philosophical and secular acceptance – faces two prominent criticisms: (1) the Social Norms problem and (2) the Social Rules problem.

The Social Norms problem results when an action violates a social norm but is nevertheless acceptable under the Rule because the actor would not object to the same action if the roles were reversed. For example, an employee who enjoys situations where other employees start frivolous arguments with him – arguments completely unrelated to an employment relationship – acts in compliance with the Rule by starting non-work-related frivolous arguments with other employees. Such argument-starting violates the generally-accepted social norm that it is impolite to start frivolous arguments with others in the workplace but also seems to comply with the Golden Rule.

The Social Rules problem results when a person commits any act that violates an established social rule – such as a state or federal statute – and would not object to a similar violation if roles were reversed. For example, assume that an actor offers non-public investment information to a friend in the form of a stock tip and that the offeror would want, or even expect, the friend to reciprocate if roles were reversed. At this point, the offeror is acting in accordance with the Golden Rule but in violation of state and federal law.

Rule adherents argue that the critics' interpretations of the Golden Rule violate its spirit; a spirit requiring an actor to consider two aspects neglected by the two problematic actors above: (1) the dignity and consent of all recipients and (2) the secondary recipients as represented by societal segments and not just individuals. Therefore, in the argumentative employee example above, the actor would not adhere to the spirit of the Rule by starting frivolous arguments because this action does not take into account the dignity and consent of the recipient – an individual who would not likely endorse this social norm violation. Just as a rational actor would not tolerate invasions of personal dignity and consent, such an actor should not treat others in an undignified and non-consensual manner. As for the insider trading example, actors must consider that company stockholders are also indirectly affected by this insider stock tip. Therefore, assuming a role reversal, the actor must ponder a reaction as a stockholder harmed by insider trading and not just as the recipient of inside information. With this in mind, proponents argue that both the Social Norms Problem and the Social Rules Problem would be eliminated if actors complied with the spirit and not merely the literal interpretation of the Golden Rule.

YOUR CHARACTER IN ACTION

At the end of the day, Virtue Ethics helps you decide whether an action is moral or immoral, but the ethical framework provides little guidance when virtues conflict. The Golden Rule, on the other hand, does not advise you on exactly how to act in any given situation other than to treat others as you would wish to be treated, but can provide clarity when virtues conflict. In tandem, however, these two concepts are tremendously effective. My advice is to utilize both Virtue Ethics and the Golden Rule to analyze each and every one of your decisions from this point forward.

Let's return to the conflict-of-virtues example encountered earlier. We are now, however, armed with both Virtue Ethics and the Golden Rule. Recall that you are trying to be more loyal and more honest at the same time. Your friend's roommate accused your friend of stealing some money out of her purse. You were not there, but you suspect that your friend did indeed steal the money judging by her past practices and her recent purchases. Refusing to side with her is a bit disloyal but hiding your true feelings is a bit dishonest. You are in a conundrum because of the apparent conflict between the virtues of honesty and loyalty.

You can now implement your second character-building tool, the Golden Rule, to help you make a decision. The rule requires you to look at the effects of your action on each individual within its sphere of influence – in this case, the people impacted by your decision are your friend and your friend's roommate. Then, you must ponder how you would feel if someone acted in a similar manner towards you in a similar situation. Let's analyze the honesty and the loyalty aspects separately. In this situation, you would not appreciate it if another person withheld her honest opinion about how $300 was stolen from your possession. This is especially true if you needed the money to pay your tuition and stay in school. Deciding that you would want an honest opinion in this situation is the easy part.

Now let's look at the loyalty issue. If you were in your friend's shoes and she suspected that you stole $300 from your roommate's purse, you can formulate two ways in which your friend may treat you: (1) she may act dishonestly and take your side solely out of loyalty or (2) she may tell your roommate the truth because genuine loyalty should not involve deception. As you sit and truly ponder this scenario, you will likely realize that option two is really the manner on which you would wish to be treated. Your thought process would also help you understand that option one requires excessive loyalty; it requires someone to become a doormat for someone else. In this case, the Golden Rule helps demonstrate that the kind of loyalty that your friend expects does not correlate very well to the Golden Mean of the virtue of loyalty.

Remember, each virtue is something that is considered good and excessive loyalty makes you a doormat rather than a loyal friend. By withholding your honest opinion in this case, you are being too loyal and letting your friend get away with an immoral act. The moral choice here is to be honest regardless of the fact that you may let your friend down.

In this case, the Golden Rule supplemented your Virtue Ethics approach and allowed you to put yourself in the shoes of the parties involved. It helped you decide to give the roommate your honest opinion. Viewing this situation from the different angle provided by the Golden Rule demonstrated that the loyalty expected by your friend is not the type of loyalty encompassed by the virtue's Golden Mean. In this case, the Rule was especially helpful because it allowed you to break a tie between two apparently conflicting virtues.

CHAPTER 4:
PRIORITIZE YOUR LIFE

> "The key is not to prioritize what's on your schedule, but to schedule your priorities."
> --- STEVEN COVEY
>
> "Wise are those who learn that the bottom line doesn't always have to be their top priority."
> --- WILLIAM ARTHUR WARD
>
> "You can never get enough of what you don't need to make you happy."
> --- ERIC HOFFER

BIG-TIME CORPORATE LAW

My weekdays commenced about eight-thirty in the morning and ended around eight o'clock in the evening. My weekends were subject to disappear into the abyss of a looming transaction. I would wake up, get ready for work and think about work – even in the shower. Then, I would go to work and think about work. Much later, I would go home and think about the tasks I needed to accomplish at work the next day. After three years of law school and $120,000 of debt, I was finally a corporate associate at a powerful law firm.

I was immediately immersed in transactions involving initial public offerings and high-profile mergers. I helped counsel prominent corporations about how to structure their most crucial business transactions. These were the deals young law students discussed in class, read about in newspapers and pondered with their peers. The money was outstanding; I earned an annual income of $110,000 plus a bonus based on the billable hours I accumulated throughout the year. I was 25 years old and had placed myself squarely in the middle of a world I had desired for years. There was only one problem – I was miserable.

As a young man, I had deliberately prioritized my life and chosen work as my top priority. Further down the list came my friends and family. Even lower were things like playing basketball – something I looked forward to daily in college and law school – and going to church. My most important personal relationships were struggling and I couldn't walk up a few flights of stairs without breaking a sweat.

I was chasing fake rabbits that had taken the form of wealth, prestige and worldly success while ignoring real rabbits such as exercise, personal relationships and religion. I felt that placing my career as my first priority was what young professionals were supposed do in order to be successful. I had always assumed that a prestigious legal career – and all the money and professional rewards that accompany it – was something to be sought after. After all, I had paid a lot of money to attend four years of college, one year of graduate school and three years of law school to get to this exact place. I had taken the SAT, ACT (twice), LSAT and the Colorado Bar Exam. I had sacrificed many evenings and weekends to studying and extracurricular activities. Knowing that I treasured my family, friends and religion, I was convinced that I could place my young career first and these other priorities a bit lower while still treating everything as if it was at the top of my list. I was wrong.

Today – at thirty years old and as a recovering lawyer – I have completely revamped my list of priorities. My religion, spending quality time with my wife and my friends and improving relationships with my family now take top billing. Exercise has moved up my list as well – although at this age I have to stretch before playing basketball. My career is now fifth in line, down four spots from its previous lofty perch.

Are my reshaped priorities acceptable for a young professional in the twenty-first century? Must I change to a less demanding field if I choose to prioritize my career in fifth place? Do I experience pressure from my employer to "reevaluate" my priority structure? The remainder of this chapter will answer these questions and encourage you to determine what your priorities are and then actually prioritize (or potentially reprioritize) your life.

PRIORITIZE YOUR LIFE

The previous story need not revolve around corporate law. If you choose to place your career first on your list of priorities, just subtract the lawyer part and fill in your chosen career field. Don't worry the results will be the same.

First, you will desire to be the best in your chosen field. This desire is actually a good thing and you should try to be very good at whatever you pick as your top priority. Second, you will want to impress your colleagues, clients and superiors. This is a natural tendency and impressed superiors often bring quality work to the employees who impress them. Third, you will need to learn the basics and the nuances of your new field. This will not come easy to you as a novice professional. Becoming fluent in the language, topics and procedures of your new career will require great energy and patience. Finally, you will feel intense pressure to put in the time and effort required to accomplish everything mentioned above. You have chosen to place your career above everything else and, both consciously and subconsciously, it will come first.

Please read this paragraph carefully and read the "A Word about Careers" section below very carefully when you get there. I am neither trying to dissuade you from placing your career first on your priorities list nor am I advocating that you do not need to work hard to succeed in the professional world. I am merely advising you that the things placed lower on your list will inevitably suffer while your attention is focused on your top priority. This is just the way priorities work. There is not enough time in each day to accomplish everything that you desire to accomplish. An illustration of these time constraints will help put this time crunch in perspective.

No matter how you frame it, each and every day is confined to twenty-four hours. At least one-fourth of that time should be allocated to sleep.[11] You now have eighteen hours from which you can divide your daily awake time. A high-powered career – your first priority, remember – required at least ten hours from me every day and you should expect a similar time commitment. That leaves eight hours of awake time in your day. But wait, getting ready in the morning, looking professional and eating breakfast combined with getting ready for bed at night and eating dinner takes time. And, don't forget your commute to and from work. Allocate at least two hours per day for these activities. You now have six hours remaining. Most young professionals have phone calls and e-mails to return every day and errands to run (i.e., picking up groceries, dry cleaning and attending various appointments) at least a few times per week. If you value exercise at all, working out can take up one hour per day.

Average all of this out and you should have around four hours each day to spend on the items lower down on your list. And, you only have these four hours if you are as efficient as you can be with your time, if your job does not keep you later than planned and if you do not allocate any time to stop and take some deep breaths. Remember, you will face the same dilemma tomorrow and the next day. Will you head to church with your extra time or will you try

---

[11] Medical research claims that adults need between six and eight hours of sleep to function correctly.

and fit in your friends/family in those few remaining hours before heading to bed? Trust me, your friends and your family will not always find it meaningful when you fit them into a two-hour "quality time" time slot. Would you if the roles were reversed?

I hope I have convinced you that your top priority will dominate your life even if you wish it were otherwise. There just are not enough hours in the day. Steven Covey, a noted expert on time management, once said: "Whatever is at the center of our life will be the source of our security, guidance, wisdom, and power." If your career is at the center, then you will derive your security, guidance, wisdom and power from your job. If your religion, spouse or personal relationships are at the center then these different sources will provide such necessities. Just keep in mind that items further down on your priorities list will merit less time. You won't have it – you'll be focusing on your top priority.

Fortunately, your life does not have to follow this script. As you build your foundation, you will begin to determine which things are most important to you in your life. You might think your career should be your number one priority until your perspective and character tell you that it should be your family. Regardless of your overall priority structure, this chapter will provide you with the tools necessary to discover the most important things in your life, craft them into a written priorities list and then stick to this list even when it is not convenient and when times get tough.

STEP ONE: SET PRIORITIES

The first step in this process is to actually set some priorities in your life. The bullet points below represent the most important things in many people's lives in no particular order. Take this list, add items to it and subtract items from it as necessary, think about what each of these things means to you and then create a written draft of your priorities. Remember, this list can change – mine did. Sit down in a place where you have peace, quiet and a piece of paper and really think about each category below and what it means to you. Try your best to keep the fake rabbits out of the picture as you jot things down – remember, we are chasing real rabbits now.

- RELIGION
- NEIGHBORS
- CLOSE FRIENDS
- CAREER
- SPOUSE/GIRLFRIEND /BOYFRIEND
- EDUCATION
- PARENTS
- EXTRACURRICULAR ACTIVITIES

- SIBLINGS
- COMMUNITY SERVICE
- GRANDPARENTS
- HEALTH & EXERCISE
- OTHER RELATIVES
- HOBBIES & OTHER FUN PURSUITS
- RELAXATION
- FINANCES
- DISTANT FRIENDS

STEP TWO: STICK WITH YOUR PRIORITIES (EVEN WHEN THE HEAT IS ON)

Okay, now that your new list of priorities is complete, go put it on your refrigerator and read on. Thus far, it has been fairly easy to nod along with the concept that you need priorities in your life. It might have been a bit tougher to recognize the implications of placing your career at the very top of the list, but hopefully you can see what happens when this occurs as well. Now is the part where this discussion becomes the most difficult. When the heat is put on you, when somebody important in your life pressures you to alter your priority structure or break your commitment to it, can you stick with your list or will you collapse and put lower priorities above higher priorities? If you bow to this pressure and cut and paste your priorities as different situations dictate, then you have not developed this crucial part of your foundation. You are like a ship lost in the sea of your life and it will be tough to find contentment on a consistent basis.

You have to stick with your priorities even if your decision is unpopular and potentially harmful to your professional life. If you place your career fifth on your list and your spouse at the top but you continually put your work first you are deceiving yourself and your list is a mere sham. A list of priorities does not work merely because you numbered and memorialized your priorities on a piece of paper. You have to stick to them in order for this process to be effective. The problem is that you can count on the application of major pressure on a rather consistent basis as a young professional. Your boss and/or your colleagues will demand that you "rededicate yourself" to your career, "take one for the team," or take your work commitments more seriously. This is likely to happen even if you are working as hard as you can or as hard as your priorities will allow. When the heat is on, you must find a way to stick to your priorities.

A WORD ABOUT CAREERS

Careers have a way of demanding much of our time regardless of their significance on our priority ladder. This is a good thing. We can and should find much fulfillment in our work and in the people we meet along the way. The vast majority of us also need to work to earn a living. Because of the significance careers have in our lives, I encourage you take your career seriously regardless of where you place it on your priorities list. While you are at work, give it a good faith effort. When you have a big project, you may have to work overtime and sacrifice a bit. I encourage you to do these things with a joyful heart. At least you have a job.

The key is for you to know where you have to draw the line – a line that you are unwilling to cross. If your employer will not let you make travel commitments because you might be needed that weekend or if you feel that you need to be home with your family for dinner most nights, it might be time to choose a different company to work for. If you feel trapped in a job, you can generally choose to leave and go elsewhere. The money and prestige may be lower but you can counter these losses with gains in the form of increased time spent on things that rank higher on your priorities list.

I joked earlier about being a recovering lawyer. While that is true – and a bit funny – I still love the law and I do enjoy working hard in my professional endeavors. As a professor of business law and ethics, I have dedicated my professional life to helping young people learn as well as pushing knowledge of the law beyond its current boundaries through my writing and lecturing. These are important tasks and they take a lot of time. Although I do not feel tied to the workplace as I did as a corporate lawyer, my current job requires me to put in significant hours during the week and on some weekends.

Here is the difference. Although the demands are similar, a glance at my revamped list of priorities gives me the strength to make better decisions about my work commitments. Today, when I have to choose between concentrating on a work-related task and seeing a movie with my wife, I will now choose the movie. I will exercise an hour a day, even if that puts me a bit behind in my to-do list.

I must admit that sometimes these choices are difficult and place me at a disadvantage in relation to my colleagues. Sometimes, I find myself drawn to the idea that I need to be more dedicated to my career so that I can be the best I can be. Old habits die hard I guess. Sometimes, I struggle to keep my priorities in their proper order and that's a good thing. If this process was not a struggle then it would be much easier to take for granted. After reading this chapter, you should be more confident in the order of your priorities and the importance of sticking to them through tough times. Now, you just have to find the guts to do it. The following discussion will help you develop some of this necessary courage.

TOUGH QUESTIONS AND ANSWERS WITH PROFESSOR C

Let's return to the three tough questions posed at the beginning of this chapter:

ARE MY RESHAPED PRIORITIES ACCEPTABLE FOR A YOUNG PROFESSIONAL IN THE TWENTY-FIRST CENTURY?

Anyone who chooses to chase real rabbits takes a leap of faith. These brave souls deliberately choose to pursue things that our materialistic world does not outwardly appreciate. One of the first things we are asked in social settings is what we do for a living or what schools we attended. People envy their neighbor's cars, homes and holiday decorations. "Desperate Housewives" is America's highest rated television drama. So, my answer to this seemingly difficult question of whether my reshaped priorities are acceptable is – "Who Cares?!" Are these reshaped priorities acceptable? Acceptable to whom? Please recall that we are working on your life here – not your parents' lives, not your colleagues' lives and definitely not your boss's life.

As long as you are comfortable with your priorities and the potential professional repercussions of sticking to them, then place them on your list and hold on tight. You can still be a successful professional and be respected in your community with work falling below family and friends on your list of priorities. In fact, this change has been a breath of fresh air in my life. I consider myself a successful young professional. I am one of the youngest and highest-rated professors in a department and a college that ranks third in the world for producing ethical graduates – and my career rests fifth on my list. Ironically, many of my law school colleagues with high-powered legal careers often joke about trading jobs with me. I work diligently; however, when it comes time to choose, I think back to my priorities and choose the ones at the top both consistently and confidently.

MUST I CHANGE TO A LESS DEMANDING FIELD IF I CHOOSE TO PRIORITIZE MY CAREER IN FIFTH PLACE?

Young professionals who rank their careers lower on their list of priorities may find themselves limited within their chosen career field. The key phrase here is "limited within" and not "banned from" their chosen field. My job as a corporate lawyer was on a collision course with my amended priorities list. It was impossible for me to place that particular job fifth on my list and, at the same time, survive long enough to become a partner. It was possible, however, for me to work within a different area of the legal profession with my career in fifth place.

While practicing big-time corporate law proved to be untenable, teaching at my alma mater presented itself as a perfect alternative. As a legal studies professor, I am able to deal with the law everyday and still structure my time around my other priorities. I continue to work very hard – between fifty and sixty hours per week – but I have the privilege of setting my own schedule. I was not forced to give up my career in law even though I completely retooled my priorities. The bottom line is that, by placing your job fifth or so on your list, you may be forced to choose a different type of job within your career field but you need not abandon your chosen field altogether.

DO I EXPERIENCE PRESSURE FROM MY EMPLOYER TO "REEVALUATE" MY PRIORITY STRUCTURE?

I have experienced pressure in the past from employers urging me to "reevaluate" my priorities. Interestingly, similar pressures came from my colleagues. It was a groupthink type of mentality – something similar to: "we're all putting in long hours, this sucks, we can't change anything, so you just need to tough it out with us." Looking back, I can see how ridiculous it sounds. When I was in the midst of it, however, I started to think that my colleagues were right and that I needed to sacrifice all else for my job. Be careful that you don't join in on such a dangerous groupthink mentality.

In my newest endeavor, I have avoided the application of this type of pressure. This avoidance stems from the fact that I have developed the ability to get difficult projects done well and done quickly. I avoid most of the heat because I have heeded my own advice from this book and developed the ability to think (see Chapter Seven) and the skill of consistent-persistence (see Chapter Eight). These qualities allow me to be successful without working the ridiculous hours I had in the past.

I guess it's an experience thing combined with more flexible job duties. I am sure that the pressure would be more noticeable if I was not as productive or if I did not care about my students as much as I do. At the end of the day, I consider it a good thing that my department and my administration expect me to be a top-notch professor. This reasonable expectation is in both my and my employer's best interests and is manageable because I possess the skills necessary to effectively achieve it.

GOALS

> "If you are failing to plan, you are planning to fail."
> --- **TARIQ SIDDIQUE**
>
> "A goal properly set is halfway reached."
> --- **ABRAHAM LINCOLN**

Your priorities are now in order (congratulations!). At this point, you need to figure out how to order your life accordingly. How, for instance, are you going to put your family first, treat your friends with more respect or excel at your education? To properly execute your priorities, you need goals. A goal is something you desire to achieve in your life accompanied by a timeframe within which you aspire to achieve it. Goals focus your mind on an endeavor and give you something to strive for.

It is time for you to set some goals. Begin the goal-setting process by utilizing your list of priorities as your guide. Your most important goals should be tied to your top priorities. You also need goals for your lowest priorities as these are still important – they merited a place on your list didn't they? Merely thinking about your goals is good but writing them down is even better. Therefore, strive to write your goals down on a piece of paper, draft them as positive statements and aim high (not astronomically high and unachievable but high enough that you will have to struggle to get there). Start this process by creating goals for the following time periods: three months, six months, one year, and three years in the future. Your goals for the one and three-month periods should be somewhat specific, while your goals for the more distant periods can be more abstract.

SET YOUR GOALS

Carefully analyze the following example. The priorities and goals stated in the charts below come from a freshman in college (let's call her Katie) who desires to attend medical school upon graduation. Katie just completed her first semester and has a 3.0 GPA. She is involved in five extracurricular activities but is not truly dedicated to any of them. She has no clue about how the medical school application process works and has poor study habits (sometimes going a full week without picking up a textbook or looking at her notes). She knows that she needs to work out for her mental and physical health but was not raised in a family that valued exercise.

The first chart indicates Katie's top five priorities. The second chart provides an example of how Katie could emphasize these priorities in her life by creating a list of goals. Notice how each of her top five priorities finds a place in each period of time on her list. Notice also that each goal is both ambitious and achievable at the same time. For instance, Katie desires her GPA to improve from a 3.0 to a 3.5 in a three-year period. This is a tough task, but one that a dedicated student can achieve. Once you analyze this chart, please try and craft your own list of goals for the same time periods. Remember to start by listing your priorities and then insure that each priority finds a spot on your list.

KATIE'S PRIORITIES

1. FAMILY

2. EDUCATION

3. FRIENDS

4. PLAYING THE PIANO

5. EXERCISE

KATIE'S GOALS (USING HER PRIORITIES AS HER GUIDE)	
TIME PERIOD	GOALS
THREE MONTHS (THE MIDDLE OF KATIE'S SPRING SEMESTER)	• Call my family twice per week • Study every night for one hour • Spend quality time with friends • Exercise one hour per week
SIX MONTHS (THE END OF KATIE'S FRESHMAN YEAR)	• Call my family twice per week • Obtain a GPA of 3.3 • Study every night for one hour • Declare my major and minor • Spend quality time with friends • Reserve one hour per week for playing the piano • Exercise two hours per week
ONE YEAR (THE MIDDLE OF KATIE'S SOPHOMORE YEAR)	• Call my family twice per week • Obtain a GPA of 3.4 • Study every night for two hours • Understand the school admissions process • Get my resume together • Spend quality time with friends • Reserve one hour per week for playing the piano • Exercise two hours per week
THREE YEARS (THE MIDDLE OF KATIE'S SENIOR YEAR)	• Call my family twice per week • Obtain a GPA of 3.5 (graduate with this GPA) • Take the MCAT test • Select ten medical schools to apply to and apply • Spend quality time with friends • Reserve one hour per week for playing the piano • Exercise three hours per week

Your list of goals will likely be longer than the illustration above. A more elaborate list is a good thing, just make sure not to write too much down about each goal – remember, these are goals and not journal entries. Make sure you update your goals often and create new goals when your current time periods expire. Also, make sure to save your old lists so that you can look back to see how much you have accomplished. If you are diligent, you will be amazed at how many of these goals you have actually achieved within the given time parameters.

At this point, you have a list of priorities, a set of goals and the motivation to stick to them when the pressure is applied. You are well on your way to developing the foundation necessary for authentic success. The only remaining foundational principle you need to adopt is the proper perspective about life. We head in that direction right now.

CHAPTER 5:
A BRAND-NEW, BIG-PICTURE
PERSPECTIVE

> "He can who thinks he can, and he can't who thinks he can't. This is an inexorable, indisputable law."
> --- **HENRY FORD**
>
> There are things I can't force. I must adjust. There are times when the greatest change needed is a change of my viewpoint."
> --- **DENIS DIDEROT**
>
> "It is the mark of great people to treat trifles as trifles and important matters as important matters."
> --- **DORIS LESSING**

YOUR PERSPECTIVE

Your perspective defines the way that you look at the world and empowers you to analyze your place in that world. Your perspective also dictates your reaction to each of the ups and downs life tosses your way as it allows you to differentiate between the important and the relatively unimportant. Finally, your perspective comprises a major part of your foundation and its orientation has a dramatic impact on your life. Most people's perspectives fall into one of the following two orientations: (1) big-picture or (2) little-picture.

A big-picture person looks broadly at life without being overly concerned with little setbacks stemming from specific endeavors. A big-picture person focuses on the entire forest of life and is able to shrug-off flaws in its individual trees. A little-picture person, on the other hand, looks more narrowly at life and is particularly concerned with specific setbacks. A little-picture person focuses on the individual trees in life and often misses the panorama of the forest itself.

I encourage you to become a big-picture person. Similar to the other three foundational principles, altering your perspective is a difficult task. If you already consider yourself a big-picture person, congratulations! However, please read a bit further and seriously ponder the attributes that someone of this nature possesses – you know, just to make sure your assumption is accurate. In fact, most of us would consider ourselves big-picture people, even though we do not fully understand the requirements underlying such an assertion. Beyond our desire to label ourselves as big-picture people, we also sense that this is the right answer to give when we are asked about our perspective in job interviews and social situations. Please keep in mind that falsely classifying your perspective will hinder the completion of your foundation-building process.

On the other hand, if you feel that you are a little-picture person, you do not need to fret too much just yet. In fact, you already possess the tools necessary to drastically alter your perspective (i.e., the development of a strong work ethic, a solid character and a list of priorities), you just need a plan to make this change a bit easier on yourself. This chapter is designed to provide you with such a plan and encourage you to make this difficult philosophical shift. As with everything else in this book, you should start right now.

Unsurprisingly, I have found that individuals lacking a strong foundation in their lives tend to be little-picture people. They overreact to trivial situations. They allow minor setbacks to get them down. Little-picture people stress out for too long about a poor test score or a minor slight by a colleague. People with a strong work ethic, solid character and clearly-defined sets of priorities, however, tend to be big-picture people. They are able to shrug off these little setbacks in their life because they understand that they have something bigger and more important to live for. How do I know all of this? I was formerly a small-picture person.

MY CHANGE OF PERSPECTIVE

My perspective changed recently and it changed considerably. Although I always appreciated the importance of maintaining a big-picture perspective, I could not shake my small-picture mindset. I would become frustrated with a sluggish classroom performance, stress-out about minor flaws in my work product and punish my friends for minor slights. Basically, I would sweat a lot of the small stuff in my life. Everything changed, however, during the summer of 2005. You see, it was over that period that I began feeling dizzy, very dizzy, all of the time. This dizziness became so bad that I could not read a magazine or stand up quickly without feeling like I was going to faint. It got to the point where my doctor worried that it might be a brain tumor. In shock, my wife and I scheduled an MRI to find out for sure.

Being claustrophobic, I was not looking forward to my appointment with the confined space that medical professionals refer to as an MRI machine. On the other hand, I understood that this was something that had to be done. I discovered that the machine was actually smaller than I had thought and that my nose was about six inches from the roof. The end closest to my head was closed while the open end was seven feet away – it might as well have been seventy feet away as far as I was concerned.

The technician told me I would be stuck in the machine for 45 minutes and that was only if I remained completely still. I was looking death – in the form of a brain tumor – right in the eye and I was losing it. I thought to myself, "I'm only 30 years old, dear God,

I feel like I still have something to offer this world" and "I just got married and will leave behind the most beautiful person I've ever known." This was it, the moment of truth. I was a disaster.

The only comforting factors I recognized were my wife's presence in the control room and the microphone in the MRI machine allowing patients to talk to the technician. In this case, and unbeknownst to me, my microphone was broken. Throughout the scan and with all of the voice I could muster, I asked my wife, "Honey, am I ok?" Honey, what's wrong with me?" There was no response. I asked again and again . . . and no response. I was sure that my wife was in tears after seeing the results and just couldn't face telling me over the microphone. These were some of the worst moments of my life.

Only later did I realize that my MRI scan was actually one of the best things that could have happened to me in terms of my perspective. After what felt like an eternity in the machine and the horrible wait for the results, my wife and I received good news – negative for a brain tumor. I cried. My wife cried. We sensed that the doctor wanted to cry. This emotional process caused me to look at the world in a different way.

After thinking I was about to die of a brain tumor, the little-picture issues in my life automatically became less important. I subconsciously stopped giving them a second thought. This process actually began while I was in the MRI machine itself. Unsurprisingly, while I was scared out of my mind during the scan, I was not thinking about my job, my possessions, any differences with my friends and family or my agenda for the week – basically, all of the stuff I used to think about constantly. Instead, I found myself thinking about my wife, my wedding, my mom and my dad, and all of the good things that had happened in my life. I thought about the people who had helped me in the past and the people that I had helped as well. I remembered all of the neat places I had visited as well as the places I wanted to visit in the future – if I was fortunate enough to have one. Finally, I remembered my grandmother's redundant piece of advice that urged me to "count my blessings."

In fact, ever since my trip to the hospital, I have been thinking about all of these genuinely important things far more often. Now, I continually count my blessings and by count, I mean I actually count them – one by one! This often takes a long time but the results are amazing. My final tally helps me realize that my grandmother was indeed correct – I am truly blessed. I am blessed even when trivial setbacks endeavor to weigh me down. Today, it is very difficult for me to stress-out about the little problems in my life; if something goes wrong at work or I otherwise have a bad day, I remember that my life was one MRI scan away from turning out much worse. I can now shrug off these minor occurrences. I have genuinely become a big-picture person.

CHANGE YOUR PERSPECTIVE, CHANGE YOUR LIFE

Welcome to the section where you learn how to change your perspective. To this point, we have defined and analyzed the idea of a perspective, discussed both little-and big-picture perspectives and illustrated the results from a major perspective shift in the life of a formerly little-picture person. As a result, you have seen what a difference a change in perspective can make and hopefully you realize that you need to become a big-picture person ASAP.

Think of this final section as a user-manual specially constructed for this exact mission. As I mentioned earlier, transitions of this nature are very difficult. In fact, if you are currently a little-picture person, one chapter in a book, even a well-written, extremely helpful chapter on perspective such as this, is insufficient to change your perspective by itself. However, this chapter should jumpstart the process by presenting you with three crucial steps you can take to change your perspective forever.

The first step requires you to discover your current perspective on life. You can make this determination very quickly using something I refer to as the "one-bad-test" analysis. The second step requires you to make a commitment that the small setbacks weighing you down should matter but not T-H-A-T much. Finally, the third step requires you to divide each of your priorities into big and little-picture components, create hypothetical setbacks for each category and then craft ideal reactions to these and similar setbacks you may experience in the future. In the end, the reactions you decide on are not as important as the process you went through to craft them. With practice and the dedication to change your perspective, you will be able to categorize your setbacks as big or little as they occur and eventually react appropriately according to your intuition.

STEP ONE: DISCOVERING YOUR TRUE PERSPECTIVE

Tinkering with your perspective before you determine if you are a big-picture or a little-picture person is silly. Accordingly, this first step requires you to discover your true perspective before moving forward. It is crucial that you take this step seriously and avoid making assumptions about being a big-picture person this early in the process. Remember, it is common for people to think that they are big-picture people when, in reality, they have adopted a little-picture mindset. I have witnessed these misconceptions many times while observing young people who are very smart, put together and seem to have a solid foundation underneath them. I listen intently when they tell me that they are big-picture people. I tend to take them at their word, at least until I witness first-hand their reactions to poor scores on their assignments and other small academic-related setbacks. It quickly becomes clear to me whether each student's assumption about being a big-picture person was accurate or way off base.

Many students merely assume that they are big-picture people because they have made it this far in life – they are in college and have promising careers staring them right in the eye. By neglecting to test their assumption, however, they will never be able to determine whether they are merely imposters posing as big-picture people. These students are proof positive that you can experience a measure of success in your life with a little-picture perspective. What they fail to recognize is that their success is associated with unnecessary stress and with insufficient time being devoted to the genuinely important things in life. These are negative consequences that are not associated with a genuine big-picture perspective.

THE ONE-BAD-TEST ANALYSIS

Fortunately, making an accurate determination of your perspective is a straightforward process. Merely apply both prongs of the one-bad-test analysis to your life and the results will scream big-picture or little-picture person loud and clear.[12]   The first part of the analysis requires you to think back to a few of the small setbacks you have recently experienced.[13]   Each setback should be small in the sense of its overall impact within the big-scheme of your life. When considering potential setbacks of this nature, think of something similar to a minor spat with a colleague, an unpleasant customer service experience, or the results of one bad test, for instance. Write three of these setbacks down on a piece of paper.

The second part of the analysis requires you to recall your reaction(s) to each setback. Did you react with shock, anger and blame? How about crying, grief and depression? When you think about it, these are major-league reactions that likely caused you a great deal of anticipation, stress and fatigue. Even worse, you

---

[12]I created this analysis from my observations of students in the undergraduate and graduate business school environment. Although the name of the analysis derives from that environment, the test will apply for any small setback in any environment where it occurs including the workplace or the home. Don't be fooled by the name, this analysis is adaptable.

[13]This series of setbacks need not be related in any way.

devoted these major-league reactions to setbacks that you purposely picked as being small in nature. What I am trying to say is that these serious reactions generate a tremendous amount of worrying directed at issues that likely do not merit it – especially when judged in the context of the big scheme of your life. These reactions will continue to manifest themselves with each little-picture setback you experience. Over time, this will literally and figuratively wear you out.

Now to the results . . . If you experienced a major-league reaction for one or more of the small setbacks you analyzed then you may officially refer to yourself as a little-picture person. If you did not experience a major reaction when considering any of the small setbacks then you are likely a big-picture person. Congratulations! The box below provides a snapshot of the one-bad-test analysis.

THE ONE-BAD-TEST ANALYSIS SUMMARY

1. RECALL A FEW SMALL SETBACKS YOU RECENTLY ENCOUNTERED:

    a. Make sure each setback is a small – but not a trivial – setback

    b. Write down the exact circumstances of each setback

2. RECALL YOUR SPECIFIC REACTIONS TO EACH SETBACK AND CATEGORIZE EACH AS EITHER A:

    a. Major-league reaction; or

    b. Minor-league reaction

3. CATEGORIZE YOURSELF AS A BIG- OR A LITTLE-PICTURE PERSON AS FOLLOWS:

    a. You are a little-picture person if you experienced a major-league reaction to one or more of the small setbacks you analyzed

    b.   You are a big-picture person if you did not experience a major-league reaction to any of your small setbacks

MEET DONOVAN: A LITTLE-PICTURE PERSON

Meet Donovan. His story provides a vivid illustration of a little-picture perspective in action. Donovan is currently an undergraduate student enrolled at a prestigious state university. He experienced a tough upbringing in a rough neighborhood and always had to work hard for everything he received. Donovan has adopted a little-picture perspective; after all, his life has been one fight after another. He believes that the chips are constantly stacked against him and, accordingly, that nothing short of straight As on every assignment is going to allow him to break free from his past and experience success. He had made it this far under this little-picture perspective and had no desire to change an approach that has worked so well for so long.

Through all of this hardship, Donovan found a way to succeed academically and graduated in the top five percent of his high school class. As you know, he was accepted to college and is doing quite well to this point. In fact, as of the second semester of his sophomore year, Donovan has a 3.7 grade point average. As he considers his upper-level class requirements, he decides to sign up for a course entitled "The Business Environment." On his first quiz in this class he receives an 80% – a score representing a B minus. Having studied for over three hours for the quiz in question, Donovan felt prepared and predicted that his score would turn out much higher.

Under these specific circumstances and considering his perspective, you can see why Donovan considered a B minus to be a significant setback in his life. Upon receiving the results, he was shocked and just stared at the paper in front of him. Soon afterwards, Donovan's shock turned to anger – first towards the course itself and then at the professor for making the questions so "tricky." After a few days, he accepted his score and pouted around campus, mumbling things like "my efforts in this class are not reflected in my grades" and "I'll never understand this stuff." Does any of this sound familiar? Have you ever reacted this way in a similar circumstance? If so, I would encourage you – along with Donovan – to run this type of setback through the one-bad-test analysis and scrutinize your results. At the very end of this chapter, I will present the actual results of Donovan's analysis and you can compare answers.

In the end, the hardest part of the one-bad-test analysis may be determining which setbacks you should consider small as you undertake part one. Notice that I did not ask you to determine the setbacks that you wish to consider small. Only picking trivially small setbacks negates the power and effectiveness of this analysis. Instead, you must determine the setbacks that you might currently consider big but that you should consider small (i.e., the types of setbacks that a reasonable person would probably consider small). This is a much tougher task. Does Donovan's B minus qualify as small? Do any of your low grades? Before you can determine whether a setback is small or big and thereby complete the one-bad-test analysis, you must move through the second and third steps in the perspective-changing process.

STEP TWO: UNDERSTAND THAT SMALL SETBACKS MATTER . . . BUT NOT T-H-A-T MUCH [14]

You may sense that I am urging you to completely ignore the small setbacks in your life and concern yourself only with matters of genuine importance. These feelings are perceptive but not entirely accurate. A big-picture perspective does not mandate the complete

---

[14] The reference to "not T-H-A-T much" comes from a great book on negotiation by Herb Cohen entitled *Negotiate This: By Caring But not T-H-A-T Much* (Warner Business Books: 2003).

neglect of small setbacks. In fact, you will experience many such setbacks over the course of your life and completely ignoring them to focus on more important things entices their reemergence in your future. Ignorance is not bliss when it comes to small setbacks. Instead of ignoring them, you must understand that small setbacks by themselves should concern you but they should never concern you T-H-A-T much. In other words, the best way to react to these setbacks is to: (1) understand their implications, (2) carefully consider how each setback occurred, (3) create a plan to avoid similar setbacks in the future and (4) then shrug them off.

This is a much better approach than neglecting the cause of the setback and worrying only about its implications. By understanding how each of your setbacks occurred and by striving to change the circumstances that brought each about in the first place, you are more likely to avoid similar setbacks in the future. I am convinced, however, that merely worrying about the results without examining the cause, on the other hand, is likely to result in a string of similar setbacks in the future. Making these types of distinctions is what being a big-picture person is about.

For example, I would argue that a poor score on a school assignment or minor criticism on a project at work should be shrugged off as a relatively unimportant setback – especially when you consider it within the big scheme of your life. Both of these occurrences can be sincerely disappointing and should matter to you, but they should not stimulate an overreaction which will cause you unnecessary stress. They should not matter T-H-A-T much.

On the other hand, you need to understand that a series of small setbacks such as these can represent a major problem worth worrying about. It would be unwise to shrug off a string of academic or professional setbacks while blaming your ambivalence on the adoption of your new big-picture perspective. So, if you find yourself continually criticized for the quality of your work product, such criticism likely matters a great deal and might even cost you your job. Similarly, if you under-perform your expectations on six straight quiz scores then these setbacks likely merit some consideration as well. Therefore, please do not confuse an individual small setback that matters a little bit with a series of small setbacks that might cause you major problems in the future. With this in mind, your final task is to divide your list of priorities and come up with your ideal reaction to potential setbacks in your life.

STEP THREE: DIVIDE YOUR PRIORITIES AND SET YOUR IDEAL REACTIONS

The final step in the perspective-changing process utilizes the priorities list you created in the previous chapter. Recall that your priorities represent the truly important aspects of your life and that you must consider these priorities every time you face an important decision. Coincidentally, your priorities list has another important attribute in addition to being a decision-making guide. It also provides an easy way for you to divide each priority into big-and little-picture categories and then think of hypothetical setbacks that might fall under each category. Allocating your setbacks in this manner allows you to craft an ideal reaction to each one depending upon the importance of the setback within your priority structure. These ideal reactions then serve as a goal for you to strive for assuming that the hypothetical setback actually occurs. Once you master this step in the process, your perspective will change from little-to big-picture in no time. The following section explains how this works.

Your priorities list should be divided into three different classes. Your top three priorities are your *summa cum laude* priorities and constitute the most important things in your life; by placing them first, you commit to honor these priorities higher than all others. Your next three priorities are your *magna cum laude* priorities and are still very important to you but not as important as your top three.

Finally, the rest of your priorities – no matter how many there are – constitute your *cum laude* priorities. These are still priorities to you but they are not as important in the big scheme of your life as the six priorities on the top of your list. Everything else in your life not meriting a place on this list is not a priority for you.

You should recognize that using the Latin terminology of *summa cum laude*, *magna cum laude* and *cum laude*, meaning "with highest honor," "with high honor" and "with honor," respectively, is a unique way of expressing that all of your priorities are to be honored in your life. That is why you classify them as priorities in the first place. These distinctions also allow you to recognize that some priorities merit more honor in your life than others. Now that you have your priorities classified into three groups, you must make one further division. Take each priority on your list and split it into a big-picture category and a little-picture category. The following chart illustrates a simple way to accomplish these divisions.

PERSONAL PERSPECTIVE CHART

PRIORITIES	PERSPECTIVE & SETBACK		IDEAL REACTION
1.	BIG-PICTURE		
	LITTLE-PICTURE		
2.	BIG-PICTURE		
	LITTLE-PICTURE		
3.	BIG-PICTURE		
	LITTLE-PICTURE		

This template represents your starting point and contains blanks which you should fill in after you have given this step some serious thought.[15]   Create three separate charts – one for each of your priority classifications – with your first chart representing your *summa cum laude* priorities.[16]

YOUR SUMMA CUM LAUDE PRIORITIES

Begin by transcribing the top three priorities from your priorities list into the Priorities section on the chart. Next, think of a few hypothetical setbacks that might occur within the context of each of these three priorities. Make sure to craft setbacks for both the big- and the little-picture components. For instance, a serious physical illness is a setback that could touch your significant other, your family and your friends. Coincidentally, a trivial disagreement could affect each of these relationships as well. Obviously, these are two significantly different types of setbacks with the illness being a big-picture problem and the spat being a little-picture problem. Keep in mind that this allocation helps you formulate your ideal reactions for each of these hypothetical setbacks. The incarnation of our template contains three hypothetical *summa cum laude* priorities broken-down into big-and little-picture categories and contains hypothetical setbacks for each category.

---

[15] I encourage you to make a few copies of this chart or create your own format and actually write out the concepts we are discussing here.

[16] Make sure to fill in the top left box indicating that we are dealing with your *summa cum laude* priorities in this instance.

PERSONAL PERSPECTIVE CHART

SUMMA CUM LAUDE PRIORITIES		PERSPECTIVE & SETBACK		IDEAL REACTION
1.	Spouse	BIG-PICTURE	Serious illness	
		LITTLE-PICTURE	Minor disagreement	
2.	Friends	BIG-PICTURE	Major relationship change	
		LITTLE-PICTURE	Minor slight	
3.	Education	BIG-PICTURE	Poor LSAT score	
		LITTLE-PICTURE	Poor quiz score	

Notice the major differences between the big-picture setbacks and the little-picture setbacks. These differences merit different reactions with the most serious reactions reserved for your highest, big-picture priorities. At this point, you need to complete the chart by determining your ideal reaction to each setback. Predicting a reaction to a future setback is a difficult task because you really do not know how you will react until the event actually occurs. It is possible, however, to craft a desired reaction to potential setbacks before they occur. If you misstep when the setback actually occurs by reacting differently from your plan, you can try to muster a reaction closer to your ideal reaction the next time. Remember, this is a long-term commitment and not a quick fix.

Keep in mind that people generally react to setbacks with (1) major-league reactions, (2) minor-league reactions and (3) shrug off reactions. Major-league reactions are emotionally-charged, drawn-out, stress-causing responses to an occurrence. Typical major-league reactions are severe shock, anger, depression and despair. Minor-league reactions are less severe versions of major-league reactions and include disbelief, frustration and pouting. Finally, shrug off reactions are mere reflections upon a setback and last for a short period of time – thirty minutes at the longest – before we forget about them completely.

Your major-league reactions should be reserved primarily for your *summa cum laude* priorities – with the vast majority reserved for your big-picture setbacks in this classification. If your spouse contracts a serious illness, for instance, you are entitled to worry about her health immensely and for as long as you need to. This setback might merit shock, anger and depression depending upon its severity. This illness constitutes a big-picture setback occurring within the context of one of your top three priorities.

On the other hand, if you are dealing with a minor disagreement between you and your spouse, you should be concerned, but this setback does not merit a major-league reaction. On the other hand, you should not just shrug off the setbacks for priorities this high on your list – shrugging off spats with your spouse can lead to long-term future damage. Instead, your reactions for setbacks affecting your *summa cum laude* priorities should merit only major-league and minor-league reactions. I advocate that you reserve your major reactions for your big-picture setbacks and your minor reactions for your little-picture setbacks – at least for this classification of your priorities. The following chart presents the complete picture and the box at the very bottom represents the types of reactions that you are allowed for this classification.

PERSONAL PERSPECTIVE CHART

SUMMA CUM LAUDE PRIORITIES		PERSPECTIVE & SETBACK		IDEAL REACTION
1.	Significant Other	BIG-PICTURE	Serious illness	<u>major</u>
		LITTLE-PICTURE	Minor disagreement	<u>minor</u>
2.	Friends	BIG-PICTURE	Major relationship change	<u>major</u>
		LITTLE-PICTURE	Minor slight	<u>minor</u>
3.	School	BIG-PICTURE	Poor LSAT score	<u>major</u>
		LITTLE-PICTURE	Poor quiz score	<u>minor</u>

ALLOWED REACTIONS FOR THE *SUMMA CUM LAUDE* CLASSIFICATION:

BIG-PICTURE = MAJOR-LEAGUE
LITTLE-PICTURE = MINOR-LEAGUE

YOUR MAGNA CUM LAUDE PRIORITIES

I hope this process is beginning to make sense. Now let's turn to your *magna cum laude* priorities. The first steps – the placement of priorities and breakdown into big-and little-picture components – remain the same as they were with your *summa cum laude* priorities. The only difference occurs when you craft your ideal reactions to this classification of your priorities. Because you are moving further down your priorities list, your *magna cum laude* priorities are correspondingly less important to you than your *summa cum laude* priorities. Therefore the universe of reactions here is increased by one: (1) major-league reactions, (2) minor-league reactions and (3) shrug offs are now acceptable. Note that the shrug off reaction was not available for your most important priorities; this is because everything in your top three priorities is too important to just shrug off. Within the *magna cum laude* classification, however, you will have some discretion as to your ideal reaction and shrugging something off is now a possibility.

Within this classification, some big-picture setbacks will merit a major-league reaction while other big-picture setbacks might only merit a minor-league reaction. Something similar occurs with your little-picture setbacks as some will merit a minor-league reaction while others will merit nothing more than a shrug off. You must choose here in a way that is different from your *summa cum laude* and your *cum laude* priorities. The following chart illustrates a hypothetical *magna cum laude* priority classification.

PERSONAL PERSPECTIVE CHART

MAGNA CUM LAUDE PRIORITIES		PERSPECTIVE & SETBACK		IDEAL REACTION
4.	Exercise	BIG-PICTURE	Unhealthy exercise habits	<u>major</u>
		LITTLE-PICTURE	Decreased exercise performance	<u>minor</u>
5.	Relaxation	BIG-PICTURE	You have stopped relaxing	<u>minor</u>
		LITTLE-PICTURE	Abandonment of a few relaxation opportunities	<u>shrug off</u>
6.	Extracurricular Activities	BIG-PICTURE	Completely uninvolved	<u>minor</u>
		LITTLE-PICTURE	Abandonment of a few activities	<u>shrug off</u>

ALLOWED REACTIONS FOR THE *MAGNA CUM LAUDE* CLASSIFICATION:

BIG-PICTURE = MAJOR-LEAGUE OR MINOR-LEAGUE
LITTLE-PICTURE = MINOR-LEAGUE OR SHRUG-OFF

As you can see, all three potential reactions (major-league, minor-league and shrug off) are included in this hypothetical *magna cum laude* chart. This does not mean, however, that you must incorporate all three in your personal chart. In fact, the ultimate decision to include any reaction type must be made on an individual basis after you ponder the implications of and the reasons for each potential setback. Additionally, notice that the big-picture setbacks here are not quite as devastating as those in the *summa cum laude* classification. This is the reason why some of them might merit a lesser reaction. The same holds true for the little-picture setbacks, with some of them only meriting a shrug off reaction. It would be strange, however, to place a shrug off reaction in any big-picture category. Remember, your *magna cum laude* classification still represents some of your highest priorities and, when you experience a big-picture setback here, it merits more than a shrug off reaction.

YOUR CUM LAUDE PRIORITIES

The final chart is reserved for your *cum laude* priorities and you will notice below how your ideal reactions should change significantly from your two prior classifications. For your *cum laude* classification, your reactions to the big-picture setbacks are allowed to range between minor-league and shrug off. Notice that a major-league reaction is not an option for this classification – even for the big-picture setbacks that occur here. Although you are allowed to choose between a minor-league and a shrug off reaction, the little-picture setbacks occurring here should be shrugged off. In fact, if you can develop a habit of shrugging off the little-picture setbacks, you will decrease your stress level and save some energy for the really important setbacks you will incur in the future.

PERSONAL PERSPECTIVE CHART

CUM LAUDE PRIORITIES		PERSPECTIVE & SETBACK		IDEAL REACTION
7.	Neighbors	BIG-PICTURE	Major disagreement	minor
		LITTLE-PICTURE	Minor disagreement	shrug off
8.	Hobbies (Hiking)	BIG-PICTURE	You have stopped hiking	minor
		LITTLE-PICTURE	Reduced time to hike	shrug off
9.	Organization	BIG-PICTURE	Your life is a complete mess	minor
		LITTLE-PICTURE	Disorganized desk	shrug off

ALLOWED REACTIONS FOR THE *CUM LAUDE* CLASSIFICATION:

BIG-PICTURE = MINOR-LEAGUE
LITTLE-PICTURE = SHRUG-OFF

PUTTING IT ALL TOGETHER: A FINAL EXAMPLE

The following example is designed to place this entire chapter in perspective. Hopefully you recall Donovan – our intelligent student currently "suffering" from a B minus quiz score. You might also remember that he was wandering the campus distraught about his recent performance. I noticed him on his walk a few days after the quiz and we began to talk. I discussed perspective and the importance of becoming a big-picture person. Donavan disagreed with my advice to take minor setbacks less seriously and claimed that he needed top grades to get into law school. Fortunately for Donovan, I would not drop my insistence that he should consider adopting a big-picture perspective. After an hour-long conversation, he reluctantly agreed to undertake the three steps of the perspective-changing process. Such a commitment was good enough for me and we headed to my office.

Donovan's first step was to conduct the one-bad-test analysis to determine his true perspective. The results were not pretty. At first, he needed to recall a little-picture setback in his life – but refused to consider his quiz score as such at this point in the process. He maintained that each assignment in college was a big deal and that a poor score was a big setback. I knew this would happen considering his little-picture perspective. Accordingly, we moved on to step two and talked about how the small setbacks in life should matter, but not T-H-A-T much. I talked about how I could not remember one of my individual quiz scores from when I was an undergraduate student.

When we reached the third step, we ran through Donovan's newly-constructed priorities list and created hypothetical little-picture setbacks. We looked primarily at his *magna cum laude* classification because this is where his education was listed. I took the time to counsel Donovan that his education was listed as his fourth priority – below his religion, family and friends. On his *magna cum laude* chart, Donovan filled in his priorities first, split each into big-and little-picture categories and then began to create hypothetical setbacks. Because he wanted to become a lawyer, Donovan and I agreed that a poor score on his upcoming LSAT test (the examination required to gain admission into law school) would constitute a major setback. Using the LSAT as the big-picture setback allowed Donovan to finally recognize that one poor quiz score might actually be a little-picture setback. We were making progress.

Finally, because Donovan was dealing with the *magna cum laude* classification of priorities, he was granted some discretion as to categorizing his ideal reactions; he was allowed to choose between major-league and minor-league reaction for his big-picture setbacks and between minor-league and shrug off reactions for his little-picture setbacks.

Donovan chose a major-league reaction for the poor LSAT score setback and was then required to choose a reaction for a hypothetical poor quiz score. After recognizing the seriousness of problems constituting a major-league reaction, such as a poor LSAT score, Donovan felt that choosing a minor-league reaction to a poor quiz score was appropriate. He was still not ready to concede a poor quiz score as a shrug off type of setback and he was not required to under this system. Remember, choosing a minor reaction for little-picture setbacks in the *magna cum laude* classification is allowed as these priorities are still very important in the big scheme of things. The following chart represents the relevant portion of Donovan's example.

MAGNA CUM LAUDE PRIORITIES		PERSPECTIVE & SETBACK		IDEAL REACTION
4.	Education	BIG-PICTURE	Poor LSAT score	major
		LITTLE-PICTURE	Poor score on an individual quiz	minor

ALLOWED REACTIONS FOR THE *MAGNA CUM LAUDE* CLASSIFICATION:

BIG-PICTURE = MAJOR-LEAGUE OR MINOR-LEAGUE
LITTLE-PICTURE = MINOR-LEAGUE OR SHRUG-OFF

Having determined that a poor score on an individual quiz was actually a little-picture setback, Donovan was finally ready to move on to the second part of the one-bad-test analysis – determining his actual reaction to the minor setback.[17] Thinking back, he recalled that, after he received his quiz score, he was shocked at first and then angry. He recalled blaming the professor for making the quiz tricky and then disliking the entire class because of this one quiz. At this point, he realized that these were major-league reactions (especially anger and blame) and that he failed to abide by his ideal reactions for this type of setback – which should have been displeasure or agitation. Donovan recognized that he had failed the one-bad-test analysis and was most likely a little-picture person. Because he promised me that he would change perspectives, Donovan began to chart out his other priorities and their big-and little-picture setbacks. He then created sets of ideal reactions and practiced honing them on a daily basis. I was proud of Donovan for undertaking this difficult task and I knew that his life would be better because he was now thinking about his perspective and committed to making a change.

My final piece of advice for Donovan was that he should count his blessings. In fact, I urged him to actually count them. He did and was impressed by their multitude. Although he grew up poor and struggled throughout his childhood, Donovan was blessed to have caring relatives, a nice group of friends and a chance to get a wonderful college education. He was truly blessed. We all are in many ways – even if life has us down at the moment. Keep this advice in mind next time a tree gets in the way of your view of the forest.

*   *   *   *   *

---

[17] It is acceptable to begin step one of the perspective-changing process, complete steps two and three, and then return to step one and complete the one-bad-test analysis.

CONCLUSIONS & CONGRATULATIONS!

My perspective-changing experience illustrates the incredible impact that shifting from little-picture to big-picture generates in a person's life. Before my MRI, I desperately needed to change my perspective but couldn't muster the guts to do it. I was haunted by the bone-headed idea that failing to micromanage everything in my life would impede my ultimate success. I was chasing fake rabbits with this little-picture mentality. Unfortunately, my terrifying episode is what it took for me to wake up, realize that my perspective was way off base and make major modifications to my life. Talk about learning the hard way. Hopefully you are not nearly this stubborn and can find a better way to transform your perspective without the assistance of an MRI machine and the threat of a looming brain tumor. Just run through the three steps of the perspective-changing process and you will be amazed by the results.

We have reached the point where congratulations are in order! You have now completed Part I and are beginning to develop a solid foundation for your life. I am so glad that you chose not to ignore this crucial phase. However, you must do more than just read about foundation-building in this book to experience authentic success. You now have to go out there and build a solid foundation for yourself by striving to: (1) develop a better work ethic, (2) solidify your character, (3) set priorities and goals and (4) obtain the proper perspective on life. If you get lazy and want to stop before properly developing your foundation, just remember what happens to structures built on weak foundations and get out of the way.

Part II moves from developing a solid foundation to preparing for authentic success. Here, you will be encouraged to act like a professional regardless of your career field. You will learn how to think at the highest of levels which allows you to learn more effectively and solve the most difficult problems you face. You will ponder the term consistent persistence and the idea that you do not have to be the smartest or hardest-working person in the room to be authentically successful. You will read about a recession-proofed life and I will urge you to become more flexible in your career choices, become a jack of many trades and become irreplaceable. Finally, you will receive a unique tool to manage your time appropriately and to consider your priorities and the effort involved with each task you undertake. It is essential that you incorporate each of these tools into your life before you attempt to achieve success in each of your daily endeavors. You are ready. Onward!

Part Two:
Get Set!

Preparing for Authentic Success

"By failing to prepare, you are
preparing to fail."
--- **Benjamin Franklin**

"There are no secrets to success. It is the result
of preparation, hard work, and
learning from failure."
--- **Colin Powell**

"You cannot escape the responsibility of
tomorrow by evading it today."
--- **Abraham Lincoln**

CHAPTER 6:
PROFESSIONALISM

> "No individual has any right to go into the world and go out of it without leaving behind . . . distinct and legitimate reasons for having passed through it."
> --- GEORGE WASHINGTON CARVER
>
> "Whatever is true, whatever is noble, whatever is right, whatever is pure, whatever is lovely, whatever is admirable – if anything is excellent or praiseworthy – think about such things."
> --- PHILIPPIANS 4:8 (NEW INTERNATIONAL VERSION)

PROFESSIONALISM DEFINED

Professions are noble endeavors which: (1) are undertaken to protect valuable assets, (2) commonly involve extreme mental and emotional pressure and (3) require a great deal of character, intelligence and training. Historically, professions represented exclusive territory and were reserved for a small percentage of people society recognized as professionals. A professional was someone with extensive academic training who was licensed in a unique field governed by its own code of ethics.[18] Doctors, lawyers

---

[18] Historically, law, medicine and theology were considered the three primary professions. Another interesting characteristic of professions is that associations are often created within a profession to provide continuing educational services and, more recently, to lobby on behalf of the profession. This has occurred in the law via the American Bar Association and in medicine via the American Medical Association. Religion has its lobbying groups, but such groups are not as organized as law or medicine.

and religious leaders constituted the prototypical professional. Professionals also possessed strong fiduciary duties, or unwritten ethical mandates, requiring them to uphold a reasonable standard of care and loyalty in all of their professional endeavors. It was socially unacceptable for a professional to take on a client solely to reap a profit. She would also be expected to accept a client based on a desire to genuinely assist a person in need and to benefit the common good. If a conflict arose, being a professional meant that truth, fairness and loyalty come before financial gain. Therefore, lawyers would concern themselves with their client's case as well as the furtherance of justice and fairness while doctors would attempt to prevent a patient from experiencing bad health instead of only treating someone once a problem occurred. Professionals were expected to incorporate high ethical standards into their lives and to continually hone their professional skills. In the past, to be a professional was to be a part of something special. This philosophy encouraged the general public to trust professionals with their most valuable assets, including their lives, their souls, their freedom and their money.

In the twenty-first century, the ranks of professionals have expanded while professional standards have diminished. Aside from doctors, lawyers and religious leaders, contemporary professionals include accountants, athletes, comedians, engineers, financial analysts, nurses, teachers, technology specialists and veterinarians, just to name a few. Today's professionals are considered as such because they are specifically trained to apply their specialized knowledge to solve practical problems. This transformation and expansion of the professional realm has been beneficial to society because more people are undertaking more specialized training in their career fields and helping people in ways that were not possible in the past. This enhanced knowledge and dedication benefits individual clients and the common good. This expansion has the potential to make the world a far better place – that is, once the historical professional standards regain their proper place in society.

Problematically, however, time has eroded some of the major characteristics that previously identified a professional. The following are some of the principles that have been greatly diminished: (1) the concept that profit should not be the only motivation for going to work, (2) the duty of professionals to conduct themselves honorably and ethically and (3) the sense of fiduciary obligations to clients and to the common good. Every time we turn on the news, we witness stories of professional athletes who play the game solely for money, accountants and lawyers who cover up evidence and shred documents in order to keep the consulting and legal fees flowing, teachers who verbally and sexually abuse students and doctors who commit insurance fraud out of blatant greed. These "professionals" are putting their self-interest in front of the public interest and they are placing potential profits ahead of high ethical standards. We now live in a world where the general public has a hard time trusting its professionals.

How did such a philosophical shift occur? I believe that things started to change when professionals were encouraged to check their moral compasses at the workplace door. A new ethical and philosophical standard has emerged recently and revolves around the idea that a good professional is someone who is amoral and who best serves a constituency by respecting the autonomy of his clients. In other words, a professional is only acting as such by allowing the client to decide what is ethical. Today's professional may have ethical reservations about how to proceed but instead defers to the will – either moral or immoral – of the client up until the point such requests cross a legal boundary. This theory claims that because the client is the one making the moral decisions, all responsibility for any immoral decisions is removed from the professional and placed onto the client.

This new philosophy is problematic in my eyes. In fact, I am convinced that being a true professional does not allow you to check your moral compass at the workplace door. Once you set aside your ethical reservations, other less important things – like the potential for profits or winning at all costs – enter to fill the void. The world does not need any more self-interested and unethical professionals. Clients should not be allowed to dictate your performance or ask you to do your job in a legal, but unethical, manner. This is your life, your character and your reputation. A major part of being a professional is living an honorable and moral life. Once this is lost, the distinction of being a professional is all but gone.

Additionally, I am convinced that you cannot be truly content if you allow yourself to act immorally at work solely because your client requests it or your profession demands it. In fact, I argue that it is extremely difficult, if not impossible, to be amoral at work and to be moral outside of work. Humans are just not built that way. If we are dishonest, disloyal and mean-spirited at work, those qualities will carry over to our home lives. Think about who we take our anger and frustration out on when we have a bad day at school or at work. That's right, we usually take it out on the people we love the most – people who had nothing to do with our bad day in the first place. The professionals of the past would roll over in their graves if they knew what was happening to their beloved callings. We have strayed from the core of what it means to be a professional and need to find our way back.

WHAT DOES ANY OF THIS HAVE TO DO WITH ME?

At this point, you might be thinking, "I am not going into any of the career areas you mentioned above and, therefore, I will never be a professional; so why is this discussion at all relevant to me?" If you are feeling this way, you are exactly the type of person this discussion is targeted towards. People who are currently professionals already have the moral obligation to uphold the professional standards of the past. You, on the other hand, are not currently a professional and are the person I want to talk to about this subject.

The major point of this chapter is to encourage people who are not yet professionals or who are not going to enter professional career fields to act like professionals anyway. In other words, you should consider yourself to be a professional and uphold the highest of professional standards regardless of what you do for a living and regardless of what other people think. Strive to be concerned with more than just money. Instead, care about the common good, endeavor to treat the people you encounter as if you owe them a fiduciary duty of care and loyalty, utilize your character to hold yourself to a high standard of ethics and values and endeavor to be as good as you can be at what you do.

My motivation for encouraging you to act like a professional stems from my belief that no person has any right to "come into the world and go out of it without leaving behind . . . legitimate and distinct reasons for having passed through it."[19] You have something to offer this world and it is your duty to offer it before you pass on. Acting like a professional will give you a better chance to create this legacy because you will be focused on a worthy goal and dedicated to achieving that goal ethically. The remainder of the chapter will describe what it means to be a professional and provide you with the tools to begin acting like a professional right now. With your assistance, society can begin to regain what it has lost in terms of professionalism.

THE STORY OF THE IRON RING

The story of the iron ring embodies the essence of what it means to be a true professional. In Canada, you will find a group of engineers who have been honoring their profession in a meaningful way for nearly one hundred years. In the early 1900s, a group of Canadian engineers felt that the engineering profession needed common ethical standards as well as some type of ceremony to help

---

[19] George Washington Carver.

engineers across the country develop a closer bond to each other and to the profession. With these goals in mind, the group enlisted Rudyard Kipling – a famous author who commonly wrote about engineering in his stories and poems – to craft a special ceremony and an ethical creed. The ceremony Kipling created is a solemn proceeding, designed to welcome new engineers to the profession and to remind them of their obligations to each other and to society in general. Today, any Canadian engineer can choose to go through the *Calling of an Engineer* ceremony upon entering the profession. During the ceremony, engineers are encouraged to read the following statement of obligation:

> I am an Engineer, in my profession I take deep pride. To it I owe solemn obligations. Since the Stone Age, human progress has been spurred by the engineering genius. . . . Were it not for this heritage of accumulated experience, my efforts would be feeble.
>
> As an Engineer, I pledge to practice integrity and fair dealing, tolerance and respect, and to uphold devotion to the standards and the dignity of my profession, conscious always that my skill carries with it the obligation to serve humanity by making the best use of Earth's precious wealth.
>
> As an Engineer, in humility and with the need for Divine guidance, I shall participate in none but honest enterprises. When needed, my skill and knowledge shall be given without reservation for the public good. In the performance of duty and in fidelity to my profession, I shall give the utmost.

A unique part of this ceremony is the distribution of the iron rings. Any engineer who passes through the Calling ritual receives an iron ring. This ring must be worn on the little finger of the engineer's working hand. On the vast majority of people, because their right hand is their dominant hand, the iron ring is placed as far away as possible from their wedding band. As wedding bands are typically made of expensive metals such as gold, the distance between the iron ring and the gold signifies that the engineering profession is not overly consumed with money and luxury. The iron ring also symbolizes membership in the engineering profession, the hard work and training involved in becoming an engineer and the tragedies that befall engineering mistakes. Legend has it that the original rings were made with the iron from the Quebec Bridge in Canada – a bridge that collapsed in 1907 killing seventy-five people. The alleged cause of the devastating collapse was poor planning combined with several major engineering errors. Following the tragedy, both the accident and the profession were scrutinized in the national media and the public trust ebbed to a low point. Canadian engineers wear their iron rings to this day in remembrance of the Quebec Bridge collapse, to symbolize the trust that the public places in their profession and to recall the terrible things that can happen if they ever stop acting like professionals.

The story of the iron ring embodies the mentality all professionals should adopt. These Canadian engineers take their profession and its tremendous obligations very seriously. By making a solemn obligation to uphold the high standards of their profession and to work diligently for reasons other than the mere accumulation of money, these engineers understand the duties, devotion and integrity that come with being a professional. They also understand that they owe obligations to all of humanity because of their calling.

Remember, I am encouraging you to act like a professional as well. As such, you owe obligations to others and you must hold yourself to high ethical standards. These requirements are hard to satisfy and require a serious dedication and commitment. Unless you are an engineer, you likely do not have a solemn ritual and an iron ring to constantly encourage you in your efforts. In place of these things, what will you use to constantly remember your professional obligations in life? What is your iron ring?

YOUR OWN PROFESSIONAL CREED

Unfortunately, it is unlikely that you have something as cool as an iron ring to reinforce your professional duties in your mind. In its place and even if you find something equally symbolic, you need a creed. A creed is a statement that codifies your feelings and beliefs concerning a certain area of your life – in this case your career. As a professional, it is important that you offer the people you interact with some commitment about how you will treat them and how you will perform the basic functions of your job. The Lawyer's Creed below provides a nice, concise example for an attorney.

THE LAWYER'S CREED[20]

TO MY CLIENTS, I offer competence, faithfulness, diligence, and good judgment. I will strive to represent you as I would want to be represented and to be worthy of your trust.

TO THE OPPOSING PARTIES AND THEIR COUNSEL, I offer fairness, integrity, and civility. I will seek reconciliation and, if we fail to achieve it, I will make our dispute a dignified one.

TO THE COURTS, AND OTHER TRIBUNALS, AND TO THOSE WHO ASSIST THEM, I offer respect, truthfulness, and courtesy. I will strive to bring honor to the search for justice.

TO THE PROFESSION, I offer assistance. I will strive to keep our profession a high calling in the spirit of pro bono and public service.

TO THE PUBLIC, I offer service. I will strive to improve the law and our legal system, serving all equally, and to seek justice through the representation of my clients.

---

[20] This is the typical language of the lawyer's creed although the exact wording varies from example to example.

Your personal creed will have some of the same elements as this lawyer's creed, but will be based on your chosen career field. Instead of legal clients, opposing parties, courts and the legal profession, your creed may include slightly different stakeholders. A stakeholder is: (1) someone with an interest in the way you live your life or conduct your business and (2) someone who is or may be affected by your professional decisions. Corporations have various stakeholders in the form of shareholders, management, employees, customers, neighbors, governments and suppliers. Although companies are not legally required to concern themselves with the interests of their stakeholders, the most successful businesses understand that caring for these groups is in their overall best interest. In fact, I would argue that companies have an ethical obligation to protect the people within their sphere of influence by refusing to pollute the air and water, responding to valid concerns and helping improve the surrounding community. Happy stakeholders also make happy customers. You should feel the same way towards the important stakeholders in your life. These stakeholders often include your significant other, family, friends, colleagues, superiors and community. Part of your duty as a professional is to avoid injuring these parties through your decisions and actions.

For most of us, many different people have an interest in our professional success. Some care more than others, some care begrudgingly and others care whether they realize it or not. For example, your colleagues have an interest in your success because the better you perform on the job, the more likely your employer will succeed and they will keep their jobs, get promoted and receive bonuses. Your neighbors have an interest in you becoming a successful member of the community rather than a burden on society. Your family and friends have an interest in seeing someone they care for succeed professionally. Professional success allows your loved ones to spend their time enjoying your company rather than supporting you financially. The way you perform on the job and your overall career success will impact each of these stakeholder groups in one way or another. While you have no legal obligation, you are a professional and you owe these stakeholders at least an explanation of how you will conduct your professional life. Let your creed serve as this explanation. Within it, you need to include each stakeholder group mentioned above and make certain commitments about how you will act towards them each and every day. This creed is designed to serve as your iron ring – your continual reminder that you are a professional.

It is now time for you to craft your creed. The following creed template is modeled off of the Lawyer's Creed and is targeted towards each of the relevant stakeholders in a typical person's life. For each stakeholder, you will need to draft a corresponding commitment. This chart is merely hypothetical and intended to show you a few of the commitments you might want to make in your own personal creed. I encourage you to ponder the commitments below and then draft your own.

STAKEHOLDER	POTENTIAL COMMITMENT
SIGNIFICANT OTHER:	I offer love, care, compassion, faithfulness, friendship and honesty. I promise to put your interests ahead of my own and to work together to build our future.
FAMILY:	I offer love and respect. I will seek to work out any differences with compassion and understanding.
FRIENDS:	I offer assistance, loyalty, support and understanding. I will strive to be an active listener and will make time to build the relationship.
COLLEAGUES:	I offer courtesy, dedication, fairness and service. I will strive to maintain the highest ethical standards as I undertake my career.

COMMUNITY:	I offer my service. I will strive to leave behind me distinct and legitimate reasons for having passed through this world. I will seek to avoid becoming a burden on society and will treat people the way that I would want to be treated.

YOU WILL BE JUDGED

Thus far, this chapter has introduced the concept of a profession and the serious responsibilities inherent in being a professional. We talked about why the traditional purposes and fiduciary duties required of a professional are so important and should be retained. In this vein, I encouraged you to bring your moral compass into the workplace and think of yourself as a professional regardless of your chosen career field. Thinking of yourself as a professional helps you prepare to be authentically successful in your personal and professional life. Part of becoming a professional is the adoption of a professional creed and you were given an opportunity to craft a creed in the previous section. This mission statement for your life is designed to aid in your transition from amateur to professional and to be something that you can refer to anytime you need to find your bearings.

Your day-to-day existence as a professional, however, requires you to do more than understand the philosophy of professionalism, think of yourself in that light and adopt a professional creed. You must also incorporate a few key professional practices into your daily routine. In fact, your peers, colleagues, superiors and clients will judge you based on certain attributes expected of a professional. The remainder of this section describes some of the most important professional attributes upon which you will be judged such as:

- The quality of your handshake;
- The way you look;
- The way you speak;

- The way you think; and
- Your character and your professional virtues.

YOUR HANDSHAKE

"The evaluators rated the handshakers in eight areas: grip, temperature, dryness, strength, duration, vigor, texture of skin, and eye contact . . . We found that handshakes were related significantly and systematically to several personality characteristics [including] extroversion and emotional expressiveness . . . [and] a negative correlation between a firm handshake and shyness and neuroticism."
--- **DR. WILLIAM CHAPMAN, UNIVERSITY OF ALABAMA HANDSHAKE STUDY**

You likely realize that your handshake is important. But would you have thought that eye contact, the texture of your skin and the grip, temperature, dryness, strength, duration and vigor of your handshake are all important factors in making your handshake a professional one? In fact, a University of Alabama professor conducted a scientific study on handshakes that was published in the JOURNAL OF PERSONALITY AND SOCIAL PSYCHOLOGY. This study found that your handshake can tell someone else a great deal about you – even if you do not realize it at the time.[21] The study found

---

[21] The study involved psychology students analyzing the handshakes of 112 University of Alabama students. The study was well-accepted upon publication. "Results from the study generated worldwide media attention, as well over 100 newspaper and television outlets, including local, regional, national and international outlets picked up on the research. Stories on Chaplin's handshake research were spotted in the Los Angeles Times, USA Today, CNN, The London Times, the Chicago Tribune, The Sydney (Australia) Morning Herald and elsewhere." Chris Bryant, *Study Suggests Handshakes and Good Impressions Really Do Go Hand-in-Hand*, UNIVERSITY OF ALABAMA RESEARCH MAGAZINE ONLINE (Volume V, 2001), *available at* http://research.ua.edu/archive2001/handshakes.html. The precise citation for this study is: William Chaplin, Jeffrey Phillips, et

that firm handshakes exude confidence and extroversion and make a better first impression than do limp handshakes. Men had firmer handshakes than women, but women with firm handshakes made as good a first impression as men with firm handshakes. This is interesting because gender stereotypes generally bring about more favorable impressions for men than women with the same credentials and characteristics. The study also found that an improper handshake is not something that you can change without practice.

We all notice how awkward it is when someone shakes our hand with a limp wrist or with the fingers instead of the hand extended. These types of handshakes never make a good, professional impression. Then, there are the people who shake hands and avoid eye contact, the people who hold on for too long and the people who clasp on with both hands. As a professor, I shake hundreds of my students' hands during each academic term. Instead of just shaking hands, however, I take note of the good and bad aspects of each handshake. This informal study consistently shows that the handshakes of my female students are less firm than the handshakes of my male students. I also discovered that, although my male students have firmer handshakes, they still struggle with all of the elements of a professional handshake. The bottom line is that young people need better handshakes.

Improving your handshake requires you to master four key concepts. First, you must understand that your handshake is often the first contact you have with another person and can be the very first impression that you make. Positive impressions are made when you are able to give a solid handshake that people are impressed with upon receipt. At the very least, you want the people you meet to shake your hand and then forget about the handshake entirely. You must avoid the situations that occur when your handshake is

al., *Handshaking, Gender, Personality, and First Impressions*, 79 JOURNAL OF PERSONALITY AND SOCIAL PSYCHOLOGY 110 (2000).

unprofessional and other people take notice. The bottom line is that a handshake, in and of itself, will not seal any deal, or get you very far, but it can set a positive tone for the beginning of the relationship.

Second, people are expecting certain qualities in a professional handshake such as firmness, warmth and simultaneous eye contact. You want to meet these expectations without exceeding them. For instance, a handshake can be too firm and too warm and you can make so much eye contact that the situation becomes awkward. Remember, you are shaking hands and not embracing in a romantic relationship. Find the middle ground with your professional handshake.

The third concept that you have to master is that developing a professional handshake requires a great deal of practice and forethought. Studies have shown that a person's handshake will not change unless that person makes a dedicated effort to change it. Like most of the important things in life, practice makes perfect. Therefore, practice shaking hands with your friends so that you get it right when it really matters. On this note, women need to firm up their handshakes in order to make as good an impression as men and men need to improve their handshakes in general.

Fourth and finally, professionals are expected to possess professional handshakes. This means that none of the advice I have just given you is optional. With this in mind, you need to begin working on your new, professional handshake today.

YOUR APPEARANCE

> "The biggest fool in the world is he who does his work
> supremely well, without attending to appearance."
> --- MICHAEL KORDA

Your appearance matters. People will judge you as a professional, for better or worse, based on your physical appearance. Your appearance includes the way you dress, groom yourself, style your hair, sit and stand. These same people will also make a determination as to whether you are pleasant to look at or not and use each of these judgments to form an impression about you. I wish I could tell you that none of these physical characteristics really matter and that what you are made of is the only thing that's important. The problem is that I just cannot say that with a straight face in the world that we live in today.

Although I personally place far more weight on the content of someone's character than on their appearance, I still believe that an individual's appearance says something about that person. Beyond my personal feelings, it is human nature for people to make these superficial judgments. And, no matter how hard we try to change this nature, these types of judgments are going to be made all of the time and are generally going to carry a great deal of weight. Neglecting your appearance under the theory of "if they can't appreciate the way I look, then I don't want to do business with them," will only cause you to suffer. Until things change, it is a good idea to present a professional image in terms of your appearance. A professional appearance requires you to: (1) be physically fit, (2) wear clothes that fit the occasion, fit you and look nice and (3) tend to your grooming habits.

YOUR PHYSICAL FITNESS

Someone who is in good physical shape generally looks good and feels good about herself. In fact, physical fitness provides many benefits such as increased energy and endurance. People think more highly of people who are in good physical condition. This does not mean that you have to train for triathlons. Rather, you may choose to exercise regularly by lifting weights, playing a sport, jogging or otherwise breaking a sweat. When you do not exercise, you automatically become less healthy and less physically fit. Over time, it becomes harder and harder to undertake typical activities, such as walking up a flight of stairs, without breathing heavily. Your muscles do not grow and you end up getting much weaker as you age. Because you do not burn the excess calories you take in, you begin to gain weight in all the wrong places.

It's not just you – if you look at the country in general, America is becoming less and less healthy. Even the United States Surgeon General has chimed into the argument in a report to Congress where he stated:

> As Surgeon General, I welcome this chance to talk [to Congress] about a health crisis affecting every state, every city, every community, and every school across our great nation. The crisis is obesity. It's the fastest-growing cause of disease and death in America. And it's completely preventable. Nearly two out of every three Americans are overweight or obese. One out of every eight deaths in America is caused by an illness directly related to [being] overweight and [to] obesity.[22]

---

[22] Richard Carmona, *The Obesity Crisis in America*, TESTIMONY BEFORE THE SUBCOMMITTEE ON EDUCATION REFORM COMMITTEE ON EDUCATION AND THE WORKFORCE, UNITED STATES HOUSE OF REPRESENTATIVES (July 16, 2003).

To counter this disturbing trend, the United States government encourages you to exercise at least thirty minutes a day, five days per week.[23] For those of you who are exceptionally busy, thirty minutes a day can be hard to come by. Each day presents new challenges and finding the time to exercise lapses into ceasing to look for the time to exercise. Over time, you will find yourself extremely out of shape. You need to bite the bullet and make the commitment to tend to your physical health and fitness – your body will thank you for it and perform well for you in the future.

Another important part of your physical fitness is your diet. If you eat unhealthy foods most of the time, you will be less healthy as your diet is a key component to your overall physical health. The bottom line is that there are a few primary reasons why unhealthy people are unhealthy: (1) they are too busy to exercise, (2) they have a physically unhealthy diet or (3) they have no desire to exercise or eat more healthily. None of these reasons inspires much confidence in the people you work with, the people you meet or the people who interview you for a job. Your goal is to present yourself as a physically fit professional and the way you get there is by exercising at least thirty minutes a day, five days a week and by committing yourself to a healthier diet.

YOUR CLOTHES

Do you have any idea what business casual means? If not, you're not alone. However, the fact that you are not sure what to wear for a specific occasion does not give you an excuse to dress poorly or otherwise neglect your appearance. Your clothes should do three things: (1) fit the tenor of the occasion, (2) fit you and, most importantly, (3) make you look like someone another person would want to associate with. People who wear a wrinkled shirt, pants that

---

[23] The President's Challenge, *Taking Part in the active Lifestyle Program*, *available at* http://www.presidentschallenge.org/the_challenge/active_lifestyle.aspx (last visited January 15, 2007).

are too short, or a dangling shoelace are saying something to the rest of the world – they are basically saying "I'm not really sure about my ability to succeed in social situations," "I do not care what people think of me" or "I do not put enough of my resources into my appearance." None of these statements will build confidence in your professional abilities. In fact, such an impression is dangerous and will encourage people to take their business to someone else – someone who is more put-together. It is also true in general that someone who dresses sloppily has other sloppy characteristics. Make sure that you dress for success.

YOUR GROOMING HABITS, PIERCINGS AND TATTOOS

You will also be judged by your grooming. Every time I interview someone, the first thing I notice when they walk in the room is their grooming habits. If they have a tongue ring, I notice it. If they have a visible tattoo, I notice it. If they are not clean-shaven, I notice it. I notice all of these things before that person ever says a word. This does not mean that someone with a tongue ring, tattoo or facial hair will not get the job. In fact, I am all for you being your own person. I am, however, looking for a professional that my clients will want to work with. I mentioned earlier that the world expects certain characteristics from its professionals regardless of how well they do their jobs. Without clients, my business is bankrupt and, therefore, I need to take their concerns into consideration. So, be careful with your grooming habits, piercings and tattoos and make sure you present yourself as a professional.

THE WAY YOU SPEAK

> "She had lost the art of conversation but not, unfortunately, the power of speech." --- **GEORGE BERNARD SHAW**

Have you ever met someone who talks a lot but has very little to say? Have you ever listened to someone with horrible grammar or poor word usage? What about someone who is so quiet that you struggle to make sense of what they are saying or someone who speaks so loudly that it hurts your brain to listen? The types of people who fall into these categories need to learn to speak more professionally. I encourage my students to practice this crucial skill constantly and to continually seek improvement. Speaking well requires you to do the following things very well:

1. Speak slowly, clearly and audibly;
2. Enunciate your words;
3. Avoid speaking in monotone by working on your voice inflection;
4. Choose your words carefully and strategically;
5. Make sure that the words you speak actually express the point you are trying to make;
6. Speak in an organized manner and with a certain flow; and
7. Use impeccable grammar and avoid misconjugating your verbs and using slang or folksy talk (including the word "ain't").

This is a lot to fix – especially if you have never thought about the way that you speak. However, you must remember that you are a professional and professionals must speak well to be successful. This takes a great deal of practice and dedication. I have personally witnessed smart students who are terrible speakers (and not just poor public speakers, but also poor speakers in one-on-one conversations) improve drastically in a ten-week period. These students focused their attention on the seven concepts listed above every time they found themselves in a conversation. Give this a try, but expect to struggle throughout this process. Fortunately, you can also expect great gains if you can meet the challenge of becoming a more professional speaker.

THE WAY YOU THINK

"What's on your mind, if you'll forgive the overstatement?" - --FRED ALLEN

Is there anything on your mind? Let me ask this question in a different way: Is there anything worth having on your mind on your mind? I have entered conversations with numerous people and then walked away when they were over thinking, "this person has absolutely nothing on his mind" or "what was she thinking?" If you are dedicated to reading this book, I assume that there is at least something important on your mind. In that case, a better set of questions for you would be: (1) do you know how to think and (2) can you critically analyze a situation and then come up with an effective solution? The ability to think is not the same as the ability to memorize and regurgitate. What I am really asking is as follows: can you take a complex intellectual or moral problem and think through its implications in such a way that you make an excellent decision? Chapter Seven is dedicated completely to honing your ability to think and, therefore, I will not belabor the issue here. At this point, I merely want you to understand that part of being a professional is the ability to think.

In order for people to respect your intelligence as a professional, you must be able to think critically and quickly to come up with the correct answer most of the time. If you are poor at thinking and forming conclusions, three things will happen to you throughout your career: (1) you will make more mistakes than you need to, (2) you will lose confidence and (3) people will stop supplying you with work or trusting in your judgment. In combination, these three things have the potential to force you out of your chosen career and into something less stimulating and challenging. We will discuss this issue in much more detail ahead in Chapter Seven.

YOUR CHARACTER AND YOUR PROFESSIONAL VIRTUES

> "Always do right – this will gratify some and astonish the rest." --- MARK TWAIN

Are you an ethical person? Have you developed a solid character as part of your foundation? These are questions that you were asked to answer in Chapter Three and I hope that your development process is well under way. There is yet another reason why you need to develop a solid character and abide by life's virtues and the Golden Rule. Simply put, professionalism requires it.

It should come as no surprise that people will judge you by your character. In fact, your character shines through just as brightly as your outward appearance. If you are dishonest, disloyal, self-interested or uncompassionate, people will sense it within a brief period of time. This feeling will quickly turn into a negative judgment of you. Once this type of negative impression is formed, it will be tough to overcome. First impressions can never be taken back and people rely on them throughout the beginning stages of any relationship. Additionally, we live in an interconnected world where people in the same field tend to know each other. For instance, I receive calls all of the time from potential employers seeking a reference for a lawyer-applicant at their law firm. They say things like, "You went to Duke, do you know so and so?" or "You worked at this law firm with Susan, is she a hard worker?" and often "What type of person is she?" I always tell the truth and sometimes all I have to go on is a first or a second impression. I am not alone; people who think poorly of you will tell other people about you and people who think you are solid will brag about you. This can make the difference between being employed and continuing your job search. Always remember my advice in Chapter Three that your character counts and it always will. This statement is especially true when you hold yourself out as a professional.

In addition to developing a solid character which people can judge you by, there are a plethora of professional virtues that you need to incorporate into your life. Similar to the virtues detailed in Chapter Three, professional virtues are virtues that everyone should strive to obtain, but which are especially important in the life of a professional. Make certain that you strive for the Golden Mean of every possible virtue and focus a bit harder on these professional virtues in the process. Examine the list below and, as you did in Chapter Three, place a mark on each virtue spectrum in the area that best describes your life:

- DILIGENCE
- TACT
- MAGNANIMITY

- PERSEVERANCE
- EFFECTIVENESS
- PRUDENCE

Extreme - not diligent

DILIGENCE

Extreme - too diligent

| CARELESS | | MICROMANAGER |

Extreme – not enough tact

TACT

Extreme – too much tact

| BLUNT | | OVER-HESITANT |

Extreme – not
enough
perseverance

Extreme – too
much
perseverance

PERSEVERANCE

| **QUITTER** | | **OVERLY-DETERMINED** |

Extreme - not
effective

Extreme - too
effective

EFFECTIVENESS

| **UNPRODUCTIVE** | | **OVERLY-AMBITIOUS** |

Extreme - not
prudent

Extreme - too
prudent

PRUDENCE

| **UNWISE** | | **SHREWD** |

Extreme – not
magnanimous

Extreme – too
magnanimous

MAGNANIMITY

| **SELFISH** | | **PUSHOVER** |

WELCOME TO THE CLUB!

Professionals possess great responsibilities and should act accordingly. They should be virtuous and shoot for the Golden Mean of as many virtues as they can as often as possible. In particular, professionals should be compassionate, diligent, effective, honest, magnanimous, prudent and tactful. Professionals should take their career obligations seriously and always act with an eye towards the common good. They should exercise the utmost care and loyalty towards the people they serve and constantly try to improve their own abilities – all while exhibiting an honorable character. They should recognize that the twenty-first century brought with it a diminished standard of professional responsibility and join the fight against further decline. Acting in this manner will make you a part of something noble, something special. You must also understand that professional qualities are qualities that everyone should possess. Therefore, I encourage you to act like a professional regardless of whether or not your chosen career field falls within society's common definition of a profession.

Start this process by understanding all that society requires of its professionals. The next step is to craft a professional creed. This is your iron ring, your mission statement for your professional life. Make sure your creed embodies high ethical standards, fiduciary duties and a desire for self-improvement. Look at your creed often and heed its advice. Then, understand that you will be judged on the quality of your handshake, the way you look, the way you speak, the way you think, the content of your character and on your professional virtues all throughout your life. Recognize that professionals are expected to excel in each of these areas. Once you master these principles and act like a professional, you will be part of the solution instead of part of the problem. Your actions will help repair the damaged reputation of noble professionalism; your presence on the scene will help revitalize professionalism to its prior lofty perch. Welcome to the club!

CHAPTER 7:
LEARNING TO THINK, THINKING TO LEARN

> "All the problems of the world could be settled if people were only willing to think. The trouble is that people very often resort to all sorts of devices in order not to think, because thinking is such hard work."
> --- THOMAS J. WATSON
>
> "An investment in knowledge pays the best interest."
> --- BENJAMIN FRANKLIN
>
> "Wisdom begins in wonder."
> --- SOCRATES
>
> "Learning is not attained by chance; it must be sought for with ardor and attended to with diligence."
> --- ABIGAIL ADAMS

THE POWER OF THINKING

Thinking is extraordinarily powerful. The ability to think allows you to shine in places where less-accomplished people stumble. When you are able to think, you are able to solve difficult problems effectively, gain the authentic respect of others and save valuable time. Thinking transforms you into an asset, someone who is invaluable to any professional community and to the world in general. And, because very few people are very good at thinking, this ability will make you a scarce asset as well. Thinkers move beyond mere memorization to higher, more challenging levels of knowledge and possess the ability to comprehend, analyze and evaluate life's toughest problems. The work product of a thinker positively influences the intellectual capital, reputation and bottom line of any company. Most importantly, thinkers help save the world. They cure diseases, save lives, interpret the law and advocate for justice, advance technology, stimulate the economy and help humanity in general. Of all the preparations necessary for authentic success, the concept of learning to think and thinking to learn is the most important.

You must first learn how to think before thinking about learning anything. Your brain is smart, but it still needs to be trained to do something with all of the information it collects on a daily basis. In other words, information continually enters your head but your brain needs to know what to do with it from that point forward. Thinking is the catalyst that jumpstarts your brain into dealing with this information effectively.

You can train your brain to conduct two types of thinking: (1) low-level thinking and (2) high-level thinking. Low-level thinking occurs when people inhale information, memorize it and regurgitate it in some form or another. Low-level thinking is basically just rote memorization. When memorizers are forced to synthesize their thoughts or apply the information to real-world situations, they find themselves stuck. Their brain tries to processes this information into a more orderly and effective manner, but to no avail. Unable to form a respectable answer, low-level thinkers lose credibility and become frustrated. The time they spent memorizing was wasted because no real learning actually took place. At the end of the day, low-level thinking is not enough. High-level thinking, on the other hand, occurs when you are able to analyze, synthesize and evaluate any piece of information that you encounter. Memorization alone is not an option in this type of thinking. In other words, high-level thinkers are able to take information and do something useful with it like solve a problem or save the world.

When I refer to the idea of learning how to think, I am talking about beginning your transition from a low-level to a high-level thinker. This is a monumental task and requires you to alter your learning behavior. This transition process begins with an understanding of the different categories of thinking and ends when you have trained your brain to think effectively in each of these different ways. Before we jump into the specifics of learning behavior, however, it is important to witness the difference between a memorizer and a thinker.

DIFFERENTIATING BETWEEN A MEMORIZER AND A THINKER

There is a big difference between someone who has learned to think and someone who has not and between someone who can synthesize and evaluate a problem and someone who can merely understand that a problem exists. People are impressed with the higher-level thinker and are disappointed with the lower-level thinker. This is just the way the real world works. Examine the cases of Maria and Theresa below and you will surely recognize the distinction between the two types of thinkers and why it is important in your life.

Maria the Memorizer

Meet Maria. Maria is intelligent and has a mind like a steel trap – information going into her brain, stays in her brain for extended periods of time. These characteristics enhance her ability to memorize facts and regurgitate them back on examinations or to her boss. In fact, her memorization skills have become so proficient that she graduated high school with a 3.7 GPA and was regarded as one of the top students in the senior class. Similar to many high school students, Maria spent very little time studying outside of school hours. On the off chance that she did study, she merely read and reread her notes and textbook until she memorized each of the key terms and concepts. During examinations, Maria would recite the definitions word for word and would solve the predictable fact patterns using her memorized information. These questions never really forced her to think. If she ever came across a question requiring some critical thinking she would usually miss it but such wrong answers were never enough to hurt her overall examination score or her GPA. Her memorization skills were more than sufficient at this level. Maria utilized a similar tactic when it came time to study for the SAT test. She spent hours memorizing definitions of different words and study tactics for the test and was able to achieve an average score. Her high GPA allowed Maria to be accepted to a private university on the East Coast a few months later. She had memorized her way through high school and she felt that college would present the same opportunity.

Because of her carefully-honed memorization system, her above-average common sense and her reputation for being intelligent, Maria was confident that she would be set up well for the future. Unfortunately, this assessment was dead wrong. Maria is in big trouble. You see, Maria has not learned to think. In fact, the thought has not even crossed her mind. Her strategy served her well in the short-term and she currently has no reason to change her modus operandi. Unfortunately, as problems in her life become much tougher – as they undoubtedly will in college and in the real world – memorization alone will not be enough.

Things started to go bad in college as Maria began to experience some academic problems. For the first three weeks of class, Maria would show up for lectures, check her e-mail for an hour on her laptop and take down a few notes – basically, everything she was accustomed to doing in her high school classes. She read her assignments through once in order to prepare for the first quiz. Throughout the text, she would stop and memorize key words and concepts. Unfortunately for Maria, her first college quiz required more than her memorization skills could provide. The questions did not ask for the recitations of mere definitions or easy concepts and all of the fact patterns were obfuscated in ways she had never imagined. These examinations were nothing like her high school tests. She blew the first quiz and vowed to study harder for the next one. Problematically and predictably, her results on the second quiz remained the same.

Things became worse during her first summer internship with a prominent clothing retailer. She was placed on a team assembled to develop a marketing strategy for her new employer. Although she was able to memorize key marketing terms, concepts and market analysis statistics in her business marketing class, she found it tough to remember this information in the summer – a good five weeks after the class had ended. She was basically useless when her group brainstormed creative concepts for a retail marketing strategy or looked at marketing in a way that she had not been taught. While the group was busy thinking, Maria felt out of sorts. She offered no assistance and worried that she would not be asked back to fill the one internship slot available the following summer. Unfortunately for Maria, Theresa was also on her project team.

Theresa the Thinker

Meet Theresa. Theresa is a moderately smart person. Unlike Maria, Theresa does not have the ability to memorize large amounts of information and definitely cannot regurgitate it back on quizzes and exams. In order for Theresa to succeed as a student, she needed to find a different strategy. After attempting the memorization and regurgitation strategy and failing, Theresa realized that she was going to have to actually understand and apply the information she was taught. Therefore, she spent hours actively reading her textbooks and intently listening to her lectures. After each class session, Theresa spent some time trying to understand what she just read or heard. She would put her notes away and, a few hours later, attempt to recall the information. She would think through the concepts and the practice examples. When faced with a different fact pattern, she was able to think through the dilemma and discover a correct answer.

She found that she scored well on her college quizzes and she even felt like the college questions were easier to answer than the high school questions requiring memorization alone. During her summer internship, she was able to assist her team in a way that Maria could not. The two interns were the same age and, on paper, Maria looked like a much smarter person. Reality proved different, however, as Theresa's ability to think made her a much more successful college student as well as a more valuable asset to her team during her internship. Maria's memorization got her through high school successfully but, in the real world, she is sure to find herself in a difficult situation. On the other hand, Theresa's ability to think will help get her through the rest of her life successfully.

LOW-LEVEL AND HIGH-LEVEL THINKING

A common way to start learning how to think is to analyze Professor Benjamin Bloom's taxonomy of learning behavior – one of the gold standards in the educational community. Created in 1956, Bloom's categories describe the different types of learning behavior and lay out the steps necessary for someone to become a high-level thinker. Bloom's Taxonomy, as it is commonly known, consists of three separate categories of learning: (1) Cognitive (knowledge), (2) Affective (attitude) and (3) Psychomotor (physical skills). Although all three categories are interesting, the cognitive category is most relevant to our discussion in a chapter all about thinking and is the only category that we will discuss here.

Bloom's cognitive taxonomy has gone through rigorous analysis and at least one reincarnation since 1956, yet it has withstood the test of time. Although a detailed analysis of its functions and implications is outside of the scope of this chapter, a brief introduction and explanation of each cognitive category is appropriate. The following chart presents the levels and categories from the original version of Bloom's Taxonomy followed by a description of each.

LEVEL	COGNITIVE CATEGORY	CATEGORY DESCRIPTION
1	KNOWLEDGE	Retain and recall pieces of information
2	COMPREHENSION	Understand and interpret meaning of knowledge
3	APPLICATION	Use knowledge and comprehension to solve real world issues
4	ANALYSIS	Analyze specific principles and interrelationships of information
5	SYNTHESIS	Create new meanings from information
6	EVALUATION	Strategically review the effectiveness of informational concepts

View this chart from the top down and notice that as the numbers increase, the learning behavior becomes more advanced. High-level thinking does not occur until you move past the first three categories. Unfortunately, you cannot move to a higher level without becoming proficient at the lower levels of thinking. You must also understand that, as you move upwards towards more advanced levels of learning, you do not leave the other levels behind. These lower levels of learning are important and remain integral parts of your thinking process. In a few situations, such as running errands or taking a message, all you need to do is memorize pieces of information. The vast majority of situations, however, will require you to utilize the higher-level categories in tandem with the lower-level categories. The tougher the problem, the more categories of thinking you will need to utilize to come up with a workable solution.

THE SIX CATEGORIES OF THINKING

You might ask, "How do all these grand concepts work in the real world?" Maybe you are also wondering how the higher levels of learning behavior build off of the lower levels to transform a person from a low-level thinker into a high-level thinker. The following real world example will help answer these tough questions. More importantly, if you thought about asking questions similar to the two above, you are already thinking about learning how to think! Congratulations!

Assume that you are a first-year associate in a law firm and have just received your first big assignment. A senior partner recently e-mailed you a lengthy article on the recent recession and the many corporate governance problems associated with the tough economic times. The article focused on corporate crime and the executives who were accused of bilking their investors and companies out of billions of dollars. The author also discussed the role of the criminal justice system and the idea of sending white collar criminals to prison for long periods of time. The article spent many pages lamenting the idea that contemporary juries seem to have a harder time convicting someone of a white collar crime then convicting someone of a crime involving violence. Your law firm feels that the laws in your state targeting white collar crime are much too lenient and much less restrictive than similar laws in nearby states. Your boss represents the State Bar Association and has been asked to write a proposal urging the state legislature to tighten up the laws punishing white collar criminals. You have been asked to read the article, assess the law in your state on the issue, compare your state to other states and craft an argument to give your boss some ammunition to use in the proposal. You need to draft a memorandum answering these questions and your deadline is tomorrow at noon.

You have a lot of work ahead of you and the first thing you do is panic. This type of reaction is normal for someone who just received a tough assignment. Once you settle down, it is imperative that you determine how to work through the various questions you have been asked and then answer them correctly and effectively. Time is of the essence. Under this type of pressure, thinkers thrive and non-thinkers perish. The following section will utilize your looming memorandum project to examine the six categories of thinking so that you can see how the process works. Through this exercise, you will also be able to determine whether you are currently a low-or a high-level thinker. We will start with category one and talk about knowledge.

KNOWLEDGE

The first category in the taxonomy is knowledge – basically, the ability to retain and recall information. Most everyone in their teens or older is relatively proficient in this level of thinking. Such people are able to memorize pieces of information and then recall this information for a period of time. In fact, this is how many people get through high school and the early years of their life. They are a lot like Maria.

An examination of your memorandum project clearly demonstrates why knowledge is the lowest-level of thinking possible. In this category, there are two tasks that you have to accomplish. First, you must read the article and highlight the author's points about white collar crime, white collar criminals and the recent conviction statistics. Second, you must read the laws of a few other states in this area. You can probably accomplish these tasks within an hour or two. While this form of thinking is acceptable under this category, it is really nothing more than rote memorization. You are not really adding anything of value to your project.

During this stage, if your boss comes to your office and asks you only for the basic facts and statistics from the article, you're all set. You will be able to recall this information and get through this simple conversation. As soon as your boss asks you something outside of the scope of the article or something requiring more than mere memorization, however, you will find yourself stuck and without an adequate answer. No offense, but much more thinking is required if you are to adequately complete this project. Besides, the chances are that your boss already knows the facts and is looking for something much deeper – your boss is looking for some good, old-fashioned, on-target advice. Once you demonstrate that you haven't got a clue, your boss will turn to someone else to complete the project and likely question why you were hired in the first place. Keep in mind that this memorandum is a relatively easy assignment to begin with – especially compared to the large cases you will be expected to handle within the next few years. Limiting your thinking to the knowledge category is not enough.

COMPREHENSION

Having conquered the knowledge category, you are now officially authorized to move on to category two – comprehension. Instead of reading and attempting to recall specific pieces of information, comprehension requires you to decipher meaning from various pieces of information. Comprehending is determining the point behind the information. In the case of our example, comprehension requires you to ask the following types of questions: "What was the article all about?" "Why was the author so concerned that corporate criminals seem to be adjudicated not guilty more often than violent criminals?" "Are white collar criminals different in any way?" "Are their victims?"

This is only the second step, but you are moving far away from the idea of memorization. Now, you are actually taking some meaning from the words and concepts that enter your brain. You should be able to summarize the article that you read without looking at it for guidance. You should begin to look beyond the actual words you read and into their implications. This is a great start to the project, but it is still not enough. You are not yet able to apply what you have learned to the public policy issues lurking behind the laws in your state and you are not even close to being ready to come up with a solution. Your boss will want much more. Therefore, we must move on to the application stage.

APPLICATION

The application category requires you to move from the ability to summarize information to the ability to solve a real world problem. You may certainly utilize your knowledge and comprehension skills at this stage, but only as tools to supplement your thought process. Neither of these lower-level categories can assist you in applying your knowledge to the issue at hand. You now need to use the information in a different way than it was provided to you in the article. The author of the article was concerned with white collar laws and convictions in general and you are concerned with white collar laws and convictions in your state as compared to other states. Problematically, the article did not even mention your state. You need to take what you have read and apply it effectively to your specific set of facts.

While a low-level thinker would be stuck here, someone proficient at the application stage will be able to detach the relevant information from the article and apply it to a different situation. If you can handle this, you are adding something of your own to the mix and are finally getting somewhere. At this stage, you can begin to think about the questions that you have been asked and cull information from the article that applies to your situation. At this stage, you are advancing but you are not fully prepared to complete the project successfully. You have yet to break down the information into different categories, synthesize it together or create a strategic plan to fix the problem. These more difficult tasks are reserved for categories four through six – the higher levels of thinking.

ANALYSIS

This high-level thinking category requires you to be able to analyze and compare specific principles and pieces of information. At this stage in the process, you must be able to break down the information into its component parts and start to make sense of the details. Which pieces of information go into which category and why? How do the different pieces of information relate to each other? How are they different? This is a good place to experiment with your opinion on the matter at hand.

In our example, you are now ready to compare and contrast the typical white collar defendant to other types of defendants. You can take the laws of different states and break them down into their individual components to determine why they were drafted in such a manner. You also need to be able to break out key concepts, such as the various motivations for white collar crime as compared to the various motivations for violent crime, to determine if the two should be punished differently. You should also be able to see the merits or demerits of the argument and either criticize or praise its author. The ability to analyze information in this fashion is a skill that is in high demand in the real world.

SYNTHESIS

The fifth category of thinking requires that you be able to piece together or synthesize new meanings from the various pieces of information you are dealing with. The goal is to find a pattern in this information where no pattern was clearly defined beforehand. You are also expected to make some predictions. At this stage, information from other, unrelated experiences in your life can be utilized to assist you.

Corporations seek to synthesize their business models and strategies all of the time in an effort to stay ahead of the competition and create cutting edge products and services. For example, a company like Nike is able to deftly create innovative new shoe designs and then package them with the endorsement of famous professional athletes while, at the same time, tailoring an advertising budget specifically towards profitable target markets. Nike is able to synthesize information concerning its customer demographics, athlete profiles and primary products into an effective marketing package. Nike seeks patterns in consumer behavior and the world of sports and attempts to predict the desires of its customers. This ability to synthesize effectively has made Nike one of the most successful companies in the world.

It is doubtful that a first-year lawyer will be able to synthesize as effectively as a big corporation. However, you are trying to craft a legal argument and not compete with Adidas. This makes your job much different and a bit easier. Your boss has asked you to synthesize the American criminal justice system and its response to white collar crime. The goal is to determine whether the laws in your state are consistent with the laws in other states and whether there is a pattern as to why juries are not convicting white collar criminals at the same rate as violent criminals. You must take this information and create a strategic plan to take to the state legislature in an effort to strengthen the laws targeting white collar crime.

You can only make an accurate judgment in this regard if you can bring together the many different factors that might make a difference in the conviction rates you learned about. A few examples you may want to synthesize are the lack of violence in a white collar crime, the difficulty of proving injury and the sympathetic nature of a white collar crime versus a violent crime. If you can find a pattern in this information and show decision-makers how the law is currently being applied, you can begin to make an argument for or against the tightening of white collar crime statutes. This is important stuff and your project is almost done.

EVALUATION

The sixth and final rung on the thinking ladder is the evaluation category. At this uppermost stage, you must be able to effectively evaluate the entire swath of information you have been presented with and create a strategic plan to move forward. Use everything you have gleaned from the other levels of thinking to formulate this argument. You must be able to see both sides of the issue at this point in an unbiased manner. Keep in mind that the more accurate and effective your evaluation is at this stage, the better. Unfortunately, creating an original plan or concept from a base of information is the most difficult part of the entire thinking process. However, if you can think well enough to come up with at least a few ideas that: (1) are cost-efficient, (2) can be executed and (3) will ultimately succeed, you will find yourself submitting a successful project.

Incorporating this final step into our legal argument example represents the most critical piece of the puzzle. Now that you have read the article, comprehended its thesis, applied the information to your situation, analyzed each different aspect and synthesized the concepts, you are finally ready to craft an argument for your partner to use in front of the state legislature. You should now be able to draft a memorandum either for or against the tightening of laws targeting white collar crime. You should also be able to use the facts and statistics you have gathered from your background reading to supplement this argument and give it the necessary credibility. You can either use the article your partner gave you as a shining example bolstering your point or as an example of a misguided argument.

This is really what your boss was looking for the whole time. You were not able to jump right to this stage, however, because it is nearly impossible to create a successful argument dealing with a difficult issue without running through the other five steps in the thinking process. There is a good reason why the creation of a unique, effective and accurate argument is the ultimate step. A bad decision at this stage can present a great deal of negative consequences – especially if your plan is based off of faulty or old information or if it gets shot down too easily by its critics. You cannot send your boss to the state legislature armed with a poor argument. By making excellent decisions in these situations, you will put yourself in good graces at your workplace and transform yourself into a key player for future projects. As you can see, there is a lot riding on your ability to think.

THE REAL WORLD EXPECTS YOU TO THINK

When you leave the protective nest of the educational environment and venture out into the real world, you will quickly encounter some harsh truths. The real world and the people who run it are not as nurturing or caring as you may believe at this stage in your life. For better or for worse, these people have jobs to do and they tend to have a low tolerance for silly mistakes or an inability to complete tasks effectively. They care about your work ethic, character and professionalism. They also care a great deal about your ability to think. Your boss, your colleagues and your clients will invariably expect you to think quickly and on your feet. They will also demand an accurate answer to any question within a relatively short period of time.

When you receive a real world assignment, merely reciting back statistics and concepts will never get the job done adequately. You are expected to be able to think far more broadly than that. This is not a double standard. People in the real world spend a great deal of time thinking. For example, Bill Gates takes two "Think Weeks" every year. During this time, he secludes himself away from his work and just thinks. He thinks about the current and future state of Microsoft, ponders suggestions for improvement from his employees and considers the future of technology.

Thinking is a habit you need to become very comfortable with. Start by locating where your current comfort level lies on Bloom's Taxonomy. If you find your ability to think hovering around categories one and two, you have some major catching up to do. Your goal is to become comfortable with the requirements at every level of the taxonomy. For every problem you face from now on, you need to be able to gather the information, understand its meaning, effectively apply it to real world situations, break it down and analyze its components, synthesize it with similar information to come up with new knowledge and be able to evaluate its short- and long-term implications and craft an argument. Only then will you be considered a valuable asset in the real world. Once you can think, you can begin to learn and to solve difficult problems. Therefore, I encourage you to be diligent, be intelligent, be valuable – become a thinker.

CHAPTER 8:
CONSISTENT PERSISTENCE

"The secret of success is constancy of purpose."
--- **BENJAMIN DISRAELI**

"Nothing in this world can take the place of persistence. Talent will not; nothing is more common than unsuccessful people with talent. Genius will not; unrewarded genius is almost a proverb. Education will not; the world is full of educated derelicts. Persistence and determination alone are omnipotent. The slogan 'press on' has solved and always will solve the problems of the human race."
--- **CALVIN COOLIDGE**

"Continuous effort – not strength or intelligence – is the key to unlocking our potential."
--- **LIANE CORDES**

"The successful person has the habit of doing things failures don't like to do. They don't like doing them either necessarily. But their disliking is subordinated to the strength of their purpose."
--- **E.M. GRAY**

"The first requisite for success is the ability to apply your physical and mental energies to one problem incessantly without growing weary."
--- **THOMAS EDISON**

"Courage to start and willingness to keep everlasting at it are the requisites for success."
--- **ALONZO NEWTON BENN**

NEVER THE SMARTEST AND RARELY THE HARDEST WORKING

I am never the smartest and rarely the hardest working person in any room. I do not pick up on things especially quickly and I refuse on principle to pull all-nighters to get something done. I am still able to achieve most of my goals, however, because I have developed the ability to work consistently hard on an endeavor for an extended period of time. I can press forward after the excessively-hard-working person burns out and after the excessively-smart person gets bored. I have developed the skill of consistent persistence. In fact, consistent persistence describes perfectly the appropriate work ethic of an authentically successful person. The concept encompasses each of the excellent attributes that come from hard work, dedication and consistency and ignores each of the negative manifestations such qualities possess at their extremes.

EXCESSIVE HARD WORK

Hard work enables you to complete difficult tasks successfully and on time. Hard work also allows you to gain valuable experience in the process. I encourage you to work hard at each of your endeavors. On the other hand, excessive hard work generates extraordinary levels of stress and eventual burn-out. People are not machines and perform poorly when they are consistently overworked. You must realize that hard work, at its extreme, is a success-killer. Consistent persistence lies near the fine line between hard work and excessive hard work.

OVER-DEDICATION

Dedication is a key component to achieving any goal successfully. A lack of dedication will cause you to do a sloppy job, lose interest and eventually give up. While dedication is a good thing, over-dedication is problematic. An overly-dedicated person is akin to an addict – she is addicted to the task at hand and cannot pry herself from it even when it is in her emotional, mental and physical best interests to do so. Overly-dedicated people expend excess energy on specific tasks and do not have the time to savor any of the other important things in life. Their dedication transforms them. At the end of the day, the endeavor they are fixated on becomes the only area where they can find meaning in their lives. Celebrations and special moments quickly pass by someone who is overly-dedicated. Too many sunrises and sunsets are missed for no good reason. At some point, this type of extreme dedication will lead to regret.

I used to work at a place where over-dedication consistently reared its ugly head. One summer day, a senior associate wanted to leave work at 6:00 pm to attend his son's birthday party. The only problem was that he was assigned to a project that was somewhat time sensitive, but something which could have waited until the next day to complete. When he asked politely if he could leave, a senior partner looked him right in the eye and asked, "How old is your kid anyway?" The associate said that his son was turning two years old, to which the partner replied, "Don't worry if you miss his birthday party. At that age, he won't remember it anyway." The associate took this advice and ended up staying late at work and missing the party. He did not want to create ill-will with the senior partner and wanted to make sure that he received a promotion to partner and a large bonus at the end of the year. In the end, he let his over-dedication to his job interfere with something much more important on his list of priorities. I could tell that he regretted his decision as soon as he made it. This story represents a prime example of over-dedication leading to regret. Consistent persistence does not require this type of over-dedication.

TOO MUCH CONSISTENCY

People who are consistent are in demand. Assuming that they are consistently good at what they do, people will trust them with similar tasks time and time again. You know what you get when you deal with someone who is consistent. However, someone who is too consistent is tempted into narrow mindedness and subject to a lack of creativity. Think of a doctor who handles hundreds of the exact same procedures every year, consistently utilizing the exact same tools and processes. Over time, these procedures will become second-nature, but will stifle the creative edge necessary to complete any procedure even a bit different from the status quo. This doctor will be trapped within a world where she can only perform the one procedure she knows. If medicine advances to the point where the procedure becomes obsolete, she must either spend years retraining or find herself out of a job. Similar to excessive hard work and over-dedication, too much consistency can hurt you in the long-run.

WHAT CONSISTENT PERSISTENCE REQUIRES

The great thing about consistent persistence is that it does not require you to work excessively hard all of the time, overly-dedicate yourself to any one project or stifle your creativity. On the contrary, consistent persistence entails working hard on a task, but stopping before you burn out. It requires you to be dedicated, but only as dedicated as your high-level priorities allow. And, it mandates consistency, but not the type of over-consistency that stifles creativity and traps you into one area. Here is how you can determine when and for how long you should consistently persist.

First, identify where your current endeavor falls on your list of priorities. Second, determine how much time and effort are required to successfully complete it and if completion is worth the price you will pay in terms of lost time, the sacrifice of other priorities and the mental and physical energy expended. Third, assuming you choose to move forward, dedicate yourself to working hard and for as long as it takes to successfully complete the task. On this note, I would argue that not even your summa cum laude priorities merit very many all-nighters or the utter neglect of your other priorities. Make sure to pace yourself throughout the process and do not give up unless you can no longer justify the effort in relationship to your list of priorities.

Let's analyze the following example to determine what consistent persistence is all about. Becoming a fully-licensed, employed lawyer is a seven-year commitment and a nerve-racking process. Over 100,000 people apply to law school each year, making the process extremely competitive. Because law schools understand supply and demand, they make the process very rigorous to ensure they accept only the best and brightest students. The path to becoming a lawyer starts in high school when you decide which college to attend. In order to help your chances of admission to law school you need to choose a school with a solid academic reputation. Then, beginning in your freshman year in college, you need to accumulate good grades, a strong resume and genuine relationships with professors who can write your recommendation letters. At the end of your junior year, you need to prepare for and then take the LSAT – a 3 and ½ hour, 100 question, pressure-packed examination required for admission into any accredited law school. The test is tedious and challenging and represents one of the primary factors looked at by law schools during the admissions process. By the middle of your senior year, you need to apply to at least a handful of law schools to increase your chances of acceptance. Law school applications are lengthy, expensive and one spelling or grammatical mistake can send your application directly to the trash.

If you are fortunate enough to gain acceptance, you must endure the law school boot-camp experience during your entire first year. This environment, where students are seated according to a pre-assigned seating chart and intentionally picked on to answer difficult questions in order to make sure that they are prepared for class, is so intense that it generally weeds out a noticeable percentage of first-year law students each year. Additionally, you have to further develop your critical thinking and analysis skills in order to achieve above-average grades on four-hour comprehensive final examinations. Because your law school GPA is really the only indication that legal employers have concerning your ability to practice law, these examinations are crucial to your future career success.[24] Performing well in your law school classes will help increase your chances of landing a job upon graduation. Unfortunately, competition for good law jobs is more intense than the law school admissions process as there are fewer good jobs than there are spots in law school classes. Once you land a job, you have to study and take your state's bar examination. As you can see, becoming an employed, bar-certified attorney is a grueling process and you cannot get through it with hard work, dedication or consistency alone. You need consistent persistence. However, you should only undertake this great effort if becoming a lawyer is something that merits one of the top spots on your priorities list. If it does, then you need to consistently persist in order to make it happen. If it doesn't, then you should focus your efforts elsewhere.

At the end of the day, preparing for authentic success requires you to understand that if something is important in your life, you cannot give up on it no matter how far away the finish line appears. This chapter will conclude with the words and actions of a famous basketball coach who exemplified the quality of consistent persistence even through the toughest times in his life.

---

[24] The vast majority of law school classes are based on your final examination grade. Therefore, a semester's' worth of work is evaluated on only one examination. There is a great deal riding on these four hours.

NEVER, EVER GIVE UP

> "Don't give up, don't ever give up."
> --- JIM VALVANO
>
> "The pessimist sees the difficulty in every opportunity. The optimist sees the opportunity in every difficulty."
> --- WINSTON CHURCHILL

An even better way of phrasing the idea of consistent persistence is that once you dedicate yourself to a task that merits your efforts, "never give up, never ever give up." This wonderful advice was uttered by a legendary college basketball coach named Jim Valvano. Over his nineteen seasons coaching college basketball, Jimmy V, as he was affectionately known, wore his emotions on his sleeve. After his North Carolina State team won the NCAA championship in 1983, Jimmy V ran up and down the court looking for someone to hug.

His passion was infectious; but it was his ability to consistently persist, even through the toughest times in his young life, that defined him. Jimmy V was diagnosed with terminal cancer in the early 1990s and died in 1993. Cancer took away many of his physical abilities and made it hard for him to walk or stand for long periods of time. However, the coach never let his medical situation take away his mind, his heart or his soul. Throughout his battle, he continued to fight for his former players and institution, he continued to fight to raise money to treat cancer, and he continued to fight for his life. At a point in life where most people would have quit and accepted their fate, Jimmy V chose to never give up.

You can see the theme of consistent persistence throughout the speeches Jimmy V gave as his health continued to worsen. Months before his untimely death, Coach Valvano received the Arthur Ashe

Courage and Humanitarian Award at the ESPY Awards Ceremony –
the most famous awards ceremony in the sports world. On that
night, everyone realized that Valvano was in considerably poor
health. The audience would have been happy just to see the beloved
coach accept the award, smile and walk off stage. What happened
instead, however, was awe-inspiring. Jimmy V, after being helped
onto the stage to a standing ovation, gave a speech. And, not just
any speech, he gave a once-in-a-generation type of speech and he
talked about consistent persistence. The following are some of the
most memorable lines from this momentous occasion:

> I am a very emotional and passionate man . . . To me, there
> are three things we all should do every day. We should do
> this every day of our lives. Number one is laugh. You should
> laugh every day. Number two is think. You should spend
> some time in thought. And number three is, you should have
> your emotions moved to tears, could be happiness or joy. But
> think about it. If you laugh, you think, and you cry, that's a
> full day. That's a heck of a day. You do that seven days a
> week, you're going to have something special.

> You have to have an enthusiasm for life, you have to have a
> dream, a goal and you have to be willing to work for it. I
> urge all of you, all of you, to enjoy your life, the precious
> moments you have. To spend each day with some laughter
> and some thought, to get your emotions going, to be
> enthusiastic every day . . . To keep your dreams alive in spite
> of problems . . . to be able to work hard for your dreams to
> come true.

> [And, finally] Don't give up, don't ever give up. . . . Cancer
> can take away all my physical abilities. It cannot touch my
> mind, it cannot touch my heart, and it cannot touch my soul.
> And those three things are going to carry on forever. I thank
> you and God bless you all.

Prior to his 1993 speech, Jimmy V talked to a packed house in
North Carolina State's gym – Reynolds Coliseum – where he also
addressed the idea of consistent persistence.

Let me tell you what the '83 team (Valvano's NCAA basketball championship team) means to me. . . . They are special . . . because they taught me and the world so many important lessons. Number One, hope . . . hope that things can get better in spite of adversity. . . . The '83 team taught me about dreaming and the importance of dreams because nothing can happen if not first a dream. If you have someone with a dream, you have a motivated person with a dream and a goal and a vision, if you have someone who never gives up and has great hope. . . and that team taught me about persistence – the idea of never ever quitting. Don't ever give up.

The crowd gave Jimmy V another standing ovation after another great description of what it means to exhibit consistent persistence. The coach talked about hope. Hope can keep even the most unreachable goals alive in your mind. Sometimes hope can get you through when you have nothing else left in your tank. He talked about dreaming. Dreams motivate actions; dreams give you the incentive to consistently persist. He talked about enthusiasm, passion and laughter. These emotions are crucial to your enjoyment of the activities you choose to persist in. He talked about thinking and working exceptionally hard. These are the same things we have been talking about all throughout this book. Each of these attributes constitutes a tool that can help you consistently persist.

Jimmy V serves as my inspiration for this chapter. His consistent persistence, even through the darkness of the disease he was forced to face, was truly amazing. His speeches at the Reynolds Coliseum and at the ESPY awards inspire me to this day. His message of hope, goals, dreams, love and consistent persistence is what life is all about. Therefore, remember to consistently persist and you will prepare yourself well for success. And, by the way, when you undertake an endeavor that you deem worthy of your efforts don't give up . . . never, ever, ever, ever, ever, ever, ever give up!

CHAPTER 9:
RECESSION - PROOF YOUR LIFE

> "It's a recession when your neighbor loses his job; it's a depression when you lose your own."
> --- **HARRY S. TRUMAN**
>
> "The best time to prepare for the worst is before it happens."
> --- **RICHARD REAM: HOW TO RECESSION-PROOF YOUR CAREER**
>
> "When the employment market takes a tumble, many people respond impulsively and tend to panic. . . . The problem, though, is that panic tends to prevent you from taking the measured steps necessary to solve the problem effectively, which only creates more panic."
> --- **WENDY ENELOW: 101 WAYS TO RECESSION-PROOF YOUR CAREER**
>
> "A wise person does at once what a fool does at last. Both do the same thing, only at different times."
> --- **BALTASAR GRACIAN**
>
> "Don't spend time beating on a wall, hoping to transform it into a door."
> --- **DR. LAURA SCHLESSINGER**

ON RECESSIONS

Do you know what a recession is? Do you recall when the last recession in the United States occurred? While you might not know the precise definition of the word or be able to recall the timeline of recent infamous recessions, you are likely quite familiar with the concept and the troubles associated with an economy experiencing such a downturn. Recessions are tough on many different areas of an economy as entire market segments, stock prices, employers and households suffer. The negative effects of a recession eventually trickle all the way down to the typical employee merely striving to make a living.

The most common definition of a recession is any decline in a country's Gross Domestic Product (GDP) for two or more successive quarters (six months) within a given year.[25] During recessions, demand for products and services is reduced as people spend less money. The reasons for this reduced demand stem from various motivations which are tough to isolate. The most common reasons given are fear of losing a job, fear of an economic downturn (decreasing consumer confidence) or basic oversupply of goods and services (too much supply for people to consume).

Economies thrive when supply and demand are equal. In a recession, supply begins to overtake demand. Companies take the revenue-hit from the reduced demand and find that their production schedule for new goods and services is becoming excessive. At this point, companies begin to discontinue investment in new employees, property, factories and equipment in an effort to reduce costs. The decrease in quarterly revenue from the reduced sales of products and services causes a decrease in stock price and a decrease in stock market averages in general.

Billions of dollars in market capitalization can disappear in a short period of time – including large chunks of the retirement funds of millions of workers nearing the end of their careers. Mass layoffs of employees are common as businesses find themselves overstaffed. Newly unemployed people dig into their savings accounts for the funds they need to pay their bills. This savings depletion continues

---

[25] An extended recession is referred to as a depression.

until they can find a new job. Problematically, new jobs are scarce as companies have no desire to hire new employees that cannot be productive due to the lack of new business. With savings accounts dwindling, many people take jobs that they would not even have considered before the recession began – they do not have a choice. Now you can see why recessions can be devastating.

From 1991 to late 2000, America's economy was growing and from 1999 to the middle of 2000, America's economy was growing at a frenetic pace. The most recent recession in the United States begin in 2001 and was spurred on by the attacks of September 11, 2001. Immediately following the tragedy, people cancelled plane reservations, delayed vacations, and generally stopped spending as much money as they had been spending over the past few years. This reduced demand took money out of the economy and businesses in various market segments lost a great deal of anticipated revenues.

The recession impacted even the country's largest businesses and caused many Fortune 500 companies to lower their earnings expectations and suffer the resulting decrease in stock price. At the same time, smaller companies began to lay off employees and/or go out of business. Employees who were terminated stopped spending as much money. Employees who thought that they might be next in line for a pink slip stopped spending as much money. Consumers in general watched the news, became concerned and stopped spending as much money. At the same time, the high-flying technology market segment began to suffer a major decline. This made the situation even worse and decreased consumer confidence even further. The first recession of the twenty-first century was officially underway.

The good news about our economy is that it is cyclical – meaning that cloudy days caused by recessions will be followed by sunny days of bull markets, plentiful jobs and productive growth. The problem is that no one can predict the timing of an economic recovery and, while the country waits in anticipation, people suffer. Fortunately, your life does not have to hit these low points just because the economy is struggling. If you can find a way to recession-proof your career, you will be able to withstand most everything that a bad economy tosses your way. Recession-proofing is like buying insurance on your professional life. If something bad happens, your insurance will bail you out and you will land back on your feet in a relatively brief period of time. This type of insurance is expensive in terms of the skills and effort required to obtain adequate coverage, but it is a cost worth paying.

THREE STEPS TO RECESSION-PROOF YOUR LIFE

It is best to recession-proof your life before a recession actually strikes. Three steps are crucial in any recession-proofing attempt. First, you must become more flexible and understand that it is acceptable for your career field to change. Second, you need to become a jack of many trades. In other words, strive to do many things very well. Third and finally, you need to be so adept at what you do that you become as close to irreplaceable as possible.

BECOME MORE FLEXIBLE

A recession may greatly impact your life at any time. You cannot predict when the United States or the world economies will tank – it's not worth even trying to do so. Because markets are cyclical – with recessions followed by expansions and on and on – it is a near certainty that you will experience at least a few recessions in your lifetime. The best way to weather the storm is to be more flexible with what your future holds. You are not locked into the career field you choose when you are in your early twenties.

This piece of advice has been especially important in my life because, although I did not grow up as a flexible person, the most recent recession molded me into one. My primary goal since I was a junior in college was to be a corporate lawyer. I was intrigued by the size and types of deals as well as the clients corporate lawyers dealt with and I wanted to be in the middle of the action. Everything was going according to plan until September 11, 2001 when our economy entered its most recent recession. As the high-tech economy collapsed, the vast majority of my firm's clients collapsed with it. When my law firm finally accepted that the demand for its expensive services was not there anymore, the partners decided to shut the doors for good.

I was devastated. In an instant, my long-term goal went up in flames and there was no other firm to turn to as hiring was stagnant. I had to fight and claw for six long months in order to find another job in corporate law. I now felt trapped in the field because that was the only area where I had years of training and at least some experience. At the same time, I was running out of money and patience. Even my desire to practice law was waning. Already $120,000 in debt, however, I forgot those thoughts and resolved to show the world that I could make my goal a reality and be a successful corporate lawyer someday and somehow. I was completely inflexible and I paid for it dearly in terms of lost time and increased stress.

A year after I found my second job in the law, I read an article on how to create a recession-proofed life and realized that I was exposed when economic downturns hit. I discovered that my inflexibility led me down one path and one path only – corporate law. If the field of corporate law was to ever go away, or shrink to a level where my services were no longer needed, my career would be in jeopardy.

From that point forward, I realized that I would be happy doing other things and that my life was not all about corporate law. I had a desire to be an entrepreneur and so I opened my own business. I enjoyed real estate and so I obtained my license. I loved to teach and research emerging areas in the law and I applied for a job as a professor. I am much happier teaching now than I ever was as a corporate lawyer. Isn't that ironic? I am now very flexible about what life brings my way. I love to teach, but if something happens and I am no longer able to do so, I will find something else I enjoy. I am now flexible and more recession-proof.

BECOME A JACK OF MANY TRADES

Another way you can recession-proof your life is to become a jack of many trades. What this means is that you should pick three or four areas within your field or from a field closely related to it and take the steps necessary to make yourself employable in each of them. Then, if a recession hits and you find yourself out of a job, you will have options. It will be tough to become an expert in three or four different areas, but you can at least become proficient enough to get your foot in the door. For instance, someone who is a journalist and loses a job has the potential to work in public relations, do freelance writing or become an author and write a book. Combine all of this with the foundation you are developing and the preparation techniques you are practicing and you might even have a leg up. Because you are a jack of many trades, even if your second choice peters out, you will still have options to pursue.

As I mentioned previously, I have my law license and my real estate license, I have written extensively on legal and ethical topics and I started and currently run a small business. If something happens and I find myself out of the teaching profession, I can run my company, start another company, practice law, write books, consult companies on ethics compliance issues or even sell commercial or residential real estate. Through a bunch of hard work, a bit of foresight and a strategic plan, I have become a jack of many trades. Although I feel that I am called to teach, I have become proficient enough in these other areas to get my foot in the door if I am ever in search of a new job. Sometimes this is the most you can ask for in the midst of a recession. Due to my various skills and newfound flexibility, I now have the advantage of not having to run around for the good part of a year looking for a job in an area that is devastated by an ongoing recession. I am a jack of many trades and can make these different trades work to my advantage.

BECOME IRREPLACEABLE

The third way you can make yourself recession-proof is by making yourself as irreplaceable as possible. The better you are at your job and the more money or clients you bring into your company, the less likely it is that you will be laid off in tough economic times. In fact, companies generally lay off employees in inverse order of their performance and worth to the firm. This makes good business sense and it is something that you must understand regardless of whether or not you think it is fair.

Top performers in today's business environment are effective, smart and personable. Being effective means that you are able to bring in business and make money for the company. This skill trumps other skills as businesses need revenue in order to survive. Being smart means that you are able to think in a way that allows you to solve complex problems, complete projects in a timely manner and make very few errors. If you are smart, employers appreciate the benefits your intelligence brings to their problems. They know that your set of business skills will help keep them on the cutting edge in the industry. Being personable means that you are able to develop relationships with clients, colleagues and superiors and that people like to have you around the office.

What I am trying to say is that you have to give your employer a reason to keep you around during a time when your company is likely losing money and when excess employee expenses and salaries are part of the problem. In hindsight, when my law firm began to lay people off, the first to go were the senior (more expensive) attorneys who did not have their own clients and who depended upon the firm for work (i.e., the least effective). Attorneys with many clients or a solid book of business were the last to be terminated. Interestingly, the smartest and most personable younger associates, even those with no clients of their own, were retained because the firm saw within them a bright future. If you can become effective, smart and personable, you can make yourself irreplaceable.

A FEW OTHER IDEAS

Becoming more flexible, becoming a jack of many trades and becoming irreplaceable are the three best ways to recession-proof your career. You can also supplement the big three with other tactics that may protect you or help you land back on your feet when a recession strikes. These tactics, in and of themselves, are not enough to recession-proof your life, but they can help. Some are little while others are bigger. Some are time consuming and some are simple. The recipe for success in recession-proofing your life requires you to focus on the big three while also mixing in a few of the following tactics for maximum effect.

1. Become proficient at conducting risk assessments – become adept at sensing that something bad is about to happen in the economy, in your company or to your job/career;
2. Keep you resume up to date and flawless;
3. Cultivate relationships across your field and in other areas that interest you;
4. Pick a career field that will always be in demand and does not take as big a hit during a recession – i.e., engineering, medicine, law, accounting and teaching;

5. Control your finances and expenses – smart savings and reasonable expenses will help get you through a recession without draining your resources;
6. Keep your priorities and your big-picture perspective in mind – this will decrease your stress level and allow you to focus on getting through the recession in one piece and emotionally, mentally and physically healthy;
7. Be prepared to move to a different place if you have to;
8. Go back to school – earning a higher degree or obtaining education in a different area can open new doors;
9. Become a better communicator – in your writing, speaking and overall presentation of yourself; and
10. Volunteer your time – you will help society and meet people who may be able to help you along the way.

Attempting to recession-proof your life is not a magic elixir destined to completely protect you through the toughest of times. Rather, your ability to make yourself flexible, to learn different areas and to be really good at what you do constitute layers of protection. Recessions, depending upon their severity, will tear off these layers and the people with the most protection in the end will be the ones left standing.

You may be thinking that this is a lot of effort for something that may not affect you in any way. However, unless you can predict the future, I can assure you that hard work now will more than pay for itself in terms of job security and financial stability in times where everyone around you is struggling just to find a job and pay the bills. Recession-proofing your life is another aspect in your preparation for authentic success. It is not easy, but preparing for something invaluable never is.

CHAPTER 10:

REDEEM THE TIME

"See then that you walk circumspectly, not as fools but as wise, redeeming the time."
--- **EPHESIANS 5:15-16 (NEW KING JAMES VERSION)**

"Lost wealth many be replaced by industry, lost knowledge by study, lost health by temperance or medicine, but lost time is gone forever."
--- **SAMUEL SMILES**

"In truth, people can generally make time for what they choose to do; it is not really the time but the will that is lacking."
--- **SIR JOHN LUBBOCK**

"Dost thou love life? Then do not squander time for that is the stuff life is made of."
--- **BENJAMIN FRANKLIN**

"Don't say you don't have enough time. You have exactly the same number of hours per day that were given to Helen Keller, Pasteur, Michelangelo, Mother Teresa, Leonardo da Vinci, Thomas Jefferson and Albert Einstein."
--- **H. JACKSON BROWN**

PRECIOUS TIME

Time is precious. We sense this axiom when we ponder life itself and acknowledge that our time on Earth is fleeting. These philosophical moments inspire us and we resolve to be better managers of our time and to dedicate more moments to our most significant priorities. Ironically, these resolutions fade away mysteriously upon the dawning of a new day. Once again, we fail to cherish our time. Once again, we waste more time than we spend effectively. A glance at our daily routine emphatically demonstrates the irony of our approach. On a typical weekday, we work long hours anticipating our next task and under constant distraction. On a typical weekend, we loaf about the house too long in an effort to recover. All the while, we squander a great deal of precious time in the process. At some point in the future, we reflect upon the time we have lost, recognize that it is gone forever and wonder why we allocated it in such a manner.

Why do our days whisk by at such a brisk pace? Why do we shortchange the moments worthy of our time and magnify the moments we should pass right by? Although there may not be a scientific answer to such an inquiry, an educated guess proves enlightening. I attribute this brisk-day phenomenon to the idea that most of us wake up each morning without a plan. We hit the alarm clock, gather ourselves, get ready and then wander aimlessly throughout each day. We only pre-schedule our most important appointments. Nothing else merits the time and organizational effort required to create a plan and, therefore, we wing it the rest of each day. We take life as it comes at us; we wait and then react. Although we may possess the desire to exercise, relax or visit friends, we only make it happen if we can "find the time." Before we know it, 10:00 p.m. is upon us and our day has wound down. The time to see our friends, relax and exercise was there, we just couldn't lasso it in. At this point, we lament the day's quick passage, regret the missed opportunities and get ready for bed destined to wander anew the next day.

It will not surprise you that such an approach does not inspire much praise on my end. It's tough for me to be too critical, however, as I have experienced my fair share of completely wasted days and found myself frustrated at their conclusion. I have winged it on many occasions and kicked myself later for doing so. The problem was that, on a few occasions, my hope-and-a-prayer approach actually produced successful results. These successes inspired me to believe that I could wing it again and expect similar results in the future. As I know now, life never works this way and, by continuing to ignore any time management system whatsoever, I found that one successfully-winged day was always overshadowed by an avalanche of lackluster days. It is not just me; everyone at some point struggles to implement an effective time management system into their daily routine. By failing to fix this problem, we make life much more complicated than it needs to be. More importantly, we waste precious time in the process.

The best way to change your current approach is to redeem your time. In general, redemption involves recovering something of value from captivity by paying a ransom. Think of your time as having been captured by the chaos of your daily life. You need to recover this time from its captivity and the ransom you must pay is of the organizational variety – you must create a time management plan specially tailored to every endeavor you undertake every day. The following section will explain the two key components of this process:

1. Planning each endeavor from a time and effort perspective; and
2. Thinking before you act.

The chapter will then conclude by providing you with a useful time management system. Your ultimate objective is to understand that proper preparation for a successful life requires you to pay the ransom required and redeem your time from its captivity.

PLAN EACH OF YOUR ENDEAVORS . . . EVEN YOUR RELAXATION TIME

"The time you enjoy wasting is not wasted time."
--- **BERTRAND RUSSELL**

"Use your precious moments to live life fully every single second of every single day."
--- **MARCIA WEIDER**

"How we spend our days is, of course, how we spend our lives."
--- **ANNIE DILLARD**

"The bad news is time flies. The good news is you're the pilot."
--- **MICHAEL ALTHSULER**

PLAN YOUR ENDEAVORS FROM A TIME AND EFFORT PERSPECTIVE

I am convinced that the process of planning out each day before it happens represents three-fourths of the time management battle. The remaining one-fourth merely requires you to execute your plan. Problematically, the planning part of the equation is much harder than its execution. Most people do not like to take the time required to formulate a plan. They say things such as, "I'll deal with this issue when and if it happens," "there is no use planning things out because everything is likely to change anyway" or the classic "it just takes too much time and effort to think ahead." These excuses are silly, frustrating and rather ironic. In fact, the time it takes to make a daily schedule is dwarfed by the time saved by executing it throughout a typical day. In addition to the time saved, the proper implementation of a plan has other fringe benefits. For instance, people who make a daily schedule tend be more efficient, more organized and accomplish more significant tasks each day. Their daily plan keeps them on track and on time. Maybe it's the foresight involved in the planning process. It could be the extra thought required to map out a day or the reinforcement a written schedule provides. The reasons why such plans work so well are a mystery, but the reality of their effectiveness is a fact. If you think that you really have this whole concept of redeeming the time down to a science, do me a favor and try the following exercise: Track your endeavors for an entire twenty-four hour period, jotting down what you did and how long it took. My guess is that you will be shocked with the amount of time that you waste during the course of a typical day. Now that we are clear that you are one of the hundreds of millions of people who need to redeem their time, we can move forward to the first step in the process.

The first step in redeeming your time is to plan out each of your endeavors. When you craft this plan, make certain you determine the approximate amount of time and effort each task will require and then allot both of these factors into a schedule. You do not want to overestimate the time any endeavor will take because you will end up wasting time on the back end. On the other hand, make sure to allocate enough time to allow you to complete the endeavor successfully. Estimating the required effort is also important because you only have so much effort to give to any endeavor over a fixed period of time. For example, you do not want to schedule two effort-intensive activities too close together. Doing so will cause you to experience fatigue. This fatigue will lead you to give poor effort to each task or to just give up altogether. To avoid this type of collapse, always keep an eye on the energy involved in each of your endeavors in addition to the required time.

PLAN YOUR RELAXATION TIME AS WELL

While you likely grasp the idea that you should plan your professional endeavors each day, you are probably shaking your head at my suggestion that you plan your relaxation time as well. Planning relaxation is an oxymoron, right? While the thought may sound crazy at first, setting aside time solely for relaxation is actually a wise decision. When we relax, the whole point is to forget about the endeavors and troubles currently occupying our minds. Checking these issues at the door and just relaxing and rejuvenating feels good and heals our body, mind and spirit. These positive feelings tend to cause us to relax longer than we should. What is supposed to be a lunch with friends turns into an after-lunch coffee and a trip to the mall to look around. Before we know it, we have taken a three-hour lunch. Then, we head back to the office and find it hard to motivate ourselves to complete a project before the workday is over. The same thing occurs in the educational environment. What is supposed to be a study session turns into friendly chatter and any studying gets put off indefinitely.

Spending time with friends is not a bad thing and my guess is that it ranks higher on your priorities list than does your career and your education. However, if you are not careful, avoiding your other required tasks to relax with your friends will cause an entire day to whisk by before you know it. You will then face the agonizing problem of trying to fit even more endeavors into tomorrow's schedule. This quickly becomes a vicious circle. A better approach is to think about the maximum amount of time you can spend relaxing each day and then allotting that amount into your schedule. Always keep in mind that relaxing is a very good thing, but your relaxation time must be planned to make sure that these good times do not overwhelm life's other responsibilities.

THINK BEFORE YOU ACT

Do you always think before you act? How many times have you wasted a trip someplace that could have been avoided with just a bit of foresight? Taking the time to think before you act can save you a tremendous amount of time. For example, assume you have three errands to run in different parts of town and that it is eight o'clock at night. Someone with effective time management skills would sit down, think about what needs to be accomplished and then map out a plan. This plan would include the order of each errand, the hours of operation for each location and the approximate time each stop should take. With this plan in mind, then and only then would this person begin the trek. Planning something as simple as a trip to the store may sound silly and appear to be waste of time but I can assure you that the time you spend thinking will double the amount of time you save at the end of the day. Recall that you have a limited amount of time each day and that you are not redeeming the time by running all over town when more effective planning could give you more time with your friends or otherwise relaxing. This is a simple point, but something that is required to redeem your time more effectively.

A TIME MANAGEMENT TOOL

> "Time = life; therefore, waste you time and waste your life, or master your time and master your life."
> --- **ALAN LAKEIN**
>
> "We must use time as a tool, not as a couch."
> --- **JOHN F. KENNEDY**
>
> "I am definitely going to take a course on time management . . . just as soon as I can work it into my schedule."
> --- **LOUIS E. BOONE**
>
> "It's not enough to be busy, so are the ants. The question is, what are we busy about?"
> --- **HENRY DAVID THOREAU**

An effective time management system is worthy of praise. Entire industries are built around the idea that people need to better manage their time and write their schedules down on fancy calendars in fancy notebooks. They even give you a ruler to graph out your daily routine. You will be happy to hear that you do not need anything quite this exotic. All you need is a piece of paper that tracks the three most important time management issues in anyone's life: (1) dates and times, (2) energy level and (3) priority placement.

Below you will find something I refer to as the Time Redemption Schedule. Think of this template as my contribution to your redemption efforts.

SAMPLE TIME REDEMPTION SCHEDULE

The beginning of your new time redemption schedule is where you list your top priorities that you created back in Chapter Four. The following six priorities are hypothetical and designed so that we can walk through this sample schedule together. This sample schedule will cover a weekday and each endeavor that must be undertaken over this period of time. Because this chapter has urged the planning of relation time – a good chunk of the day will be reserved for that as well.

MY PRIORITIES

1. FAMILY
2. SIGNIFICANT OTHER
3. RELIGION
4. EDUCATION
5. FRIENDS
6. EXERCISE & HEALTH

SAMPLE TIME REDEMPTION SCHEDULE

TUESDAY --- JUNE 12, 2007			
TIME ▼	ENDEAVOR ▼	PRIORITY (Classification / Rank) ▼	EFFORT LEVEL ▼
8:00 AM	BREAKFAST	HEALTH (*magna* / 6th)	Mental → LOW Physical → LOW
9:00 AM 10:00 AM	BUSINESS LAW – READ CHAPTER 5	EDUCATION (*magna* / 4th)	Mental → HIGH Physical → LOW
11:00 AM 12:00 PM	MARKETING CLASS – PAPER DUE	EDUCATION (*magna* / 4th)	Mental → HIGH Physical → LOW
1:00 PM	LUNCH	HEALTH (*magna* / 6th)	Mental → LOW Physical → LOW
2:00 PM 3:00 PM	STUDY – READ FOR MATH MIDETERM	EDUCATION (*magna* / 4th)	Mental → HIGH Physical → LOW
4:00 PM	WORKOUT	EXERCISE (*magna* / 6th)	Mental → MED Physical → HIGH
5:00 PM			Mental → Physical →

6:00 PM	**CALL MY PARENTS (6:00 – 6:15)** **DINNER WITH FRIENDS (6:15 – 7:00)**	**FAMILY (*summa* / 1st)** ------------------------ ------------ **FRIENDS (*magna* / 5th)** **HEALTH (*magna* / 6th)**	Mental → MED. Physical → Low
7:00 PM 8:00 PM 9:00 PM 10:00 PM	**RELAX – WATCH DUKE BASKETBALL GAME WITH MY GIRLFRIEND**	**HEALTH (*magna* / 6th)** **SIGNIFICANT OTHER (*summa* / 2nd)**	Mental → Low Physical → Low Mental → Low Physical → Low
11:00 PM	**GO TO SLEEP**	**HEALTH (*magna* / 6th)**	Mental → Low Physical → Low
RESULTS →		**FORGOTTEN PRIORITIES:** **RELIGION (*summa* / 3rd)**	**AVG. DAILY EFFORT:** Mental → MED. Physical → Low

This hypothetical schedule resembles something that you might find in a professional day-planner, but it is much more functional and effective. The schedule is divided into four columns. Down the far left-hand column, you will find slots reserved for each hour you are awake during a typical day – there is nothing unique in this column. The second column describes the task that you wish to accomplish during the relevant time slot. The third column associates each of your tasks with one of your priorities. For instance, a recreational basketball game will be associated with your priority of exercise. The boxes in this column show the priority classification and its rank on your list. The bottom of the third column allows you to see which priorities you have forgotten to incorporate into your day.

Diligently scan this information to determine if you are spending too much time on your low-level priorities and too little time on your most important priorities. For instance, if you find a bunch of *summa cum laude* priorities in the "forgotten priorities" box over the course of a week, you may want to reevaluate your daily routine. Last but not least, the far right-hand column tracks how much energy – both mental and physical – you will be required to expend on each task you list. A day too full of high mental energy endeavors will cause you stress and hinder you from completing each task successfully. The same principle holds true for a day too full of high physical energy activities.

A perceptive quotation on time management reads, "It's how we spend our time here and now, that really matters. If you are fed up with the way you have come to interact with time, change it."[26] Consistent utilization of this Time Redemption Schedule will help you change the way you interact with your time. Although this schedule seems complicated upon first glance, it will become second nature once you begin to complete it every day. Keep in mind that the information within each category is only helpful when considered alongside the information within the other two categories. An effective day requires that you analyze everything on this chart as a whole to determine if you have the time to meet your important priorities and expend the energy that will be required to complete all of the tasks you have planned. Make sure to fill out your chart the night before and then fill in any blanks as endeavors come up. Trust me, the time you take to fill out this chart everyday will save you a great deal of time in the long run.

* * * * *

---

[26] Marcia Wieder.

CONGRATULATIONS ALL OVER AGAIN

You are now prepared to experience authentic success while living your life in real time. You have developed a solid foundation. You no longer rely on luck to experience success. You posses a strong character whereby your actions are determined via a moral compass comprised of virtues and the Golden Rule. You set priorities and goals and are on your way to becoming a big-picture person all of the time. Above and beyond this foundation, you have prepared yourself for success by becoming a professional in all you do. You have learned the importance of learning to think and then thinking to learn. You are ready to consistently persist in your endeavors and strive to never ever give up. You have learned the secret of recession-proofing your professional life. The flexibility that accompanies recession-proofing gives you a much better chance to succeed even in the worst economic times. Finally, you have changed your daily routine and shifted from winging your days to utilizing an effective Time Redemption Schedule. Again, congratulations are in order. You are now ready to experience success in real time – the topic comprising the final part of this book – and complete your journey to authentic success.

PART THREE:
Go!

LIVING LIFE IN REAL TIME

"This is not the beginning of the end; it's
the end of the beginning."
--- **WINSTON CHURCHILL**

"Success will not lower its standard to us.
We must raise our standard to success."
--- **RANDALL R. MCBRIDE, JR.**

CHAPTER II:
CULTIVATE RELATIONSHIPS

"Lean on me
When you're not strong
And I'll be your friend
I'll help you carry on
For it won't be long
Till I'm gonna need
Somebody to lean on"
--- **BILL WITHERS: LEAN ON ME**

"In order to have friends, you must first be one."
--- **ELBERT HUBBARD**

"The most important single ingredient in the formula of success is knowing how to get along with people."
--- **THEODORE ROOSEVELT**

"A real friend is one who walks in when the rest of the world walks out."
--- **WALTER WINCHELL**

CULTIVATING RELATIONSHIPS VERSUS NETWORKING

Networking stinks. Such a sentiment is harsh, but true. More specifically, the kind of networking you will encounter in the high-tech, no-time world of today really stinks. The concept of networking revolves around the idea of people meeting people, as many people as possible, in social or semi-social situations and in anticipation of contacting them for a professional or personal favor in the future. The immediate goal is twofold: (1) to obtain contact information (usually in the form of a phone number and e-mail address on a business card) and (2) to make a positive impression during the encounter. All of this must be done in the short time span governing each interaction and before moving on to speak to another potential contact. The ultimate goal of networking is to utilize these contacts to seek job opportunities, advice and additional information at some point in the more distant future. Envied networkers maximize not only their list of contacts but also their ability to obtain them. These few sentences describe networking in as positive a light as possible and it still stinks because meaningful relationships are rarely formed. The remainder of this chapter explains why and, more importantly, demonstrates how to cultivate relationships in a much more effective manner.

NETWORKING IS BOUND TO BACKFIRE

Networking is encouraged by big-time business schools, non-profit organizations and corporations alike. These institutions create networking opportunities by providing e-mail lists and websites, sponsoring formal events and coordinating informal meet-and-greets. Aspiring networkers who attend these events dream of making an appearance, meeting important people and collecting a slew of business cards. To them, this constitutes a successful evening but, in realty, their assumption is way off base. If you could somehow become invisible and hover just above all of the B.S. floating around at these events, you would see phony conversations and people looking ahead to the next person they can meet instead of engaging with the person to whom they are speaking. You would see business cards and handshakes exchanged. You would see many people near the V.I.P.s such as the executives and directors and very few people around everyone else. Most importantly, you would not see any meaningful relationships forming. In fact, interactions which may seem meaningful to the parties involved in the networking experience would appear utterly ridiculous to a neutral third party hovering above.

Think about this flawed logic of networking in the following example. Assume you are a first-year business student looking for a job on Wall Street. Assume also that during your freshman year you attended an alumni networking event and met a prominent bond trader who was also an alumna of your university. After the encounter, you placed her contact information into your cell phone and sent a nice-to-meet-you e-mail a week later; this e-mail constituted the extent of your correspondence. However, you are now a college senior and look forward to June and your graduation at which point you will contact her again to ask for a job. Nice work. You have successfully networked according to contemporary standards. Everything will come up roses in the end, right?

Unfortunately, unless the two of you are somehow related, my guess is that the bond trader will have a tough time even recalling your name. Remember, it has been four years since you met her and you have had no contact in the interim. You have thought about her and what she can offer you a great deal, but she has worked seventy-hour weeks in the heat of battle on Wall Street over the same period of time. The last thing on her mind is one of the hundreds of young recipients of her business card. And, even if your name actually rings a bell, nothing has occurred that would incline her to expend any effort on your behalf. Although you have networked with her, the two of you lack a meaningful relationship. I am sorry to say that you will likely be disappointed with the results of this networking "success." You should have seen it coming.

Your alma mater, previous employers and even your hometown can give you a networking advantage in certain situations, but such an advantage is minimal. These commonalities between you and your potential contacts may perk up some ears, but it will never get you as far as a meaningful relationship will. Hopefully, you are now beginning to recognize why focusing on networking as it is preached and practiced today is likely to backfire. You will introduce yourself and interact with many people for sure. You will also obtain a large collection of business cards and nametags, get a chance to practice your etiquette and eat some good meals. However, when you really need help, you will find yourself crossing your fingers and hoping that someone you do not really know at all will help you. You are relying on luck and you know better. What you really need to do, in lieu of networking, is to cultivate relationships.

CULTIVATING ALL DIFFERENT KINDS OF RELATIONSHIPS

Relationships come in many different shapes and sizes. We have relationships with our families, best friends, close friends, acquaintances, colleagues, supervisors, neighbors and fellow human beings. We have religious relationships, work relationships, professional relationships, service relationships and on and on. Every day generally provides a chance for you to form one of these relationships and I encourage you to take advantage of these opportunities. But, in doing so, you must recognize that different types of relationships require different types of cultivating. You have already seen that exchanging a business card and a silly e-mail is rarely enough. On the other hand, you do not need to make every person you encounter a friend or even an acquaintance. Instead, you must cultivate each relationship by adopting an attitude comprised of (1) care, (2) concentration and (3) sincerity without regard to its classification on your relationship spectrum. Always remember that the human relationship, not the contact information or the potential favor, is what's really important.

CARE ABOUT THE CONVERSATION

When you do not care about speaking with someone, it shows. In fact, people are generally adept at recognizing whether someone is truly engaged in a conversation with them or not. Ignoring someone, simultaneously thinking about other things and generally being disengaged in a conversation treats people as a means to an end. What you are basically saying is, "Look, I am only interested in what you can do for me and not interested in what you are all about as a person." Additionally, effectively faking interest in someone is tough to do and often takes more energy than it would take to actually be interested. Cultivating a relationship requires much more than this. It requires you to actually care about the conversations you take part in. Finally, if you find yourself uninterested or otherwise having trouble caring about a conversation, just exit the situation rather than being phony.

Caring about a conversation does not mean that you have to tend to every need of the speaker, kiss up or feign interest. Instead, caring requires you to concern yourself with another person's points, feelings and emotions throughout a conversation. Put yourself in the shoes of the speaker and see if you can comprehend his perspective. Dig deeper in your responses to determine the feelings underlying the speaker's points. Even if you are not interested in the topic at hand, care enough about the speaker as a person to learn something new. By doing this, you will begin to cultivate an actual relationship. Remember, if you expect people to care enough about you to help you in the future, you should care about your conversations with them. Stop treating people as a means to an end and start caring.

CONCENTRATE ON THE CONVERSATION

When you are not mentally and physically into a conversation, it shows. You need to concentrate your mind and body language and attempt to focus on every conversation you have. The last chapter of this book elaborates upon the importance of listening, but an effective conversation requires much more than just listening. When you talk to someone, make sure to actively listen, respond intelligently and concentrate your attention on the speaker and on the point at hand. Try not to let your mind wander to the next person you'll meet or to other goings-on in your life. Remove your preconceived notions about the speaker, her profession or the way she dresses and speaks. Each of these thoughts will distract you from the point the speaker is trying to make. When it is your turn to speak, concentrate on being confident, never dominating the conversation, alternating your vocal tones and speaking intelligently.

Whether you are the speaker or the listener, keep in mind that your body language is also very important. Body language is the way you position your body and your physical reactions when you speak and when you listen. Even if you neglect tending to your body language, you will subconsciously project your interest level during a conversation. This will tip off the other party as to your overall engagement loud and clear. To avoid such a subconscious reaction, be very attentive to your body language. Along with caring about the conversation and being sincere, your body language should consist of standing/sitting up straight, making eye contact, avoiding fidgeting of all sorts, continually nodding and gesturing when you agree or hear something particularly interesting, developing appropriate facial expressions and otherwise positioning yourself in close enough proximity to listen intently. Although this seems easy, concentrating your mental and physical attributes when you are in a conversation takes practice.

BE SINCERE

When you are insincere in your actions and reactions, it shows. Sincerity is basic honesty and earnestness in a situation. Sincere people mean what they say and say what they mean. We all tend to like and trust sincere people much more than insincere people. The problem is that people are afraid to be sincere, especially during initial encounters, because they do not want their true feelings and personalities to negatively affect them. So, instead of being judged negatively, they act phony. This decision is not any better.

A more effective tactic is to be sincere in all of your conversations – and all of the time for that matter. If someone holds your sincerity against you, that person is probably not someone you wish to associate with in the first place. I deal with this dilemma all of the time as a Christian. Over the course of the past decade I have entertained many requests for my resume through college and law school applications, scholarships, job interviews and other miscellaneous requests. I have encountered many people with negative connotations of religion and sincerely religious people in general. Some of these people would pass over a resume describing a candidate with sincere religious beliefs. Because of this, intelligent people and other advisors have counseled me to take all religious affiliations off of my resume and play it safe. I never do. My feeling is that this would be insincere. At the end of the day, any relationship with people exhibiting this type of intolerance will be difficult. My decision to be sincere in my resume likely cost me a few opportunities but not nearly as many as my sincere character has provided.

THE NEXT TIME YOU NETWORK, CHANGE YOUR APPROACH

To end this chapter, let me make an important point: you should attend as many networking events as possible. This is a great way to meet people you need to meet. However, while you are there, just forget about the networking tactics you've been taught and begin to cultivate relationships instead. When you meet someone, make sure you actually care about your conversation, focus your mind and body language on the other party and be sincere. By all means, exchange contact information and then follow up periodically with correspondence unrelated to your future plans. Carefully judge the other party's responses to determine how often to keep in contact as you do not want to be a bother. Only after you have cultivated a meaningful relationship should you even think about asking for a favor. If a need arises, however, you will have a solid relationship in your corner rather than a hope and a prayer.

Chapter 12:
Make Excellent Decisions & Take Personal Responsibility

> "Insanity is doing the same thing over and over again and expecting different results."
> --- **Albert Einstein**
>
> "A sign of wisdom and maturity is when you come to terms with the realization that your decisions cause your rewards and consequences. You are responsible for your life, and your ultimate success depends upon the choices you make."
> --- **Dennis Waitley**
>
> "The willingness to accept responsibility for one's own life is the source from which self-respect springs."
> --- **Joan Didion**
>
> "Man must cease attributing his problems to his environment, and learn again to exercise his will – his personal responsibility."
> --- **Albert Schweitzer**

MAKE EXCELLENT DECISIONS

Your decisions distinguish your journey through life. Wise choices beckon success while poor choices breed struggle. If you think about it, your entire life can be broken down into its individual decisions. Waking up, tucking yourself into bed and every endeavor in-between requires you to make a decision. This continual bombardment of choices can be segregated into two major classifications: (1) moral decisions and (2) life-management decisions.

Moral decisions are primarily ethical dilemmas involving your values, ethical compass and the moral distinction between what's right and what's wrong. Your moral decisions determine who you are as a person – they define your character. Examples of moral decisions include whether to break a promise, blow the whistle or bend the rules. Life-management decisions, on the other hand, involve choices that move your life forward and which do not necessarily involve an ethical dilemma as their primary component. Life-management decisions range from structuring your daily schedule to choosing a college, job or career. Think long and hard and then choose wisely in both types of decisions and you will prosper.

Problematically, we struggle to find the time to think long and hard about either our moral decisions or our life-management decisions. Because wise decisions take time and much thought to make, our neglect brings about more negative outcomes than necessary. If we only thought much longer and much harder about each of our decisions, the circumstances surrounding them and their implications, we could benefit greatly over time.

The action plan presented in this chapter encourages you to make every decision an excellent decision. Excellent decisions maximize benefits to your life, minimize harms, adhere closely to moral duties, embody virtues and contemplate the potential impact your actions have on others. Strive to fill your days with as many excellent decisions as possible in both the moral and the life-management realms. As you make these efforts, you will find that the majority of decisions you make will be relatively easy, some will be tougher and a select few will be extremely difficult.

EASY DECISIONS

Easy decisions are reserved for simple matters that: (1) are not found on your list of priorities, (2) do not require significant brainpower and (3) will have little impact on your future if you happen to choose poorly. You will be surprised as to how many easy decisions you are faced with each day. Choosing where to eat for dinner or what to wear to work are perfect examples of such decisions. Although you may be slightly flummoxed when deciding between restaurants or about what business casual actually means, these decisions do not impact any of your priorities and require no more than a few moments of thought. An easy decision made wisely will make your life better but a poorly-made easy decision will not negatively impact your life for more than a brief period of time (i.e., a few hours at most if you get food poisoning or appear at a function under-or over-dressed). You should be able to move on from these setbacks rather quickly.

TOUGH DECISIONS

Tough decisions: (1) involve your lower *magna cum laude* and all of your *cum laude* priorities, (2) require a careful balancing of pros and cons and (3) can set you back emotionally, mentally and/or physically if you choose poorly. Tough decisions are harder to make than easy decisions but not nearly as hard to make as extremely difficult decisions. Tough decisions represent the middle ground in your decisional universe. Typical tough decisions include scheduling your time, picking a college or graduate school, choosing a major, developing an intimate relationship or close friendship or making a significant financial investment. Choosing poorly on a tough decision presents negative consequences that will set you back for a brief period of time (between a month and a few years in duration). Such consequences, however, are not likely to prove devastating to your life. For example, think about a recent friendship in which you devoted much time, energy and emotion to a person that did not reciprocate or otherwise let you down. Entering into a relationship of this nature is a tough decision, not to be taken lightly, because (1) close friendships should be high on your priority list, (2) you must balance the experiences, love and relational benefits of a close friendship with the trust, time and emotions at stake when you invest yourself in such a relationship and (3) the emotional letdown you experience when such relationships end can really hurt. We all have experienced friendships that did not work out and we think about them all of the time. It's sad, it sets us back, and it's proof that we need to be very careful when making the tough decision to devote ourselves to a friendship. Other tough decisions occur often in our lives and have consequences similar to a broken friendship. Therefore, you must dedicate the time and thought necessary to become adept at making as many tough decisions as excellently as possible.

EXTREMELY DIFFICULT DECISIONS

Finally, extremely difficult decisions constitute the hardest decisions that you will ever make. These decisions: (1) involve your *summa cum laude* and your highest *magna cum laude* priorities, (2) take a significant amount of time and mental struggling to make and (3) occur in situations where choosing poorly will have a long-term, detrimental impact on your life. Extremely difficult decisions include choosing the person you will marry, buying a home or pursuing a career. A poor choice here can negatively impact your life for a long period of time – likely longer then a few years in duration. Although it is extremely difficult to make these decisions, you need to choose as wisely as possible in order to be successful. If you choose to marry, you must avoid a hasty, lustful or shallow decision and only marry someone you love, know extremely well and trust. Think of each of these attributes as prerequisites to marriage and recognize that obtaining each of these feelings for another person is extremely difficult – and it should be – because you are making a life-long commitment in a marriage. Your spouse should be a *summa cum laude* priority and a poor decision will haunt you through an unhappy or unfaithful marriage and potentially a divorce. Marriage is an example of an extremely difficult decision you cannot afford to fumble. But it's not just marriage, every single extremely difficult decision you face will require a significant time commitment reserved for thinking (much longer than an easy or a tough decision). These types of decisions will also require a great deal of reasoning, input from those you love, a balancing of pros and cons and, in the end, the guts to make them. Fortunately, you will not face these immense decisions very often, but, when you do, you must choose wisely.

At the end of the day, making excellent decisions requires you to nail the easy decisions, become adept at successfully making a large majority of tough decisions and choose very wisely in your extremely difficult decisions. This is a Herculean task. Fortunately, you are young and have the time and hopefully the motivation to follow through on this advice. The remainder of this section will assist you in this process by introducing three major ethical frameworks you can consult to make excellent moral and life-management decisions: (1) Utilitarianism, (2) Deontology and (3) Virtue Ethics.

UTILITARIANISM AND ANALYZING POTENTIAL CONSEQUENCES

Utilitarianism is an ethical framework which provides you with an excellent way to analyze a decision. The framework is unique in that it applies neatly to your moral and life-management decisions alike. Utilitarianism judges how wise a given decision is by analyzing the consequences of each action under consideration. A utilitarian analysis is simple – weigh the potential positive consequences of your desired action against the potential negative consequences. Make sure to consider the impact of such consequences to you and to other people within your decision's sphere of contact. If the benefits outweigh the harms, then the decision is considered to be morally acceptable.

You must become adept at predicting the consequences of your actions in order to maximize the benefits and minimize the harms of your decisions. Although it is impossible to predict the future with any certainty, you can make educated guesses by using your prior experience, rationality and intuition as a guide. Pondering potential consequences allows you to: (1) balance the pros and cons of any action, (2) analyze the impact of an action on yourself and others and (3) take the time to think through your decisions in a way that is impossible when you act spontaneously or without any deliberate thought. Despite these benefits, too many people progress through their days without even thinking about consequences. Then, they become upset when things don't work out as planned or when an unexpected result occurs. Let's view the framework of Utilitarianism through the lens of two examples – a moral decision and a life- management decision.

A MORAL DECISION

Assume you are standing on the street in front of your apartment late one evening. You notice a disturbance down the block and see a man point a gun at another man and fire. The bullet misses and the victim flees past you and scrambles into your apartment building. A few minutes later the shooter approaches you and asks if you've seen anyone come by in the past five minutes. You are now faced with a moral decision. You can tell the shooter the truth and give away the location of the victim or you can lie and potentially save a life. In this case, your moral dilemma revolves around whether or not you should lie in order to attempt to save a life.

Lying in general is universally considered immoral, and for good reason, as trust underlies so many human relationships, obligations and institutions. It is morally unacceptable to lie in the vast majority of situations. Additionally, every lie you tell makes it much easier to lie in the future – lying is habitual and chips away at your character. Lying also ruins trust and causes people to avoid dealing with you in professional and personal situations. But, you have to be able to lie in this unique situation, right? You cannot be morally required to tell the truth to someone trying to kill someone else, right? You have a tough decision to make; you want to lie and need some moral guidance.

Under the ethical framework of Utilitarianism, you must analyze the benefits and harms to you and to others that will likely be associated with your decision – in this case, to lie. Unfortunately, you cannot predict the future and have no idea what will happen if you lie versus if you tell the truth. Making things even tougher is the fact that you have to make this decision in the brief moment you have before the shooter really gets angry.

For instance, you can lie and claim that you have not seen anyone pass by. This lie will make it more difficult for the shooter to locate the victim. You have potentially saved a life – surely constituting a large benefit to the person whose life you saved and to society in general. However, if you lie, the shooter may perceive the lie and harm you and/or find the victim regardless. Under these circumstances, harm will occur to someone else and you would have lied in the process.

After weighing the benefits and detriments, a utilitarian analysis would likely find that potentially saving a life outweighs the negative aspects of you telling this one lie and the slim chance that the shooter takes the lie out on you and/or finds the victim. In this case, a utilitarian analysis seems to show that lying to the shooter is the best decision. Unfortunately, Utilitarianism cannot provide you with a definitive and final answer. You have to make the ultimate decision as to whether or not you will lie in this instance. Additionally, just because you may choose to lie in this instance, such a decision does not mean that you are free to lie at will all of the time. Instead, you must run another analysis for each decision and then act accordingly.

A LIFE-MANAGEMENT DECISION

In addition to using Utilitarianism for moral decisions, you can also use this ethical framework to determine whether a particular life-management decision is wise. Assume that you are the president and founder of a small business that teaches tennis to children across your state. Business has been good, customers are satisfied and you are chomping at the bit to grow. With the future in mind, you are trying to decide whether to expand your sports offerings to include basketball. Jumping into another sport is risky because you will have to spend money and time on resources and trial runs in order to effectively compete in this new market. You will need to hire more employees and purchase additional insurance. You will also need to develop relationships with important individuals in the basketball world. Currently, you are making a good living on tennis alone and have some free time to spend with your family, but you worry about losing market share and you feel that you can potentially double your profits with this expansion. Although this situation has a few moral dilemmas – such as more money versus time with family, etc. – it is primarily a life-management decision. This choice is one of the many that move your life forward every day. How should you decide using a utilitarian approach?

Start by listing all of the benefits to you and to others that could stem from expanding into basketball. For example, you could make more money and cushion your business if tennis begins to fade in popularity. You will grow and become more of a player in the overall sports market. Other people would benefit by having the opportunity to learn basketball. Next, determine the potential harms to you and to others from the expansion. For instance, you could waste precious time and money on a venture where you lack experience and might not be able to compete effectively. Your business could suffer injury from bad publicity if your camps stink and other people could suffer if they waste money on a poor basketball experience. These are just a few pros and cons and you would need to spend much more time deliberating the issue and conducting the balancing test that Utilitarianism requires. As with the example involving the shooter, this ethical framework will not provide you with a final answer. It can only start your analysis and provide you with guidance. You have to make the ultimate decision and this is a tough one because much is at stake. On the other hand, making tough decisions of this nature is what life is all about. Consider it a challenge — but one where you must strive to choose wisely as often as possible.

While Utilitarianism is useful for both moral and life-management decisions, the remaining two ethical frameworks only work well with moral decisions. This is not to say that you are stuck with Utilitarianism in making all of your life-management decisions. You also have your common sense, prior experience, family, friends and colleagues to help guide your decisions. Utilitarian reasoning is just another tool to slap onto your decision-making belt. Now, let's move on to Deontology.

DEONTOLOGY AND UNDERSTANDING YOUR DUTIES

Each of us has duties. A duty is an obligation to act in a certain way in a certain situation. While many philosophers over the ages have talked about duties, Immanuel Kant is the most prominent philosopher to do so. Kant's categorical imperative (CI) is a test you can use to determine if you have a duty to act or to refrain from acting in a given situation. As an ethics professor, I am fully aware that philosophy-talk causes most people to bog down and miss important concepts completely. Therefore, just think of the CI as a test you can use to determine how you need to act in specific situations in order to abide by your duty (i.e., to act morally).

According to Kant, you must follow your duty in order for your actions to be considered moral.

The CI is based on the rationality of human beings and dictates that actions contrary to your duties are immoral and, thereby, irrational. Kant views a good person as a person who acts according to certain moral standards out of a sense of duty rather than a desire to impress others or gain an advantage. In other words, you should act out of duty for duty's sake.

Kant claimed that there are certain moral obligations that we must undertake as rational human beings. These are duties that we cannot opt-out from performing – they are universal and apply to every rational person. This section defines my interpretation of Kant's CI and then applies the test to a hypothetical moral decision.

The following three-part test presents a particularly simple method you can use to determine if you have a duty under the CI. Although this is not exactly how Kant would phrase his version of the CI, this test allows people without a PhD in philosophy to actually determine and follow their duties.

1. Determine the specific action under deliberation;
2. Ask yourself if people could live rationally in a world where everyone is allowed to act in the same way you desire to act without society collapsing; and
3. Then ask yourself even if people could live rationally in such a world, would you want to live in it.

If you fail step two, you have a perfect duty to refrain from acting according to your specified desire. Perfect duties have no exceptions. If you pass step two and then fail step three, you have an imperfect duty to refrain from acting according to your specific desire. An imperfect duty is still a duty but a duty with limited exceptions. Only if you pass step two and step three can you safely assume that your desired action is moral. The remainder of this section will analyze each of these prongs in more detail using the following moral dilemma as an example.

Assume that you own a company that sells a light-weight MP3 player that you invented. You have always provided a two-year warranty on your machines and have built up a loyal customer base by doing so. Even though the fine print at the bottom of your written warranty allows you to charge your customers half of the repair costs when they make a warranty request, your sales staff always promises your customers when they buy your machines that the company will pay for all of the repair costs.

It has come to your attention, however, that the newest version of your machine has a tendency to break down after five months. Your data shows that this will happen to one out of every twenty machines that you sell. It will be cost prohibitive for you to go back and redesign a new machine without this flaw. In the same vein, allowing your customers to return the machines under your two-year warranty with you paying for all of the repair costs will make you unprofitable for the year. Unfortunately, you know that if you take away the warranty completely, you will lose customers. Therefore, you are trying to decide whether it would be ethical for you to keep the warranty in place and make your free-repair promise at the point of sale, but then make the smaller amount of customers who send in faulty machines to pay half of the repair costs under the terms of the fine print.

STEP ONE: DETERMINE THE ACTION UNDER DELIBERATION

Determining the potential action involved (i.e., the decision you have to make) is the first step and also the easy part of the categorical imperative. The key here is to whittle the totality of a situation down to the specific action you wish to undertake. This action serves as the foundation for your duty-based analysis.[27] Try to formulate this statement into a question. In our example, the action under deliberation can be broken-down in the following manner: "Can I make a promise to a customer through a product warranty and then break that promise in the future when breaking the promise is the only way I can remain profitable and stay in business?" This is the question we will use throughout the other two steps of the CI.

STEP TWO: WOULD SOCIETY COLLAPSE IF EVERYONE ACTED IN THIS MANNER?

The categorical imperative does not allow you to make exceptions for yourself and then hold others to a standard whereby they cannot take the same exception. This is a real bummer as we do this type of thing all the time. We think that we should be able to butt ahead in line and then get mad when others butt in front of us. We justify breaking the rules because we've "earned it" or because "life just isn't fair." We want special treatment but couldn't care less if others receive special treatment. The more you think about this hypocrisy, the more you will realize that it is morally unacceptable.

Step two of the categorical imperative requires you to imagine a situation where the exception you were going to take for yourself is available to everyone else in the same situation. In other words, would the rational functioning of the world break down if everyone could break a promise when it suited their interests? This set of circumstances would constitute a world where people's promises would have no meaning and where businesspeople could not be trusted. In such a world, anyone could make a promise but nobody would expect the promise to have any meaning. This is a logical contradiction and irrational when viewed as a universal rule. If everyone acted this way, institutional and relational social structures

---

[27] When considering two actions, you need to run this exercise separately

would quickly break down as people lost trust and stopped doing business with each other. You do not even need to get to the third step with this example; you have a perfect duty to keep the promises that you make even if this decision forces you out of business. You are never allowed to make a promise to your customers that you know you intend to break in the future. Recall that it is never morally acceptable to break a perfect duty. Therefore, you must always tell the truth when you are faced with a situation similar to the situation in this example.

STEP THREE: WOULD YOU WANT TO LIVE IN SUCH A WORLD?

If you determine that the world would not break down if everyone could take the same exception you desire, then move on to the third and final step in the CI analysis. In step three, you must ask yourself if you would want to live in a world with a universal rule allowing the exception you want to take. If you would not, then you have an imperfect duty not to undertake the contemplated action. If you would not mind living in such a world, then you do not have a duty to undertake or refrain from undertaking the action you contemplated in step one. The answer you come to in step three depends a bit on subjective preferences and the imperfect duty that may arise here is not as strong as a perfect duty.

Since the broken promises example does not make it to step three without breaking down, let's look at a different moral decision. Assume you are wondering if you have a duty to be charitable – to give time, effort and/or money to causes or people in need of such assistance. Use the CI and start with step one and the following maxim: "Is it acceptable for me to never do anything charitable in my life?" Step two requires you to think of a world where everyone took this approach and refrained from undertaking any form of

---

for each one.

charity. These thoughts paint an unhappy picture to most of us, but we can imagine a situation where the social structure would stay intact without charity. People would suffer and happiness would erode but the world could logically continue. This is much different from our previous example where the social structure would completely break down due to a lack of trust and a plethora of broken promises.

Having passed step two, you move on to step three and ask yourself if you would want to live in such a world. If you would not, you have an imperfect duty to be charitable at least some of the time. This duty reflects a human desire to be assisted when in need. The idea that you likely want people to give you charity when you are in need but do not want to give charity to others in need is an unacceptable contradiction. This is irrational. Therefore, you have an imperfect duty to help people when it is possible for you to do so – even though you are not compelled to do so all of the time. This is much different from the perfect duty you discovered about making a promise you intend to break in the future.

VIRTUE ETHICS AND UTILIZING YOUR VIRTUES

You will recall that the ethical framework of Virtue Ethics was introduced in Chapter Three. As we have already covered this area extensively, let me only remind you that Virtue Ethics requires the consultation of your virtues before you make any moral decision. You are also required to determine which extreme you fall closest to and continually strive to reach the Golden Mean. Because Virtue Ethics encourages you to act consistently with individual virtues, the framework functions much better for your moral decisions than it does for your life-management decisions. In any moral decision, make sure to ponder which virtues are implicated and then act as closely to the Golden Mean of each as possible. In situations where two or more virtues seem to conflict or where you need a bit more guidance, the Golden Rule can assist you.

Let's analyze a moral dilemma with conflicting virtues involving being a loyal friend and being an honest person. Assume that you and your best friend are taking the same English class together in college. Assume also that your friend is as smart as you but does not have as strong a work ethic. You have studied for hours for today's quiz and she has hardly studied at all. As time is running out, she looks over to you and asks for the answer to the last question on the test. You are now torn between being a loyal friend – a virtue – and being an honest person – another virtue. How should you decide this moral dilemma?

Because loyalty and honesty are both virtues, you need to be loyal and honest to act morally and live the good life. Looks like you have a problem as these two virtues apparently conflict in this instance. If you ignore your friend and keep your answer to yourself, you are being honest and refusing to cheat. This is close to the Golden Mean on the honesty virtue spectrum. However, your friend will surely think you disloyal for failing to provide the answer in her time of need. As you will recall from Chapter Three, Virtue Ethics struggles to provide answers about how to act when virtues conflict.

Therefore, I urge you to consult the Golden Rule to determine which virtue holds sway in the given situation and act according to that virtue. In this case, it appears that the loyalty your friend requires is not the kind reflected in the true virtue of loyalty; you are not straying far from the Golden Mean of loyalty by refusing to help your friend cheat. In fact, I would hope that you would not want someone to cheat in order to help you succeed. You can also use the other two ethical frameworks and your judgment and common sense to assist you in making your final decision. Keep in mind that actually combining each of these frameworks with the Golden Rule, your common sense, your intuition, your gut feelings and the opinions of people you trust would take much longer than you have to make a typical decision. My advice is to take as long as you have to decide and then make the best decision that you can. As you become better at using these tools, you will be able to implement them more extensively in a short period of time.

✕✕

TAKE PERSONAL RESPONSIBILITY

> "No alibi will save you from accepting responsibility."
> --- **NAPOLEON HILL**
>
> "Hold yourself responsible for a higher standard than anybody else expects of you, never excuse yourself."
> --- **HENRY WARD BEECHER**
>
> "I believe that every right implies a responsibility; every opportunity an obligation; every possession, a duty."
> --- **JOHN D. ROCKEFELLER**
>
> "When a man points a finger at someone else, he should remember that four of his fingers are pointing at himself."
> --- **LOUIS NIZER**

The unthinkable has happened; you've just made a mistake. It seems that one of your decisions has produced unsavory results. Out of nowhere, you find yourself bombarded with repercussions including the consequences of your actions and the silent stares and biting words of others standing in judgment. The shock and awe of the whole situation forces you to sit down and determine how this could have happened. Your disbelief eventually subsides into frustration and then something predictable happens . . . you search far and wide for someone else to blame. If that special someone does not immediately appear you dig deeper until you find at least one person who was tangentially involved in the situation.

There had to have been someone who did something to set off the chain of events that caused your mistake. If only my mother hadn't called to check on me, I would have studied harder for my test. If my professor hadn't assigned so much reading, I would have had time to digest the material properly. If only my boss was more specific in my assignment instructions, I would have nailed that memorandum. If only it hadn't rained, I would have mowed the lawn or cleaned out the garage or made my bed. Bingo, with just a little effort you have discovered someone or something responsible for your mistake. With this task complete, the pressure is off and the rain cloud hovering over your head will just evaporate, right? Wrong. Although passing the buck may provide you with an easy out in the short term, misplacing blame will haunt you in the long run. In fact, chronic blame-placing hinders success by promoting the same mistakes in the future and engendering ill-will amongst family members, friends and colleagues.

You need to readjust your mindset and start taking personal responsibility for your actions. But beware, this is one of the most difficult challenges you face in becoming authentically successful. Can you even count the number of times that you blamed someone else for a poor decision that was primarily your fault? Can you even imagine what taking some personal responsibility would look or feel like? Am I touching on a sore subject or have you deluded yourself into thinking that this is not really an issue for you?

I suggest that you spend some time reevaluating these questions and then decide how good you really are at taking personal responsibility for bad decisions. Then, wipe the slate clean. From this point forward, you should etch into your mind this one crucial fact – this is your life. You made the decision, you chose to act upon it, you have everything to gain from taking blame and everything to lose from the repercussions. Most importantly, you are the responsible party. You can learn to take personal responsibility for your mistakes by swallowing the following three bitter pills. First, accept that you actually made a mistake. Second, accept that others will judge you because of your mistake. Finally, accept the consequences of your mistake and move on with your life.

ACCEPTANCE

Acceptance is the first step in the responsibility-taking process. You will make mistakes and some will sting more than others. By continually dodging responsibility, you accumulate a string of unresolved issues inside of yourself. You also anger the other people you falsely blamed or who are sick and tired of your problem-management approach. Acceptance of faults can be liberating; acceptance allows you to drop your guilt off of your back like a ton of bricks and come to grips with the regret, angst and fear caused by the poor decision.

Acceptance also allows you to move forward. All you have to do is recognize that you made a bad decision and that other people, although they may have helped bring the bad decision about or made it worse, are not primarily responsible. Acceptance of this sort will be much easier to undertake after you read Chapter Fourteen and stop fearing failure, but, in the meantime, let me offer you some advice. Understand that it is okay to make a mistake and that you will make many more over the course of your lifetime because, let's face it, life is tough and you are not perfect. You will never bat 1.000 when making decisions and you shouldn't expect to come close. As mentioned in the previous section, making more excellent decisions will increase your batting average, but you will never be perfect. Just accept that fact, keep swinging for the fences and learn to accept your mistakes as they come.

JUDGMENT

People will judge you negatively whenever you make a mistake. They will say that they anticipated the problems and that your decision was ill-conceived to begin with. They will claim that they never would have made such a poor decision and that you must now face its consequences. This is human nature and these judgments are no big deal – they might even be accurate.

What we need to do is get away from the stigma associated with judging people's mistakes and accept the reality that people will always judge people. I have become very tired of hearing people say, "don't judge me" or "that is so judgmental." Under this flawed logic, anytime anyone has an opinion about anyone or anything, such an opinion can be considered judgmental and, therefore, something to be avoided. This is nonsense. Do we really want to live in a world where people cannot have or express opinions about other people's decisions? Should we just bite our lips and keep our advice to ourselves? These questions are natural extensions of the "don't judge me and I won't judge you" mindset.[28]

Although criticism from others can be hurtful and never feels great, this dialogue can be very positive and bring to light things you did not think about previously or cause you to think harder before acting in the future. It serves as a brutal second opinion of sorts. The judgers may express their opinion poorly or be completely off base, but either way, you can hear their input and take their advice or choose to ignore them completely. Although you should never let someone's judgment force you into a decision, taking the time to ponder the thoughts of your critics can be beneficial.

---

[28] On a side note, now that you are okay with the idea that you will be judged negatively from your mistakes and that such judgments can hurt, be kind in the manner in which you evaluate others on their mistakes. By all means tell someone if you think they are making a mistake but do so out of

At the end of the day, it is irrelevant what other people think of your decision. They might not have made the same choice, and they will not have to face the consequences if it goes bad. However, as long as you sincerely felt that your decision was an excellent one, you can rest your mind. Remember, your days are filled with decisions that you have to make and sometimes the best laid plans... well you know the rest.

Do not think that the negative feelings you experience when people judge you ever go away completely. If I had a dollar for every time someone judged me based on one of my decisions, either before or after it was made, I would be happily retired in Key West and Vail – depending on the season. As a lawyer, professor and small business owner, I am constantly faced with tough decisions and the corresponding criticisms that come with such decisions. It is still frustrating when someone thinks I am not competent enough or that my choice was ill-advised. I am the type of person who wants people to think I am an intelligent, great decision-maker all of the time – even though that is not true. I have to accept that people are people and that life is tough. I have also come to realize that some of the people judging me might even be trying to help me from making a bad decision and hurting myself in the process. This remains true even if it turns out that they were wrong.

CONSEQUENCES

Accepting the positive and negative consequences of your actions is the third and final step in your personal responsibility challenge. At this stage, you must be able to determine and digest the consequences of your actions and then effectively discard any lingering thoughts on the matter. This process is something that you need to get comfortable with because every action you ever undertake will result in a consequence or a set of consequences.

---

compassion and not out of spite or jealousy. If you sense that your comments are motivated by such anti-virtues, then just keep quiet.

Some of these consequences will be positive, such as earning acceptance to medical school after working extremely hard in college. Others will be negative, like having to face your final grade when you chose to go out with your friends repeatedly rather than study. Much like taxes, consequences cannot be avoided. Therefore, you need to learn how to deal with them by enjoying the positive variety and understanding that even negative consequences can have some positive attributes. Negative consequences can teach you about the typical outcomes of certain actions and help you tailor your actions to produce different results in the future. If you fail to pin mistakes on yourself, you are less likely to take their consequences seriously.

One final thought to keep in mind about consequences is that really bad decisions will present you with really bad consequences. I cannot emphasize this point enough. For instance, a decision to drive drunk could cost you: (1) a DUI ticket including a court date, a felony and a potential jail term,[29] (2) an accident and loss of your vehicle during repairs, (3) a great deal of money for your car, other cars involved, increased insurance premiums, your court costs, potential lawsuit judgments and your lawyer, (4) physical and mental pain and, maybe (5) your life or the life of another. Driving while under the influence of alcohol is a terrible choice and a decision that is destined to present you with horrible consequences that will haunt you for a long period of time.

Hopefully, the first half of this chapter, your common sense and your intelligence in general, will provide you with enough ammunition to banish the most remote thought of acting in such a

---

[29] While most states classify a DUI as a misdemeanor, the offense can be raised to a felony if someone else was injured during the course of the DUI or if it constituted a second offense. If that injured person dies, the charge can be raised to reckless homicide – a very serious felony. After all of the horror stories I have heard as a lawyer and as a professor, I am convinced that driving after drinking is one of the worst decisions that a human being can ever make.

stupid manner. But, there are less horrible decisions that you can make that still result in really bad consequences. It is crucial to remind yourself every day that one really bad decision is all it takes to significantly set you back.

Making excellent decisions and taking personal responsibility are like two peas in a pod. Excellent decisions lead to positive consequences and effectively dealing with negative consequences leads to excellent decisions in the future. With this in mind, strive to make as many excellent decisions as possible and then take personal responsibility for your mistakes. These two actions in combination will lead you closer to authentic success.

CHAPTER 13:
UNDER THE INFLUENCE OF STRESS

> "Who of you by worrying can add a single hour to his life?"
> --- **JESUS OF NAZARETH: THE GOSPEL OF MATTHEW 6:27 (NEW INTERNATIONAL VERSION)**
>
> "If people concentrated on the really important things in life, there'd be a shortage of fishing poles."
> --- **DOUG LARSON**
>
> "Sometimes the most important thing in a whole day is the rest we take between two deep breaths."
> --- **ETTY HILLESUM**
>
> "The reason why worry kills more people than work is that more people worry than work."
> --- **ROBERT FROST**

During a typical week, dozens of students drop by my office. Throughout these meetings, I look each of them in the eye while we discuss life and other less important things. As they talk, I consistently notice a disturbing trend; by and large, young people are too stressed. Young people today are so busy with school, work, extracurricular activities and social events that they barely notice the days pass by. Instead of enjoying the best time of their young lives (i.e., a period without a full-time job or a family to feed), they stuff each day full of running from activity to activity without truly investing themselves into anything. Most students become overly-involved because they feel that their future endeavors (i.e., graduate school, the top employers in their field and a successful career) require a resume full of hustle and bustle upon graduation. They chase false expectations and quickly become chronically over-stressed. Doesn't this sound a lot like the story of a certain racing greyhound we met in the Preface?

MEET LAUREN

This phenomenon of excessive busyness merits an answer to the following crucial questions: Are you truly investing your best into your current pursuits? And, if not, why are you involved? Serious deliberation of these questions allows you to sit back and determine, for each activity you pursue, whether the endeavor is truly worthwhile to your life and priorities or mere resume padding. I once asked a super-involved (and very intelligent) student named Lauren these questions in that order. We began with her role in the seven extracurricular groups she listed on her resume. Lauren responded that she wasn't really sure what each of the groups did specifically and that she only had time to attend the mandatory meetings. Astoundingly, she was a Vice President of one of the groups and had no idea of its current goals or what her role as V.P. entailed. This situation smelled of resume padding as well as the chasing of fake rabbits – in this case the chance to document more campus involvement than her peers.

Lauren was over-stressed but she could not understand why. She also had no clue about how to change her current situation. She told me that she was not investing her best in the majority of these activities, but could not muster the guts to tell me the true reason why she was involved in so many of them. Even without her admission, however, the point was clear to both of us. We talked about how excessively-involved people tend to burn out. Over time, these students begin to fade from each of their activities while simultaneously spending less time in class and little or no time talking to their families or hanging out with their friends. Lauren asked how I could predict that burn-out was looming on her horizon. I responded that I had stood in her shoes back when I was a college student.

MEET COREY

In college, I consistently took an overload of classes, joined a plethora of student groups and always tried to find something else that would differentiate me from the pack. I wanted to be the best. The problem was that I was not able to think effectively in my classes because I was always thinking ahead and making lists as to what I needed to do the rest of the day/week. I could rarely give my all to my extracurricular commitments because I needed to get home and study for my classes the next day or run to another activity. Above and beyond all of that, I spent ridiculous amounts of time trying to find more to do to provide me with that crucial edge I felt I needed.

In the end, I became chronically overstressed. I found myself suffering from some of the physical and mental ailments associated with stress; my neck was always sore, I lived with a minor headache over long periods of time and I had trouble sleeping at night. I ended up dropping most of my extracurricular commitments and struggling to keep up in my classes. I was too busy; I took on too much. The stress Lauren and I experienced nearly a decade apart produced a similar symptom – the breakdown of our ability to function as healthy human beings. We both needed to refocus; I did and I hope Lauren will. In fact, each of us can benefit from refocusing from time to time. How should you refocus to reduce your current stress level? It's simple. Ask yourself these simple questions: Are you investing your best in your current pursuits? If not, why are you involved?

DEFINING STRESS

This lead-in is designed to focus your attention on the infamous concept that comprises the subject of this chapter: STRESS. Amazingly, those six little letters embody an unhealthy state of mind and very serious implications. The word stress has two pertinent definitions of interest in this chapter:

1. STRESS: "A specific response by the body to a stimulus, as fear or pain, that disturbs or interferes with the normal physiological equilibrium of an organism."

2. STRESS: "Physical, mental, or emotional strain or tension."[30]

My first-grade teacher used to tell me that "dictionaries don't lie." Well, I don't need Mrs. Brown for this one; I can tell you from first-hand experience that the dictionary is telling the truth when it comes to defining stress. As these definitions indicate, stress causes two major problems in our lives. First, a stress-filled life makes it tough to function in a mentally-sound fashion and second, stress takes a tremendous toll on our physical bodies.

PAYING THE MENTAL AND PHYSICAL TOLL OF STRESS

Most succinctly, to stress is to be worried about someone or something in your life. Stress is problematic because it makes it nearly impossible to function properly from a mental and physical standpoint. Interestingly, the word "worry" is derived from the Old English word wyrgan and the Old High German word wurgen both meaning "to strangle" or "to choke." This derivation is remarkably appropriate as stress does make you feel as if you were drowning

---

[30] Stress. Dictionary.com. Dictionary.com Unabridged (v 1.0.1), Based on the *Random House Unabridged Dictionary*, Random House, Inc. 2006. http://dictionary.reference.com/browse/stress (last visited November 24, 2006).

and unable to breathe. Stress causes you to constantly worry about a multitude of issues all of the time. In fact, you spend more time worrying about the troubles in your life than you do on fixing the problems that cause such troubles in the first place. Stress overwhelms your thoughts and emotions – you are figuratively choking. Things would be so much better if only you could come up for air and find a way to stay up and breathe. Ridding your life of unnecessary stresses provides you with the opportunity to fully breathe in the air of a healthy life.

The second major problem with stress is the toll it takes on your body. As an involuntary reaction to stress, your body automatically increases: (1) blood pressure, (2) heartbeat, (3) breathing, (4) metabolism and (5) blood flow. Stress can cause "physical, emotional and behavioral disorders which can affect your health, vitality, peace-of-mind, as well as personal and professional relationships. Too much stress can cause relatively minor illnesses like insomnia, backaches, or headaches, and can contribute to potentially life-threatening diseases like high blood pressure and heart disease."[31] Yikes!

TAKE A STRESS TEST

Are you too stressed? Let's find out. The following stress test will pronounce your current stress level loud and clear.[32] Answer each of the following twenty questions with a "yes" or a "no." Give yourself one point for every "yes" answer and zero points for every "no" answer. Be honest and beware that this test is designed to really open your eyes.

---

[31] Mental Health America, *Stress: Coping with Everyday Problems*, *available at* http://www.nmha.org/go/information/get-info/stress (last visited November 24, 2006).

[32] Awakenings Homepage, *Stress Test*, *available at* http://www.lessons4living.com/stress_test.htm (last visited January 5, 2007). This stress test has been reproduced with permission.

ARE YOU TOO STRESSED? FIND OUT BY TAKING THE TEST BELOW		
	YES	NO
(1) DO YOU FREQUENTLY NEGLECT YOUR DIET?	❏	❏
(2) DO YOU FREQUENTLY TRY TO DO EVERYTHING YOURSELF?	❏	❏
(3) DO YOU FREQUENTLY BLOW UP EASILY?	❏	❏
(4) DO YOU FREQUENTLY SEEK UNREALISTIC GOALS?	❏	❏
(5) DO YOU FREQUENTLY FAIL TO SEE THE HUMOR IN SITUATIONS OTHERS FIND FUNNY?	❏	❏
(6) DO YOU FREQUENTLY GET EASILY IRRITATED?	❏	❏
(7) DO YOU FREQUENTLY MAKE A "BIG DEAL" OF EVERYTHING?	❏	❏
(8) DO YOU FREQUENTLY COMPLAIN THAT YOU ARE DISORGANIZED?	❏	❏
(9) DO YOU FREQUENTLY KEEP EVERYTHING INSIDE?	❏	❏
(10) DO YOU FREQUENTLY NEGLECT EXERCISE?	❏	❏
(11) DO YOU FREQUENTLY HAVE FEW SUPPORTIVE RELATIONSHIPS?	❏	❏
(12) DO YOU FREQUENTLY GET TOO LITTLE REST?	❏	❏
(13) DO YOU FREQUENTLY GET ANGRY WHEN YOU ARE KEPT WAITING?	❏	❏
(14) DO YOU FREQUENTLY IGNORE STRESS SYMPTOMS?	❏	❏
(15) DO YOU FREQUENTLY PUT THINGS OFF UNTIL LATER?	❏	❏
(16) DO YOU FREQUENTLY THINK THERE IS ONLY ONE RIGHT WAY TO DO SOMETHING?	❏	❏
(17) DO YOU FREQUENTLY FAIL TO BUILD RELAXATION INTO EVERY DAY?	❏	❏
(18) DO YOU FREQUENTLY SPEND A LOT OF TIME COMPLAINING ABOUT THE PAST?	❏	❏
(19) DO YOU FREQUENTLY RACE THROUGH THE DAY?	❏	❏
(20) DO YOU FREQUENTLY FEEL UNABLE TO COPE WITH ALL YOU HAVE TO DO?	❏	❏

Tally your final score and let's take a look at the results. After deliberating and answering these twenty questions, you likely sense that this is not a normal quiz and that a perfect score of twenty is not a good thing. In fact, the higher your score, the more stressed you are at this point in your life. As I have given this test to many of my students, I have become adept at reading and translating their scores into four individual stress levels that I have named "A-OK", "Just Breathe", "Over-Stressed" and "Watch Out". The following chart correlates your stress test score to one of these four categories.

SCORE	STRESS LEVEL
< 5	A-OK
6 – 10	JUST BREATHE
11 – 15	OVER-STRESSED
> 15	WATCH OUT

Your goal is to keep your overall stress level at a score of five or below. At this point you will be A-OK and can worry about (just kidding, I mean move on to) another area in this book. A score between six and ten indicates that you are on the verge of being over-stressed and you need to just breathe a little and do so more often. You are vulnerable to moving up the stress scale if you do not tread cautiously. Be careful. Any score between ten and fifteen indicates that you are currently over-stressed. This means that you are having a tough time dealing with the troubles in your life and are experiencing an unhealthy amount of stress every day. If you are here, you really need to refocus your energies on de-stressing. Any score higher than a fifteen means you are at serious risk of long-term mental and physical damage due to stress. Things need to change in your life and they need to change quickly.

Keep in mind that your score will fluctuate over time. Your goal is not to keep a consistent score every day; rather, strive to keep your score as low as possible all of the time. There will be times in your life when a major stress event occurs that places you in the over-stressed or watch out range. The key here is to understand where you stand during these times and then make genuine efforts to lower your stress level as quickly as possible. As we will discuss shortly, you cannot control the major stress events that occur in your life, such as a death in the family or a car accident. The only thing you can do is to deal with them slowly and methodically. It will likely take you some time to recover from these incidents and to decrease your stress score in these cases.

The most important way you can be proactive, however, is to focus on a quick recovery from the troubles that cause minor stress in your life. You should be able to bring your score back down rather quickly after experiencing these minor stress events. The remainder of this chapter will give you a sense of the difference between major and minor stressors and provide some guidance in attacking your minor stressors. From here on, you should continually tally your current stress score and, more importantly, keep these twenty questions, and their implications, in mind.

A LINE IN THE SAND OF YOUR LIFE

Just like a twelve-step program designed to help people recover from addiction, the best first step to de-stressing your life is admitting you have a problem. Once you admit that you are overly-stressed and that such a state of being is not acceptable, you have a solid chance at recovery. Otherwise, you risk continually being stressed and experiencing some or all of the mental and physical symptoms described above. How can you begin your recovery? The answer is both extremely easy and extremely difficult at the same time: you must minimize the influence of stress in your life.

That's it, just minimize stress. No problem, right? Although this is much easier said than done, you have to give it a good faith effort. To begin the stress-minimization process, you need to divide the types of stresses in your life into major stressors and minor stressors. Major stressors occur when something big and bad happens in your life. These are events that touch upon something in your highest priority classifications, are too important to be ignored and are primarily out of your control. Examples of major stressors include deaths in the family, losing a job, facing a serious illness or ending a serious relationship. Minor stressors, on the other hand, stem from more trivial happenings, affect your lowest priorities if they affect your priorities at all, are primarily within your control and can be set aside by adopting a different, big-picture perspective as described in Chapter Five. Examples of minor stressors include a poor score on a test, a run-of-the-mill bad day or a bad encounter with a mean or otherwise rude person. It's acceptable to stress about major issues in your life, it's unacceptable to stress about the minor issues in your life for more than a very brief period of time and it's damaging to stress both the major issues and the minor issues at the same time. Your mind and body cannot take this kind of beating.

Start the healing process by visualizing each and every one of your stressors. The easiest way to do this is to draw a line in the sand of your life. Go ahead and physically jot this line down on a piece of paper. Place the major stressors that are currently troubling you on the left side of the line. Then, on the right side of the line, place the minor stressors that are currently troubling you.

YOUR LIFE

MAJOR STRESSORS	MINOR STRESSORS

Your job is to eliminate as many stressors from the right side of the line as you can. This feat is possible because the power to eliminate the cause of each minor stressor is within your control. All it takes is the motivation and the effort to obliterate each one from your life. With these minor stressors out of the way and off your mind, you can deal with the stressors on the left side of the line – the stressors outside of your control – more effectively. In order to function as a healthy human being, you must give your mind and body a break from the beating caused by experiencing both kinds of stressors at the same time. The following section provides an example of a major stressor and an example of a minor stressor. As you read each paragraph, the distinction between the two will become quite obvious.

I recently talked with a student whose dad was diagnosed with kidney failure. The student had to decide whether or not to donate a kidney to his father – who was on a three-year waiting list. While most of us would claim that we would donate one of our two kidneys in a heartbeat, it's stressful when we really sit down and think about the process of what's about to happen and actually going through with it. This was a major stress event that was outside of my student's control, but an event that affected him immensely. His family is at the top of his list of priorities and this situation is very worthy of stress. This is a major stressor and should be placed on the left side of his line. Prior to this medical diagnosis, my student had been stressing about his grade in my Constitutional Law course. He knew better, but was preoccupied with getting an A. This obsession with his grade caused him to cut corners in the learning process and attempt to memorize only the topics that he thought I would place on the examination. After his father's diagnosis, things changed. Can you even imagine my student stressing about an upcoming Constitutional Law test while visiting his father in the hospital on dialysis and also having to decide when to schedule his kidney-donation operation?

The second story deals with a situation involving a group of students and the same Constitutional Law examination. Imagine a smart group of students who are struggling to acclimate to the college lifestyle. Each student has a decent moral background and can generally differentiate right from wrong. Problematically, the students became caught up in extracurricular activities and socializing at the same time as the university's examination period. Time ran out, the students were stressed about their grades and decided to "work together" on their Constitutional Law final. This activity violated course policy and constituted a serious Honor Code violation. Eventually, word spread about the cheating and their classmates and I all learned of the incident. I had sensed a problem a few months prior when I entered final grades and found that their scores and the questions they missed were very similar. As the word of the cheating spread, the students involved become more and more stressed, worrying about my personal and professional opinion of them, the impressions of their classmates and the potential scars on their academic record.

Although the students were in complete control of their cheating, they were unable to control their reputations after the fact. A harmed reputation can caused immense personal and professional damage and constitutes a major stressor. The Constitutional Law final, while marginally important in the short-term, is of little to no importance in the big scheme of things. These students should have adopted a big-picture perspective. They should have realized that obtaining a good score on one examination was not worth the negative consequences associated with cheating. This would have eliminated the minor stressor in their lives and, more importantly, prevented the major stressor caused by their actions.

YOUR LIFE	
MAJOR STRESSOR	**MINOR STRESSOR**
KIDNEY DONATION FOR FATHER ON DIALYSIS	CONSTITUTIONAL LAW EXAMINATION
REPUTATION AS A CHEATER	CONSTITUTIONAL LAW EXAMINATION

DE-STRESS FROM YOUR DISTRESS

As you can see, stress in your life brings about distress in your life. Now is the time to clear your mind and recharge your body by de-stressing. This chapter has demonstrated that the best way to start this process is to draw a line in the sand of your life and classify each of your worries as either a major or a minor stressor. This is the easy part. Then, you must begin to eliminate your right-side (minor) stressors one by one. This is the hard part. Although you may find it difficult to dispense with every minor stressor right away, consider any elimination as a step forward on the path to an eventual victory. Before you know it, you will be able to scratch the vast majority of the minor stressors off of your list and hinder new troubles from being added. This entire process will become much simpler if you can adhere as closely as possible to the following pieces of advice:

1. MAKE EXCELLENT DECISIONS

The previous chapter encouraged you to make excellent decisions and to make them as often as possible. Decisions also prove crucial in the de-stressing process as poor decisions cause negative consequences and negative consequences cause stress. If you are currently experiencing worry produced by minor stressors, it's likely that you made some poor decisions somewhere in the recent past. Strive to make better decisions and remember that the causes of minor stressors are primarily within your control. Also remember that you can eliminate anything that you can control. That doesn't mean it will be easy, but the opportunity exists. Keep this equation in mind as you journey through each day:

EXCELLENT DECISIONS = LESS STRESS

---

2. DEVELOP PRIORITIES AND ADOPT A BIG-PICTURE PERSPECTIVE

Once you have spent the time required to create a solid list of priorities, eliminating minor stressors is much easier. A clear set of priorities will show you why it's important to worry about major stress events affecting your highest priorities and why you should just shrug off minor stress events. Take some time to think about some of your minor stressors and how low the issues that are causing them fall on your list of priorities or if they even make your list in the first place. For instance, if you find yourself constantly stressed about slow drivers and other issues involved with your daily commute, take a look at your priorities and determine where "driving to work" falls. I hope that this activity does not even merit a place on your list. Realizing the unimportance of this activity to your life will allow you to recognize that something so trivial should not cause you so much stress. You can control your reactions on the road and I encourage you to give it a try.

Additionally, Chapter Five urged you to develop a big-picture perspective. As you do, you will begin to see that some of the small issues currently causing you stress fade into oblivion. Little-picture perspectives, on the other hand, make you feel like every little setback in your life is important. You end up micromanaging your life instead of living it. As soon as you realize that there are more important things in life than a poor quiz score or a slow driver in the fast lane, you will eliminate some minor stressors rather quickly.

3. AVOID PURSUING TOO MANY WORK/SCHOOL/SOCIAL-RELATED ENDEAVORS

Are you too busy? I used to be. Do you run from one activity to another and then repeat the process throughout a typical week? I used to do that as well. In fact, a few years ago, I found myself so busy pursuing my work-related endeavors that I did not have time to spend time on my family, my friends or my relaxation. I felt compelled to join the boards of directors for a few non-profit organizations and serve on several of my employer's committees in order to get ahead in my professional life. All that happened, however, was that I allowed my job and these work-related commitments to dominate my existence. With the few moments I had to dedicate to deep thinking, I became depressed that this type of existence is what my life had boiled down to. Even worse, all of this hustle and bustle caused me to experience tremendous amounts of stress. The symptoms of this stress were similar to those I experienced in college.

Fortunately, my prior experiences allowed me to quickly realize that I needed to slow down. There really was no reason for me to pursue so many work-related activities, even if they would have helped me advance at my job. I was cheating the people and things that ranked higher on my list of priorities. I finally heeded the advice that "the time to relax is when you don't have time for it" and dropped some of my commitments.[33]

While it may be difficult, sometimes the answer to your problem is to whittle down your list of activities. This was the second time in my life that I had to abandon commitments I did not have time for

---

[33] Sydney Harris.

in the first place. This looks terrible and I felt terrible about it. Quitting an organization that you have committed to hurts your reputation, the other people involved and the organization itself. Today, I am much more careful about the groups I join and commit my time to. Now that I have finally incorporated this important maxim in my life, I'll pass it on to you. Keep this advice in mind every time you think about pursuing another endeavor and you will save yourself from some unnecessary stress.

4. AVOID SEEKING PERFECTION FROM YOURSELF AND FROM OTHERS

Are you a perfectionist? So am I. Actually, I am a recovering perfectionist. I gave up my perfectionist tendencies after discovering that my many mistakes made it impossible to achieve such a lofty goal. I would bet big money that you will face the same problem if you attempt to adopt perfection as your standard. It's not your fault; you can blame it on human nature. It seems that you and I and humans in general are not designed to be perfect. Aside from my mother-in-law,[34] we all tend to make mistakes and we make them quite often. If humans are pre-wired to make mistakes each and every day, the only thing you will find on your quest for perfection is stress. Therefore, stop striving for perfection and settle for close-to-perfect or above-average performance instead.

If you choose to stop seeking perfection for yourself, remember that it is unfair to demand perfection from others. This concept seems so obvious, but we often operate under double standards. For example, how often have you gossiped about a friend's big mouth without recognizing that, by gossiping behind your friend's back, you are doing the exact same thing? You are expecting your friends to be

---

[34] This is a funny story -well, kind of. My mother-in-law once claimed to have only made two mistakes in her entire life. We all should be so lucky but I strongly doubt that we will.

perfect and that is unfair. Your gossip also functions as a double standard as you are expecting perfection from someone else knowing that you are nowhere close to being perfect yourself.

5. DON'T WORRY TOO MUCH ABOUT BAD THINGS THAT COULD HAPPEN

Over 200 years ago, Thomas Jefferson adeptly commented "How much pain they have cost us, the evils which have never happened." This prescient comment remains valid in the twenty-first century. Think of the predicted Y2K computer meltdown. What was supposed to be a disaster of epic proportions turned out to be a trivial event. We worry and worry about potential happenings, far off in our future, that have not happened and may never happen at all. For instance, because previous relationships have caused us emotional damage, we worry that someone will hurt us in the future and are reluctant to develop fresh relationships. This attitude causes us to miss out on beneficial opportunities to meet someone who may actually care about us. These future encounters have not hurt us, yet we worry that they will. This is not to say that you should jump into a new relationship without a care, but you should definitely stop worrying about something bad that has not yet happened and may never happen.

You should prepare for the future by all means, but don't spend this preparation time worrying that things will go bad in your life. The time that you save can be spent on more productive things. This new approach will reduce your overall level of stress right away as you drop these worries from your mind. If you find this task difficult, then try and heed Mark Twain's advice to "Drag your thoughts away from your troubles . . . by the ears, by the heels, or any other way you can manage it."

6. IMPROVE YOUR LIFESTYLE

Your lifestyle is a main contributor to your overall stress level. Your lifestyle is comprised of the activities you undertake during your non-working hours on a typical week. Do you hang out with your friends, family or by yourself in your spare time? Do you go to restaurants, bars, parties, movies, plays, sporting events, or concerts where you have good, clean fun or do you frequent sketchy bars, parties and other establishments where trouble lurks? Do you spend a lot of money on your nights out? Do you overindulge on alcohol, cigarettes or drugs on weeknights and weekends? Are you primarily involved in healthy or unhealthy relationships in your personal life? The answers to these questions can reveal a great deal about your lifestyle. If you find that any of these activities are causing you stress, it's a safe bet that your lifestyle needs improvement.

Let me give you an example of a lifestyle choice that usually causes stress and should be eliminated. For some reason, young people tend to think that their late teens and early twenties constitute their prime years to drink alcohol – and not just drink, but get completely wasted on special occasions such as Fridays and Saturdays. It is no surprise that people who are drunk make stupid decisions such as driving, fighting and generally acting stupid. They also tend to say foolish things to people they do not know and hurtful things to their friends. These people invariably regret many of these decisions after they sober up. I am very concerned about this problem and have determined that young people choose drunkenness as an integral part of their lifestyle: (1) because of peer pressure, (2) to mask personality flaws and/or (3) to escape from their troubles. Each of these is a horrible reason to undertake any activity, especially something that can be as dangerous as excessive drinking.

Bowing to peer pressure shows that a person is spineless and shows why your mother likely asked you "if everyone jumped off a bridge, would you?" Apply this logic to your drinking habits and ask yourself if you are drinking excessively because you feel pressure from your peers or because everyone around you is drinking excessively? If so, go ahead and locate the nearest bridge just in case your peers decide to jump. If you are inhibited or otherwise fear talking to people without the assistance of this "liquid courage," try to work on these personality traits themselves instead of being phony and masking them by drinking. Finally, if you are drinking to escape from stress, then use the tips from this chapter to eliminate your minor stressors and the urge to drink for this reason will dissipate.

7.   BE MORE FLEXIBLE

One of the toughest aspects of being human is that we cannot predict the future. Anything could happen tomorrow. You could win the lottery and retire or get struck by lightning and die. You could get promoted with a raise or lose your job via downsizing. With unpredictability a near certainty, you need to be flexible as to the direction in which your life takes you. Throughout my life, I have wanted to be a doctor, a basketball coach and a partner in a law firm. I had a hard time passing high school chemistry and knew then that being a doctor was out. I never played varsity basketball in college and so my dream of coaching was gone. I tried being a lawyer in a law firm and realized that the job was not worth the personal agony involved. I do not work in any of the fields I thought I would and yet I am as content in my life as I ever have been. I have found that teaching and writing are both my calling and my passion and I am so glad that life led me in this direction. I have learned to be flexible with the things that life tosses my way, which has helped me accept and excel in my current situation.

Problematically, many people panic when something does not go the way they think it should have gone. This inflexibility leads to a great deal of stress as life will inevitably veer away from your plan. Instead of stressing, you must let go of the unrealistic expectation that everything will go your way all of the time. You must begin to be more flexible.

8. TALK AND BE OPEN TO TALKING

Have you ever been to a restaurant and witnessed two people eat an entire meal together without speaking to each other? I cannot imagine how damaged the relationship must be when two people can spend one hour facing each other and not talk. Open communication between people really makes a difference between a relationship that struggles and a relationship that prospers. I have seen so many relationships fail because the people just cannot or will not talk to each other.

Small talk is not enough and you must become comfortable telling the people you love about your innermost feelings. This is especially true when it comes to discussing something that another person did to you that makes you angry, hurts your feelings or otherwise upsets you. When we keep things inside of us, we have no outlet for these emotions and we get irritated and stressed. Practice expressing your deepest feelings, anxieties and angers to the people you care about and then be open to, and even encourage, these same people to share these things with you.

9. WATCH A SUNRISE AND THEN WATCH A SUNSET

Wake up early and watch the sun come up. Then, in the evening, turn around and watch the sun say goodnight. This will show you that there are much bigger things going on in the world than your minor stressors.

10. GO TO BED A BIT EARLIER AND TAKE A FEW NAPS

Sleep deprivation is extremely stressful. While I am not an expert on the symptoms of chronic sleep deprivation, I have experienced long periods of time without sleep. I have learned that pretending that you can make up for lost sleep is a myth. You may get more sleep than you need when you attempt to catch up, but you will not be able to make up for the long-term damage the previous lack of sleep has caused. I can tell you that someone who is tired is generally more stressed and irritable than someone who gets adequate amounts of sleep each night. If you find yourself lacking the sleep you need, try to go to bed a bit earlier and take a few naps here and there.

11. WATCH A CARTOON

"Sometimes it's important to work for that pot of gold. But other times it's essential to take time off and to make sure that your most important decision in the day simply consists of choosing which color to slide down on the rainbow."[35] Enough said.

12. SAY AND DO SOMETHING NICE FOR SOMEONE ELSE – ESPECIALLY SOMEONE WHO CAN NEVER PAY YOUR BACK

Socrates said, "Beware of the barrenness of a busy life." When we are excessively busy, we have a hard time saying or doing anything nice for other people. This lack of compassion leads to a pretty barren life filled only with thoughts of yourself and what you are trying to accomplish. Instead, we need to take the time to really say or do something nice for someone else. For example, a friend of mine named Loren tells a story about how his best friend always calls him at the airport before he travels in order to wish Loren a safe trip. This is amazing. How many of you call your best friends to bid them safe travels? To the guys reading this book, I am referring especially to you. Have you ever done something like this? Ladies, although you may be more likely to make such a call, have you? It seems strange to act this nice because we have not done anything like it in the past. In fact, if my best friends started calling me at the airport, I might feel awkward and laugh it off – at least initially. Then, after pondering the call, I would be appreciative and

---

[35] Douglas Pagels, *These Are the Gifts I'd Like to Give You* (SPS Studios, Inc., 2000).

feel loved for the rest of my trip. When you do or say something nice to someone else, it feels good. Good feelings help to eliminate stress. Additionally, it is often more fulfilling to do something nice for someone who could never pay you back. Either way, you should strive to say and do something nice for someone else every single day.

13. LAUGH, GIGGLE AND SNORT

Have you ever heard someone laugh so hard that they snort? Oftentimes these snorts are funnier than the joke itself. My wife – bless her heart – has a tendency to snort when she laughs exuberantly. When my wife snorts, I find that I am happy for at least the next hour or so. When she snorts more than once, my happiness doubles. Laughing, giggling and snorting are stress relieving for the laugher, giggler and snorter as well as for everyone in her presence. So, laugh, giggle and snort away and reduce stress in the process.

14. PET A DOG

It is impossible to pet a puppy, or any dog for that matter, without smiling. Impossible! If you don't have a dog, run over to a neighbor's or to a puppy store or to the park and pet a dog (please ask first if it's not your dog). If you happen to be a cat person, and you can actually get your cat to come over to you, pet it and this should produce the same result – a stress-relieving smile.

15. TAKE A WALK

In a world where we take a car, bus or subway everywhere we go, walking often takes a backseat. Walking is a stress-relieving activity and unfortunately, something that we do not do often enough. We would walk everywhere when we were kids, but, once we obtained our driver's licenses, that stopped immediately. So, drive to someplace pretty and then take a long walk. On this walk, make sure to think about the really important things in life and not about the minor stressors that are troubling you.

16. READ SOMETHING UNRELATED TO WORK OR SCHOOL

I have a friend who hates to read and brags about not having read a book from cover to cover since high school. I cannot understand why this "accomplishment" is something to brag about. Reading not only helps you build your intelligence and general knowledge, opens up doors to unknown places in your mind and allows you to live vicariously through different characters, it also reduces stress. Oftentimes all it takes to eliminate minor stress from your life is to direct your mind to an unrelated, enjoyable and productive activity. I enjoy reading the Bible, legal thrillers, books on American history and the works of Mark Twain. For you, it might be the latest murder mystery, biographies of world leaders or even the fantasy football report. Whatever you choose, take time to read something unrelated to school or your career at least three times per week.

17. GIVE SOMEONE A HUG AND THEN ASK SOMEONE FOR A HUG

Hugs are powerful stress relievers. It is tough to give someone a hug and then immediately go back to worrying about your minor stressors. More often than not, the hugger and hugee will get to chatting about their lives, old memories or common acquaintances. So, ask for a hug and then give a hug in return – or vice versa.

18. PLAY WITH A KID

I have taught tennis to children for over fourteen years. No matter what is going on in my life, the hour I spend teaching a kid how to hit an overhead smash causes my worries to fade away. The vast majority of kids are kind-hearted, innocent and idealistic – basically, everything that adults should be.

Spending quality time with kids with this demeanor will de-stress you in a heartbeat. Give it a try and find out how well it works.

19. CLEAN UP YOUR ROOM

Messy surroundings make most people feel like their lives are disorganized. This adds stress to the right side of the line. Fortunately, this minor stressor can be easily eliminated. How? Just clean up your primary living areas and other personal property such as your apartment, car and wallet/purse without stuffing things under your bed or in your closet. Give away things you do not need anymore and trash stuff that you have a tough time even giving away.

20. STRETCH AND TAKE FIVE DEEP BREATHS

When was the last time you touched you toes? Can you even touch your toes? Remember, stress causes your muscles to tense and tighten up. Stretching relaxes these muscles.[36] You should plan on stretching every day and, eventually, you will find yourself less stressed and even able to touch your toes!

Additionally, you need to stop and take five deep breaths several times each day. I have an idea; please put the book down right now and take five deep breaths — just to get a head start. Make sure that each breath is indeed deep and that you do not rush through this exercise. Five seriously deep breaths and you're on your way to removing the chokehold stress has on your life.[37]

---

[36] Stretching also possesses other benefits such as increased flexibility, improved circulation, better posture and enhanced coordination. Mayoclinic.com, *Stretching: Focus on Flexibility* (November 24, 2006), *available at* http//www.mayoclinic.com/health/stretching/HQ01447.

[37] There are many other de-stressing activities that you could have placed on your list. Think about placing a silly ring-tone on your cell phone and then calling yourself in front of other people. You could also see a funny

"FOR FAST-ACTING RELIEF, TRY SOWING DOWN"[38]

This chapter detailed the numerous negative attributes of stress, gave you a stress test, advised you on how to decrease your stress score and introduced twenty activities you can undertake to de-stress your life. You cannot control when and where your major stressors occur so you need to work on eliminating your minor stressors instead. Doing so can and will lower your overall stress test score. Fortunately for you, the majority of the activities mentioned above can be implemented in your life ASAP. So, start right now and go find the nearest dog to pet or child to play with. Watch the sunrise and take a nap. Stick to your priorities and always remember your perspective. De-stress your life from the distress you currently find yourself embroiled in and you will be more content. As a parting note, I would encourage you to heed Dale Carnegie's advice and understand that "if only the people who worry about their liabilities would think about the riches they do possess, they would stop worrying."

---

movie or watch *America's Funniest Home Videos*. Be creative and throw some new ideas against a wall to see what sticks.
[38] Lily Tomlin.

CHAPTER 14:
FEARLESS FAILURE

"I am grateful for all my problems. I became stronger and more able to meet those that were still to come."
--- **J.C. PENNEY**

"Success is how high you bounce when you hit bottom."
--- **GEORGE S. PATTON**

"Success is to be measured not so much by the position that one has reached in life as by the obstacles which he has overcome."
--- **BOOKER WASHINGTON**

"You may have a fresh start any moment you choose, for this thing that we call 'Failure' is not the falling down, but the staying down."
--- **MARY PICKFORD**

"So, first of all, let me assert my firm belief that the only thing we have to fear is fear itself – nameless, unreasoning, unjustified terror which paralyzes needed efforts to convert retreat into advance."
--- **FRANKLIN D. ROOSEVELT**

FAILURES, MISTAKES AND DOUBT, OH MY!

Do you aspire to lead a life free from failure? Dream on. Each of us fails. We all make mistakes and we make them all of the time. Human beings are just not designed to stroll through each day displaying utter perfection in every endeavor. Instead of being perfect, we tend to mess things up. We forget, move too quickly, act negligently and otherwise make poor decisions. Our failures cause us to fall down and we are often too frightened to get back up. Doubt enters our mind and begins to rattle around, leaving the fear of failure in its wake. If we can muster the courage to rise again, it is possible to learn important lessons from each of our setbacks. After having failed more times than I can count and having learned so many important lessons in the process, I remain thankful that I do not live in a world without challenges. How boring and unfulfilling!

You will make mistakes. You will fail. This is something that is basically out of your control. What you can control is the way you respond to each of your challenges, mistakes and failures. Your reactions to setbacks will determine the amount of authentic success you ultimately experience. Take something positive from each setback and you will grow. Learn how to avoid similar setbacks in the future and you will be able to move on more effectively. React negatively to your setbacks and you will learn the hard way. Make similar mistakes anew and you will find yourself stuck in a rut spinning your wheels.

Unfortunately, and as you know, changing our reactions to anything is a difficult process. We seem pre-programmed to doubt, sulk, blame others and feel sorry for ourselves when we fail – something I refer to as the "doubt and pout syndrome." We tend to feel bad about letting ourselves down and guilty for letting others down. We have failed enough times in our lives that these reactions have become second nature. Now, you can see why altering this type of ingrained mindset is a tough task.

OVERCOMING MY FAILURE RITUAL

I recently attempted to change my reactions to my mistakes and it has paid off immensely. I am thirty years old and readily admit that I have been failing consistently for the past three decades.

Unfortunately, I have only been learning from my setbacks for the past five years or so. Before I was able to alter my mindset, I would doubt and pout after failing at something without giving much thought to what caused me to fail in the first place. This attitude led me to make similar mistakes in the future. Upon making the same mistake anew, I would learn the hard way and doubt and pout all over again. This was my failure ritual.

After a dedicated effort and much practice, I have been able to adjust my attitude to accept my failures and take something positive away from each experience. I still make dozens of mistakes each day – and that's just before lunch. But, when I experience a major setback, I sit down and analyze what went wrong and why. I think about how I could have improved upon some of my decisions. I also look at the consequences of the failure and try to determine the fallout. Finally, I reframe my mindset and set my fear of future failures aside. I invariably get up and try again.

You too can learn to stop fearing failure. You can get to where I am right now much sooner by heeding each of the lessons presented in this chapter. The first lesson to learn is the ability to differentiate between a failure and a mistake.

MISTAKES AND FAILURES AND OUR REACTIONS TO BOTH

Although we tend to associate failures and mistakes, these two types of setbacks are a bit different. Mistakes occur on a smaller scale than failures and involve the individual decisions that you make on a daily basis. You make a mistake when you make a sub-optimal decision instead of an excellent decision. A string of mistakes often leads to a failure. Although a mistake generally is less serious than a failure, this is not always the case. For instance, making the decision to drive drunk is a mistake that could cost you your life and/or your freedom. This poor decision is properly classified as a mistake, but it is a very serious mistake indeed.

However, most mistakes are generally easier to recover from than most failures because the negative consequences stemming from a mistake are smaller and less damaging to your psyche. Be prepared to make a lot of mistakes over the course of your life. If you think about it, the fact that you are faced with so many decisions each and every day almost ensures that you will make some mistakes.

A failure, on the other hand, occurs when you attempt to achieve a difficult and time-consuming goal and are unsuccessful. At the end of the day, your goal remains unmet within the required timeframe. The type of things that we typically fail at have many moving parts and are made up of many individual decisions. Generally, one bad decision here and there might not be a problem. However, a string of bad decisions will generally result in a failure. That being said, there are times when we fail regardless of the quality of our decisions and the effort we put forth.

Failures are just a part of life and we need to understand that some things are just not meant to be. A few examples of failures would be: (1) running a small business that does not generate the revenue necessary to meet expenses and is forced to close or (2) applying to graduate school and getting rejected. It is important to remember that you are not a failure after experiencing such setbacks. Rather, you have failed at an endeavor you chose to undertake. There is a difference and failing is merely a part of life.

Failures and mistakes have a wide range of negative consequences ranging from trivial disappointments all the way to major adversities. No one likes to experience the negative emotions created by these consequences. In response to these emotions we typically: (1) doubt ourselves, (2) become frustrated with our efforts, (3) blame others (4) lose interest and quit and (5) fear future failure. It is easy to understand why we react this way after we have put our heart and soul into something and then miss the opportunity to experience a successful outcome. These feelings are natural and there is no need to ignore them. Rather, the key is to manage your reactions to your failures so that you can avoid the doubt and pout syndrome and, instead, take something positive from each experience. You will notice that none of the five typical responses to failures mentioned above allow you to take anything positive away from your setbacks. The next few sections explain why in a bit more detail.

DOUBT, FRUSTRATION AND BLAME

Failures produce doubt, frustration and blame just as lightning produces thunder – and it happens just as quickly. Ironically, these types of reactions can be just as dangerous to your life as lightning. When you find yourself in doubt, frustrated and blaming others, you will also find these emotions occupying the vast majority of your time. It is tough to take something positive from an experience when your mind is focused on these negative emotions. Let's look at the repercussions of each negative emotion in order.

Failure and doubt are intimately related, with the former causing the latter. Failures cause us to doubt ourselves because we did not accomplish what we thought we could accomplish in the first place. Even worse is the fact that when we doubt, we also lose confidence in our future decisions and actions. A person operating without confidence in life is a person without a chance to experience authentic success. The real world is primed and ready to prey off of people who lack confidence because they doubt themselves. We must be very careful when we begin to doubt ourselves and our abilities.

Our failures also produce frustration. When we experience a failure or make a mistake, we become frustrated with the negative outcome, with our decisions throughout the process and with our lives in general. Similar to someone who is experiencing doubt, a person who is frustrated cannot function correctly. As soon as I become frustrated, I begin to do things too quickly, lose focus, cut corners, say stupid things and invariably end up damaging someone or something in the process. Oftentimes what is damaged is a relationship I care about deeply. Ironically, the thing or person who is hurt by my frustration is rarely responsible for causing the setback. I was responsible. When I am frustrated, the furthest thing on my mind is taking something positive from the setback I am currently experiencing. This type of mindset and approach to failure is unacceptable.

Blaming others for our failures is one of the easiest things to do and also one of the most common. We talked about this issue at length in Chapter Twelve, but it deserves a brief mention here as well. When we point the finger at someone else, we are not taking responsibility for the failure. Because we are not taking responsibility, we neglect to take anything positive from the setback and are destined to learn the hard way and blame others the next time. This quickly becomes a vicious circle.

LOSS OF INTEREST

It is common to watch someone fail and then watch the same person assume the objective that he was trying to achieve was too difficult or too time consuming. This person then loses interest in the endeavor. The problem with this approach is that once we lose interest in something, giving up is right around the corner. And, who can blame us? With this type of negativity, it is easy to convince ourselves that quitting presents the best decision. Ironically, we did not believe that the endeavor was too difficult or too time consuming at the very beginning of the process. If that were the case, we wouldn't have attempted the endeavor at all.

It is tough to change our minds once they are made up and we invariably end up losing interest, quitting and moving on to the next thing in our life. Down the road, we tend to remember that we gave up on something that we desired to accomplish and regret it bitterly. In fact, it is very difficult to be happy with your life if you have just given up on something that you desired to obtain. Most importantly, when we lose interest in a goal, we also lose interest in understanding why we failed to achieve that goal. Again, nothing positive comes from this type of reaction to a failure.

ADOPT A MINDSET OF FEARLESS FAILURE

Fear is one of the negative emotions that we all feel when we experience failure. Fear comes from doubting ourselves and our abilities, losing confidence and an unwillingness to disappoint anyone else. Fear paralyzes our life. When we are scared, we only think about protecting ourselves and not about being successful. We no longer desire to take risks and put ourselves in danger of additional setbacks. Instead of taking something positive from our situation, we cower for cover and play it safe. When we fear failure, we let this fear dominate our lives.

Let me encourage you to look at each of your setbacks in a different light. Instead of doubting yourself, becoming frustrated, blaming others, giving up or becoming overtaken with fear, you must develop a mindset of fearless failure. The American philosopher Elbert Hubbard remarked that "the greatest mistake you can make in life is to be continually fearing you will make one." Mr. Hubbard nailed it. By continually fearing another failure, you will be hesitant to endeavor too far outside of the comfort zone you have artificially created. This fear will keep you safely at square one for the rest of your life. Unfortunately, nothing worth having in your life exists at square one.

By urging you to adopt an attitude of fearless failure, I am not advising you to run head-first into failure or act recklessly just so that you can learn something from the experience. Never mistake fearless failure for foolhardy actions. On the contrary, you should always strive to act cautiously and make excellent decisions in each of your endeavors. The concept of fearless failure is something quite different. It requires you to be courageous in your life, take action towards your goal rather than sit on the sidelines, and take calculated risks instead of no risk at all. Then, whenever you experience a setback, fearless failure requires you to: (1) determine its causes, (2) understand its implications and (3) take something positive from the experience. After that point, wish the setback *bon voyage* and summon the courage to get up and get on with your life.

The chances are very good that you will meet failure again. However, during your next encounter, you will be ready to look it right in the eye, take the punch squarely in the chops, get up and walk forward with confidence and without fear. That is what fearless failure is all about and this is the only way to experience authentic success on a regular basis.

ABRAHAM LINCOLN AND FEARLESS FAILURE

Abraham Lincoln remarked that "success is going from failure to failure without losing your enthusiasm." In fact, enthusiasm and fear make poor bedfellows. If you continually fear failure, it will be impossible to be enthusiastic about your next action – something with the potential to produce another failure. Either enthusiasm or fear will ultimately win out in your mind as you ponder future decisions. I encourage you to take Lincoln's advice and be enthusiastic in the face of failure. I give Lincoln's thoughts in this area great credence mainly because of his vast experience with the subject. In fact, the man who was arguably America's greatest president was a complete failure for a good portion of his life.

As a young man, Lincoln opened up a retail store named Lincoln & Berry. This venture quickly failed and left both Lincoln and his partner deeply in debt; Lincoln spent the next two decades working to pay off the money he owed. After failing in his efforts to be an entrepreneur, Lincoln subsequently attempted to be a farmer. However, he was never able to make a decent living and eventually decided that agriculture was not for him. After this second big career failure, he decided to run for office in the Illinois State Legislature. When the results came in, Lincoln had finished in eighth place.[39] This was followed by the death of his fiancée in 1835 and a nervous breakdown a year later. Additional failures were yet to come, however, as Lincoln subsequently campaigned for the United States Senate and lost, was denied an appointment to the United States General Land Office and failed in his bid to become Vice President of the United States in 1856.

Lincoln accumulated quite the laundry list of failures! Most people would have a tough time recovering from any one of the setbacks that Lincoln dealt with throughout his short life. Yet, he rose to his feet each and every time and pressed forward. Can you imagine if Lincoln would have experienced any one of these setbacks and been overtaken by the doubt and pout syndrome? What if he became frustrated and blamed others like we often do or merely lost interest and gave up? Had Lincoln taken the approach that we generally take when we make a mistake or fail, he never would have:

1. Won four seats in the Illinois Legislature;
2. Passed the Illinois Bar Examination and become a lawyer;
3. Obtained a patent for an invention that lifted boats over shallow spots in bodies of water;
4. Won a seat in the United States Congress;
5. Won election as the sixteenth President of the United States of America;
6. Won election for a second term as President of the United States of America;

---

[39] There were thirteen candidates in the race and the election results placed Lincoln in the bottom half of the pack.

7. Helped emancipate millions of slaves;[40] or
8. Saved the United States of America from the secession of its southern states.

These accomplishments are awe-inspiring and, to this day, Abraham Lincoln is a hero to millions upon millions of people around the world. Thank goodness that the sixteenth President of the United States did not give up after he experienced more than his share of big-time setbacks. Lincoln experienced bankruptcy, other business failures, personal tragedy and humility at the hands of the electorate. Through all this, he must have been fearful of trying again. Something inside of this great man, however, urged him to learn from his mistakes, get over his fear of future failure and rise again. His great efforts eventually led to great successes. In fact, none of Lincoln's eight awe-inspiring accomplishments listed above would have occurred had he let his doubts and fear hold him back. These accomplishments will be remembered forever, however, because he adopted an attitude of fearless failure.

YOUR EIGHT GREAT ACCOMPLISHMENTS

This chapter concludes with eight blank lines designed to represent the major accomplishments you will be remembered for over the course of your life. At this point, it is likely that the majority of your lines are blank. This is okay. Your job is to fill each one of them in as you accomplish great things in your life. That is, assuming that you can overcome your fear of failure along the way. If you give up, you will never know what accomplishments these blank lines could have represented. They will remain blank forever.

---

[40] Lincoln's reasoning for advocating freeing of the slaves was summed up in his statement, "as I would not be a slave, so I would not be a master. This expresses my idea of democracy. Whatever differs from this, to the extent of the difference, is no democracy." Lincoln would not want to be

Imagine watching Abraham Lincoln sit down and fill in his list of eight accomplishments! His list changed the world. Will yours? You may not have the opportunity to save the United States from breaking apart, serve in Congress or be the President of the United States, but you may greatly influence someone's life by being a mentor, add value to the economy with your diligence and creativity or benefit your community by volunteering much of your valuable time. Actions of this nature surely belong on your list. At the end of the day, remember that your list will remain blank if you let your fear of failure get the best of you. Your life deserves and authentic success demands more than just a blank page.

1._____

2._____

3._____

4._____

5._____

6._____

7._____

8._____

treated as a slave and so would not treat others as his slaves - this is a form of the Golden Rule (see Chapter Three for a recap of character).

CHAPTER 15:

HUSTLE, FIGHT, LISTEN AND LAUGH (EVEN AT YOURSELF)

> "Success is this:
> To laugh often and love much,
> To win the respect of intelligent persons and the affection of children,
> To earn the approbation of honest critics and endure the betrayal of friends,
> To appreciate beauty, to find the best in everything,
> To give of one's self, to leave the world a bit better, whether by a healthy child, a garden patch, or a redeemed social condition,
> To have played and laughed with enthusiasm and to have sung with exultation,
> To know even one life has breathed easier because you have lived."
> **--- RALPH WALDO EMERSON (ATTRIBUTED)**[41]

---

[41] There is an argument that this quotation was not written by Ralph Waldo Emerson but is instead an adaptation from a poem written by Bessie Stanley. Ms. Stanley submitted a similar poem to the Lincoln Sentinel and it was published in the November 30, 1905 edition. The poem won first prize for the best definition of success and Ms. Stanley won $250. Both poems are wonderful and deserve mention in a book about authentic success. Here is Bessie Stanley's winning poem:

> He has achieved success who has lived well, laughed often and loved much; who has gained the respect of intelligent men and the love of little children; who has filled his niche and accomplished his task; who has left the world better than he found it, whether by an improved poppy, a perfect poem, or a rescued soul; who has never lacked appreciation of earth's beauty or failed to express it; who has always looked for the best in others and given them the best he had; whose life was an inspiration; whose memory a benediction.

FINAL CHAPTER . . . FINISHING TOUCHES

Hustle, fight, listen and laugh. Embed these activities into a daily routine and you can round out your transformation into an authentically successful person. Although you have reached the final chapter of this book, now is not the time to skip ahead to its moving conclusion. While you should anticipate the completion of your arduous journey, your present focus should be on its final leg as you summon a bit of hustle, fight, listening and laughter into your important endeavors. This last step is essential because the contentment that accompanies success is quite difficult to achieve without consistently and appropriately exhibiting these virtuesque qualities.

The verbs hustle, fight, listen and laugh embody simple actions, so simple that you may wonder why they are of such great importance. This chapter offers an answer by elaborating upon each one and emphasizing their importance in your life. With practice, each action will solidify into a habit strong enough to rely upon even during your toughest days. Because habitualization takes time, you should start forming these habits right now. To start, please ponder the following questions and then jot down your responses.

1. Think back to last week and describe each worthwhile endeavor that required you to expend much emotional, mental or physical effort. Next consider the amount of effort you actually put into each task and grade your performance on an A to F scale with an A representing significant effort and F representing lackluster effort.

2. Have you ever truly placed your career, comfort, health or reputation in jeopardy (i.e., gone out on a limb) for

anyone or anything truly important to you or to the common good? If so, please describe the circumstances.

3.   Have you ever tried to speak with someone who would not stop talking long enough to actively listen to what you had to say? Have you ever been the speaker in such a conversation?

4.   Describe as many situations as possible from the past week in which you laughed so hard that you teared up, doubled over and/or snorted – or, in other words, experienced a healthy kind of laughter. Reflect upon this past week and compare the number of times you experienced healthy laughter to the number of times you faked amusement or found humor in someone else's misfortunes – an unhealthy kind of laughter.

These questions are designed to produce a bit of internal anxiousness as you think about how to answer them truthfully. Do not be alarmed, but this feeling will likely grow worse as we analyze the implications of each of your responses.

If you lack hustle, the substandard results accompanying your lackluster effort will shine through in your response to the first question. We will determine the amount of hustle you display in your life when we discuss your hustle grade point average momentarily. Your willingness to fight for things or people that are important to you surfaces in the second question. It is likely that you have gone out on a limb at some point in your life, but your venture was probably very brief or was conducted when you had little to lose. The third question challenges your current capacity and desire to be an active listener. Were you honest enough to admit the frequency in which you were the speaker in a one-sided conversation?   The fourth question causes you to think about the last time you experienced a healthy episode of laughter. A fake giggle here and there or laughing at someone's misfortunes is a form of unhealthy laughter. Does your unhealthy laughter overwhelm your healthy laughter? If you have carefully deliberated these four questions for a while and are dissatisfied with any or all of your responses, you need to allocate more hustle, fight, listening and laughter into each of your days.

These four questions also accomplish another important lesson by demonstrating the discontentment that occurs when you do not fill your life with some hustle, fight, listening and laughter. For instance, you surely recognize that breezing through trivial tasks and failing to exhibit any hustle in the process is not a noteworthy experience. Additionally, it is relatively easy to help someone in need when the negative consequences to you are minimal. It takes little effort to talk and talk and talk about yourself when you are not concerned about the person who is listening. Finally, it is easy to fake a laugh and muster a smile in situations where you should actually laugh and smile but cannot find the energy or the willingness. Any sustained period lacking at least some hustle, fight, listening and laughter is considerably unfulfilling and leaves you feeling like you are missing out on something in life. You are.

MOVING FORWARD

Therefore, in order to move forward on this journey, make an extra effort to hustle, fight, listen and laugh (especially at yourself) at least once every single day. Make an initial attempt today rather than tomorrow. In doing so, I challenge you to break a sweat, focus your mind and energy on a task, go out on a limb for something or somebody, actively listen for a change, belly laugh and make fun of yourself. Think it will be easy? I would be willing to wager that you cannot accomplish half of these things during the course of a typical day. I am confident in my prediction because we often go a week without laughing heartily, months without exhibiting hustle or fighting for something important and a lifetime without actively listening. My feeling is that we subconsciously understand the importance of each action but find ourselves extremely unprepared when the rubber of our life meets the road of the real world.

HUSTLE, FIGHT, LISTENING AND LAUGHTER AS QUASI-VIRTUES

It is helpful to think of each action listed above as a quasi-virtue. A quasi-virtue looks like a virtue and smells like a virtue but is actually something else – in this case, an action rather than a moral principle. Quasi-virtues are just like regular virtues in that they require purposeful honing in an effort to reach the Golden Mean located between the extremes (see Chapter Three for a refresher on virtues).[42]   As with the virtues related to your character, development of quasi-virtues requires practice and also requires you to stay away from the troublesome extremes. This means that you can hustle, fight, listen and laugh too little, too often and at inappropriate moments. We will borrow the following chart from Chapter Three to visualize each of these four quasi-virtues.

EXTREME	QUASI-VIRTUE (GOLDEN MEAN)	EXTREME

---

[42] Please review Chapter Three for a discussion of some key virtues which are helpful in development of your character.

Feel free to start with baby steps if you need to. For instance, if you have to cheat and watch a funny movie in order to laugh so hard that you snort, that's okay. If you need to join an exercise class that forces you to work up a sweat instead of working-out on your own, go for it. You might even need to place a small towel in your mouth the next time you are in a conversation – whatever it takes! The remainder of this chapter details each of these four critical actions and provides a game plan designed specifically to jumpstart the process of appropriately incorporating each quasi-virtue into your life. Altering your mindset to aspire to incorporate these quasi-virtues, however, is a formidable process. With this in mind, you must understand that even though this is the last chapter and even though these actions seem so simple that a child could master them, consistently incorporating each one into your life is much easier said than done.

HUSTLE

> "Everything comes to him that hustles while he waits."
> --- **THOMAS EDISON**
>
> "You may delay, but time will not."
> --- **BENJAMIN FRANKLIN**
>
> "You can't do everything at once, but you can do something at once."
> --- **CALVIN COOLIDGE**
>
> "The pride of success is hard work, dedication to the job at hand, and determination that whether we win or lose, we have applied the best of ourselves to the task at hand."
> --- **VINCE LOMBARDI**
>
> "Always bear in mind that your own resolution to success is more important than any other one thing."
> --- **ABRAHAM LINCOLN**

THE GOOD KIND OF HUSTLE

Hustle. This word carries two primary connotations, only one of which is apt for discussion in a book of this nature.[43] The type of hustle I refer to is the exertion of great effort guided by a sense of purpose and bountiful enthusiasm. To hustle is to break an emotional, mental or physical sweat while endeavoring upon a task. This section demonstrates that the ability to hustle is a key component of success in individual activities and in life in general. Think back to the question posed previously:

---

[43] Hustle can also mean a dishonest way of making money such as a con. I'll leave it to you to use this meaning of the word in a sentence.

> Think back to last week and describe each worthwhile endeavor that required you to expend much emotional, mental or physical effort. Next consider the amount of effort you actually put into each task and grade your performance on an A to F scale with an A representing significant effort and F representing lackluster effort.

Recall the anxiety you experienced as you contemplated this question. This type of reaction is a natural response as questions of this nature are designed to shine light on endeavors marred by insufficient effort. Insufficient effort is nothing more than a lack of hustle and a lack of hustle is certain to produce a less than desirable outcome. On the other hand, hustling allows you to outperform your own and others' expectations. Hustling in worthwhile activities is a no-brainer.

Think of hustling as expending at least 60% of your available supply of effort during your important endeavors. Superior performance in certain ventures will require a 60% effort, while others may require a higher percentage – 60%, however, represents a good target percentage. If you are befuddled by my calculations, you're in good company. People ask me all the time how I dare claim that hustle does not always equal giving 100%. Oh yes, the good old, "you have to give it 100%," line. Since we were little, we've been indoctrinated with advice claiming that nothing less than an all-out-effort is acceptable. However, there is a fallacy in this admonition. It is a rare occasion where anyone actually gives 100% effort in any endeavor. 100% effort requires every bit of energy you can muster as well as all of your concentration and intelligence. Think about these requirements and ponder whether you have really ever given something a full 100%. Not too often, if at all, I'd bet. I haven't either.

It bothers me even more when people brag about giving more than 100%. I once heard an athlete described as having given

200% in a game.[44]   This is pure nonsense as well as physically impossible. Distributing 100% of anything, by definition, means everything is gone after the distribution. 100% represents the works, the whole enchilada, the entire kit and caboodle, the big shebang or the whole nine yards, however you want to refer to it . . . it's as much as you can give. You rarely need to give this much effort to something in order to obtain a successful outcome.

Now that we have that cleared up, let's also consider another problem with giving your all. Exerting 100% effort towards an endeavor means that you have 0% left to give to other important events occurring at the same time. It is simple math really: 100% (effort available) – 100% (effort expended) = 0% (remaining). Because life involves many commitments and ventures occurring at the same time, you have to portion out your effort in order to get by successfully. You cannot afford to give one task your all and have nothing in your tank to utilize for your other commitments.

For example, when writing a paper for my class, I never encourage my students to work as hard as they possibly can. In fact, I would worry a great deal about their sanity if they did. I understand that my class is important, but also that it only makes up a small portion of the things students should be doing in college at any one time. I ask for at least a 60% effort when they actually sit down to research and write the paper. If they can give me that, I am confident that they will learn all they need to know about the subject and receive a solid grade in my class.[45]   I

---

[44] "He was a hustler beyond anything." Jones said. "He gave it 200 percent every play." Tom Keegan, *Spot-on for over 5 Decades*, November 18, 2006, *available at* http://www.KUSports.com.

[45] Please keep in mind that a 60% effort will not correlate into a 60% final grade in my class. These are two entirely unrelated concepts. I

want them to think about the topics covered in the course, but I also want them to maintain relationships with their family and friends, stay involved in their extracurricular activities and maintain their overall physical and mental health. These are tradeoffs that would be neglected if students focused 100% of their effort on my assignments. Forget about it - I'm terribly happy with a 60% effort on everything I assign in class.

The following chart illustrates the quasi-virtue of hustle and its two extremes. It's my opinion that giving at least a 60% effort is all that is required to reach the Golden Mean.

EXTREME – too little hustle	**HUSTLE** **(GOLDEN MEAN)**	EXTREME – too much hustle
LAZY		**OBSESSIVE**

A FINAL EXAMPLE OF APPROPRIATE HUSTLE

Let's look at another example – this time from the environment of athletics. Professional basketball players make a living off of their ability to play basketball at the highest levels. I have observed professional basketball for years and even purchased Denver Nuggets season tickets located two rows from the court. I have never – not once – witnessed a professional basketball player running as fast as he can or exerting his maximum level of effort during the entire course of a 48-minute game. Remember that the tradeoffs with the quasi-virtues mentioned above come into play when an athlete hustles too much during a basketball game. For example, an athlete running as fast as he can for a

---

would guess that anyone who actually puts in a 70% effort will receive a solid grade in my class.

long period of time is subject to serious injury and fatigue. These players are trained to hustle – but in a way where they can measure their exertion and stamina and to make sure that their supply lasts the entire game and in a way that is not reckless. Additionally, any player who runs, passes and rebounds as hard as he can on every play is destined to get injured. Sometimes the best play is to relax a bit, still give a substantial effort and let the game develop. The tradeoffs of injury and fatigue are not worth the 100% effort that traditional definitions of hustle require. With this in mind, a better way to measure your hustle is to be realistic and dedicate at least 60% of your effort to worthwhile tasks (tasks that encompass priorities in your life). In my mind, this type of effort surely embodies what it means to hustle.

SOME FINAL THOUGHTS BEFORE WE GRADE YOUR CURRENT LEVEL OF HUSTLE

Hustle does not involve merely moving quickly. The quickest of motion without a purpose is useless. Hustle also does not involve working tirelessly. An all-nighter spent on a project while distracted by the television is a waste. Make sure you hustle with a purpose. If you are in class, make sure and focus your mind and energy on the day's topic and do not just study or read mindlessly. If you are drafting a memorandum for work, dedicate your time to making sure the information you present is accurate and mistake-free. If you are relaxing at the beach, make a great effort to relax and purposefully forget about thoughts unrelated to the beach and the loved ones you are with. If you are exercising, exert yourself to the point where your stamina and strength can actually increase without doing damage to your heart or your body.

One last point revolves around hustle and enthusiasm. The key to hustling everyday is that you must undertake each of your endeavors with great enthusiasm. A lack of enthusiasm will lead to boredom and eventually to burn out. If you are going to take the time and exert the effort to undertake an endeavor, you might as well make the best of it. Becoming enthusiastic merely requires a mental reset. Take some time to analyze the benefits of the activity and how these benefits will assist you in the long run. Change from an "I'm just wasting my time" mindset to a "this will be beneficial to me" mindset and your hustling will really pay off.

GRADING YOUR HUSTLE

Hustle is hindered by a deficiency of desire and not by a lack of ability. Although most of us are emotionally, mentally and physically able to give at least a 60% effort to our important endeavors, we find it difficult to muster the motivation. A bright spot within the dilemma is that desire is easier to strengthen than ability.

With this in mind, you need to first gauge your current level of hustle and then determine if you need to increase it. Your hustle level can be approximated with a formula resembling a grade point average. The inputs are: (1) specific endeavors within a predetermined time period, (2) your effort level, (3) a grade and (4) a priority factor. The resulting output presents a unique way to determine whether you need to incorporate more hustle into your life. This formula constitutes your Hustle Grade Point Average (HGPA).

Your HGPA should be calculated as follows. First, recall each of your most worthwhile endeavors over the previous week. Second, grade your effort level for each endeavor on an A to F scale, with an A score representing at least a 60% effort and an F score representing a completely lackluster effort. Third, determine the point value of the grade you assigned using the chart below.

EFFORT LEVEL	GRADE	DEFINITION	POINT VALUE
Over 60%	A	EXCELLENT	4
Between 50% and 59%	B	ABOVE AVERAGE	3
Between 40% and 49%	C	AVERAGE	2
Between 30% and 39%	D	BELOW AVERAGE	1
Below 30%	F	FAILING	0

Fourth, determine where each endeavor you chose fits within your list of priorities. The higher the priority the more the endeavor counts towards determining your overall level of hustle. Remember, I am encouraging you to hustle first for the most important things in your life. This determination helps you decide when you need to hustle and when you can take it a bit easier. For instance, you need not hustle as you empty the dishwasher. This activity is not found anywhere on your list of priorities – hopefully! On the other hand, trying hard on your English midterm is important as your education likely falls within your *summa* or *magna cum laude* priorities. I capture the essence of this distinction with an input I call the priority factor – the higher the priority, the higher the priority factor.

PRIORITY CLASSIFICATION	PRIORITY FACTOR
summa cum laude priorities	4
magna cum laude priorities	3
cum laude priorities	2

The fifth step in calculating your HGPA requires you to plug your chosen endeavors and assigned grades into the chart reproduced below. Sixth, multiply the point value of each grade by the priority factor. This will give you the grade points for each endeavor. The seventh, and final, step requires you to add up all of your grade points and divide this total by the sum of your priority factor numbers. The example below details the hypothetical calculation of an HGPA.

SPECIFIC ENDEAVOR (*PRIORITY LEVEL*)	REASON FOR GRADE	PRIORITY FACTOR	GRADE	GRADE POINTS
FAMILY VACATION (*summa cum laude*)	I thought about work a lot and only dedicated 50% of my efforts to relaxing	4	C	8.0
ENGLISH MIDTERM (*magna cum laude*)	I was not as focused as I should have been and missed some easy questions	3	C	6.0
EXERCISE (*cum laude*)	I worked out twenty minutes longer than my goal	2	A	8.0
WORK PROJECT (*magna cum laude*)	I did the required research but didn't carefully proofread before submission	3	B	9.0
OVERALL HGPA ▶ ▶ ▶				**2.58**

SUM OF ALL GRADE POINTS ———————————— SUM OF ALL PRIORITY FACTOR NUMBERS	=	$\dfrac{8+6+8+9}{4+3+2+3}$	=	$\dfrac{31}{12}$	=	**2.58**

This hypothetical individual has a 2.58 Hustle GPA. A 2.58 indicates a C grade or an average level of hustle. In other words, this person is dedicating between 40% and 49% of her available effort, on average, to each important endeavor in her life. This person can do better. Now, use this information to determine your HGPA from last week and then decide whether you need to incorporate a little more hustle into your life. You should accept nothing less than a 3.5 HGPA.

FIGHT

> "It's not the size of the dog in the fight, it's the size of the fight in the dog."
> --- **MARK TWAIN**
>
> "There would be no passion in this world if we never had to fight for what we love."
> --- **SUSIE SWITZER**
>
> "Twenty years from now you will be more disappointed by the things that you didn't do than by the ones you did do. So throw off the bowlines. Sail away from the safe harbor. Catch the trade winds in your sails. Explore. Dream. Discover."
> --- **MARK TWAIN**

OUT ON A LIMB

Fight. The word itself conjures up powerful thoughts of exertion, struggle and overcoming fear. Similar to hustle, the verb "to fight" also has its positive and negative connotations. Authentic success requires plenty of the positive and little of the negative. The type of fight you need requires you to go out on a limb and potentially put your career, comfort, health and/or reputation at risk in a struggle to obtain something desirable or to do the right thing. Fighting can be both an internal and an external struggle. Although the concept of fighting sounds similar to the concept of hustle described above, fighting differs from hustle in the following way. Hustle is a decision-neutral act. Once you choose to do something worthwhile, you should automatically hustle. A lack of hustle will lead to a poor result in most instances. Fighting, on the other hand, requires a serious decision before you decide to undertake an endeavor. Even if you choose to do something, you do not have to choose to fight while doing it – at least not all of the time.   Instead, you must decide that the situation merits a fight before deliberately placing yourself at risk. Also keep in mind that the type of fighting I refer to here is not only the knock-down, drag-out kind found in a boxing bout or a screaming match – although that is always an option when merited. I also refer to a more subtle kind of fighting that requires you to go out on a limb and potentially put yourself in jeopardy.

Why not fight all of the time? The act of fighting itself requires a great deal of emotional, mental and physical exertion. The emotional exertion involved includes modifying your mindset to accept the risks involved. The mental exertion includes summoning the motivation and dedication necessary to succeed and the willpower to press forward. Finally, the physical exertion involves executing your battle plan even when physical exhaustion sets in.

Fighting is also a risky activity fraught with consequences such as angst, injury and fatigue. Anyone who expends a great deal of energy and takes on so much risk in a venture ultimately gains a stake in its outcome. None of us want to undertake this type of endeavor and fail. Unfortunately, this heightened desire creates a drive within fighters to sacrifice personal and institutional relationships to obtain a victory. These sacrifices would not be made in the absence of the fight. Therefore, even upon a victory, many fights result in all parties losing something valuable in the long run. This is why fighting is different from hustle and not to be engaged in lightly. You must pick and choose your battles wisely and then fight effectively to avoid many of the consequences inherent in fighting itself. The rest of this section details a way to determine when to fight and when to stand pat and also analyzes some of the tradeoffs involved when you make such a decision.

WHEN TO FIGHT

Fighting is appropriate when something truly important is at stake and when your efforts are the only way that you can make a difference. Fighting is not appropriate when you act solely out of anger, impatience or selfishness. Because of the tradeoffs involved in any fight, the risk is not worth the reward over something you do not consider important (something located somewhere on your list of priorities). I think that we would all agree, at least after the fact, that a conversation with a customer service representative disputing your cable bill is not important in the big scheme of things. In such an example, an hour-long fight, the mental agony and the lost time devoted to the process is not worth the credit on the next bill that you may receive. Additionally, if your efforts cannot make a difference, fighting is a bad decision. For example, at the end of every academic term, I receive numerous e-mails requesting me to recalculate a student's final grade. These students realize that I utilize a computer program to calculate final grades and that assignment scores are posted online for student review as they are completed. Although students know their grades as the term progresses and computer programs do not make simple mathematical errors, a few students cannot accept that their grade is lower than they desired. They feel compelled to fight. The problem is that these fights never make a difference in a final grade and are not worth the effort and lost credibility.

Reflect upon your priorities and the circumstances surrounding a situation when deciding whether to fight. The higher the priority implicated by any situation, the stronger your incentive is to fight. But, even with your highest priority, if the circumstances of the situation indicate that the fight cannot make a difference or that the fight is not worth the long-term consequences, don't engage. Some typical things worth fighting for include relationships, education, career advancement and physical and emotional health. The following two examples demonstrate this distinction.

FIGHTING FOR A *SUMMA CUM LAUDE* PRIORITY

My buddy is in the dating market and wants to find someone special to share his time with. He is a nice, good-looking, young lawyer and seemingly a good catch. He meets plenty of people around town and they exchange a few words and their phone numbers. Instead of talking too much on the phone, however, both parties prefer text messaging to electronically chat and to set up dates. This works fine at first and represents a non-intrusive way to kick-off a budding relationship. The problem is that no real communication occurs and whenever something requiring a personal touch arises, text messages do not suffice.

In the end, one or the other just stop texting each other and the relationship is over. I asked my friend one day about a particular girl he had been seeing and he told me that they had not seen each other or talked in over a week. I implored him to, "just give her a call." My friend replied, "I'd rather not; I'll just text her and see what happens." He then went on to tell me that he really was starting to like her and that it was a shame that it was over. My buddy needed to put up a fight to save a potential relationship. Instead of texting he should have made an effort to talk in person or at least over the phone. Although it takes more guts to talk in person to someone, the effort is worth it. Overcoming fear is crucial in any fight and it's worth it.

FIGHTING OUT OF ANGER

Contrast the previous example with an example where I chose to fight, not to save a relationship, but solely out of anger. The following is a rather humiliating situation where I made a poor choice to fight when I shouldn't have. During December 2006, Denver, Colorado received over thirty inches of snow. People were having a very difficult time driving on the city streets – especially on the side streets – and everyone was on the edge. As I drove one wintry evening, a truck ran a stop sign and pulled out safely in front of me. For the next ten or so blocks, I was forced to drive a tad under the speed limit as I followed the truck down the one-lane road. In addition to the slow driving, I thought that the rolling stop was a dangerous move and, at the next stoplight, I pulled next to the truck and gestured for the driver to roll down her window. We then spent the next few moments in great agitation over the incident. She told me that she had to get a running start to avoid getting stuck at the stop sign and did not just negligently run through it. I told her that it was a dangerous move even though she was safely ahead of me. Even though the fight lasted only a few minutes, I was upset about the confrontation for the next few hours. How silly! I undertook this battle only because I was angry about having to drive so slowly and not for an important purpose. The other driver could have had a weapon or followed me home. It was a foolhardy move on my part and it occurred only because I was angry.

FIGHTING INVOLVES TRADEOFFS

EXTREME – too little fight	FIGHT (GOLDEN MEAN)	EXTREME – too much fight
FEARFUL		FOOLHARDY

The virtue chart above illustrates the tradeoffs that accompany every decision about whether to fight. Keep in mind that too little fight and too much fight can both be problematic. If you never fight for anything, your fearfulness will make it difficult to lead a fulfilling life. As Mark Twain reflected, you will be very disappointed by the things that you could have done but didn't. A failure to fight will cause disappointment. On the other hand, if you fight too often or for the wrong reasons, your foolhardiness can cause serious emotional, mental or physical injury. A perfect example of the tradeoffs stemming from over-fighting are found in my story but are more readily apparent in the story of Mark Inglis.

Inglis is a professional mountain climber who experienced the thrill of victory and the bitter taste of victory's tradeoffs. In his twenties – when he was just a kid – he lost both of his legs below the knee to frostbite. This occurred after spending fourteen days in an ice cave in a failed attempt to summit the highest mountain in New Zealand – Mt. Cook. Having dedicated his life to climbing the world's most challenging mountains, Inglis chose to continue fighting when most others would have given up. He continued to climb mountains using his prosthetic legs. His fight led him to successfully summit Mt. Cook. Then, his journey took him to Nepal and an attempt to climb Mount Everest – the tallest mountain in the world at over 29,000 feet. His wife stated that Mark dreamed of summiting Everest his entire life and, to him, this was something worth fighting for. The trek was not easy but, in May of 2006, Mark won his battle and became the first double amputee to summit Mount Everest.

Mark's successes came with great tradeoffs. He climbed some of the world's tallest mountains and became the first double amputee to summit Mount Everest. However, these ventures at first cost him his legs and subsequently cost him five of his fingertips due to frostbite. His fight was a bitter one and defied the realms of possibility. Professional climbers with two fully-functioning legs find it difficult to summit Everest. Inglis definitely found himself on the far right end of the virtue spectrum and suffered for his decision. The following paragraph from a news article about Inglis' most recent feat illustrates these tradeoffs and Inglis' apparent satisfaction with his decision.

> "It's very painful," says Mark Inglis, his entire face beaming. The juxtaposition of scarred body and radiant smile is unsettling. "From time to time, I close my eyes and then I'm back again at the summit, it's 7a.m., and the sun is shining on the roof of the world." It's been only two weeks since the 46-year-old mountain climber fulfilled his life's dream of scaling Everest. . . . Although he's been back for a week now, he hasn't left the hospital, where he faces the amputation of five of his fingers. "You have to sacrifice a few fingers to get to stand on top of Mount Everest as a double-amputee. So for me it's not a biggie to lose some fingers," he says in a booming voice.[46]

As you can see, these tradeoffs are real. To avoid them, you need to seek the Golden Mean of this quasi-virtue. Fight when it's truly important and, during the other times, just stand pat.

A KEY QUESTION

This section developed what it means to fight, how to choose your battles wisely and why tradeoffs are associated with both excessive fear and foolhardiness. With this in mind, let me reiterate the question posed earlier in this chapter. Have you ever truly placed your career, comfort, health or reputation in

---

[46] Ulrich Bentele, *A Disabled Man Caught between Fame and Disgrace*, SPIEGEL ONLINE INTERNATIONAL, June 1, 2006, *available at* http://www.spiegel.de/international/0,1518,419238,00.html.

jeopardy (i.e., gone out on a limb) for anyone or anything truly important to you or to the common good? If you have a difficult time formulating your response, I urge you to rededicate your efforts and begin to fight for something truly important.

LISTEN

> "If A is a success in life, then A equals x plus y plus z. Work is x; y is play; and z is keeping your mouth shut."
> --- **ALBERT EINSTEIN**
>
> "I know that you believe you understand what you think I said, but I'm not sure you realize that what you heard is not what I meant."
> --- **ROBERT MCCLOSKEY**
>
> "A wise old owl sat on an oak; the more he saw the less he spoke; the less he spoke the more he heard; why aren't we like that wise old bird?"
> --- **AUTHOR UNKNOWN**
>
> "It is the province of knowledge to speak, and it is the privilege of wisdom to listen."
> --- **OLIVER WENDELL HOLMES**

TWO EARS AND ONE MOUTH

Listen. In case you have failed to notice, humans are built with two ears and only one mouth. I believe that this physiological design is intentional and provides a not-so-subtle indication that we should listen twice as often as we speak. Our daily conversations rarely go down that way however. In fact, it is much more common for us to speak more often than we listen. We like hearing our own voice, even in cases where we say too much, speak nonsense or otherwise offer very little to a conversation. Excessive speaking is problematic because it is impossible to listen to someone when you are talking their ears off. Spending more time talking and less time listening will hinder the potential benefits of a conversation because:

1. You will miss an opportunity to glean more information about what the other party to the conversation is trying to say (through the other party's words and body language);
2. You will have a harder time understanding the speaker's perspective and underlying motivations making it more likely that you will overreact; and
3. People will find you rude and annoying.

A LOST OPPORTUNITY TO GLEAN INFORMATION

People in a conversation rarely get right to the point. Typical conversations are usually comprised of a handshake/hug, followed by introductions, followed by some small talk and maybe a joke, followed by the major purpose, followed by more small talk and concluded with a handshake/hug. There is nothing you can do to alter this conversation structure without appearing awkward, impatient or disinterested. Therefore, you must take the time to go through the formalities and then listen for a little bit longer when the main point part of the conversation is reached before you respond. If you interrupt the normal flow of the conversation by skipping a few steps or by taking your turn to speak before the other party arrives at the point, you lose a valuable opportunity to glean more information and the benefits such information provides. People may assume that you have heard all you need to hear when you stop listening and start speaking. This thought process may cause them to withhold other information that could have been obtained because they feel like you do not need it or that it is not worth interrupting you to provide it.

This rule applies to both professional and personal situations. If your boss is giving you an assignment and you talk quickly instead of listening to the entire set of directions for any additional pieces of information, you are likely to miss a critical component of the project. Such a misunderstanding has the potential to negatively impact the value of your submitted work product and your job performance in general. In the personal realm, if you are spending time with a friend who is going through a tough time, your inability to listen will hinder your friend's ability to deal with the emotional issues involved. You will also glean less information about the situation which you can use to formulate a helpful response.

OVERREACTIONS

Spending more time on the listening aspect of a conversation can also keep a person from overreacting. When we are talking with someone and hear something that makes us angry, we immediately want to respond in kind. We take an eye for an eye approach to being wronged by someone's words. If only we listened for a bit longer we could give the speaker a chance to: (1) apologize, (2) explain why the offensive or irritating comments made it into the conversation in the first place or (3) continue to act like an idiot and indicate to us that this is a person that we do not want to be involved with. A little extra time also gives us a chance to gather our thoughts before responding. If the speaker continues to insult or otherwise anger you, you can always walk away and avoid saying anything silly or worse in return.

RUDE AND ANNOYING

The act of listening should be considered a quasi-virtue. When you listen, you are more likely to gain the trust and respect of the people you listen to. People instinctively feel more comfortable with people who listen to them. You also come off as caring, well-mannered and polite when you listen more than you speak.

These same impressions are much harder, if not impossible, to make when you speak more than you listen. What is more likely to happen is that most people will find you rude and/or annoying.

One of my biggest pet peeves occurs when I am talking to someone and they are obviously doing something else or thinking about something else at the same time. I rarely receive an intelligent response from someone multi-tasking in this manner and, even worse, I feel insulted that they do not consider my thoughts to be important. It is something that I consider to be very rude and annoying.[47]

ACTIVE LISTENING

I hope that the preceding discussion has made it fairly clear that we all need to listen more often. However, merely listening to someone talk is not enough. Instead, you must hone your active listening skills to reap most of the benefits that listening can provide. Active listening requires you to listen carefully and think critically about what is being said and then formulate an intelligent response.

You may notice that active listening does not require you to listen all of the time and never speak. In fact, speaking at some point in every conversation is very important. Successful people

---

[47] On a student evaluation of my teaching about one year ago a keen observer wrote something to the effect of "please listen to me more and don't rush through our meetings." This comment really made me realize that I multi-task when I should be listening intently. And, this was only one brave student who made the comment in the evaluation — there are likely others who feel betrayed by me in this way. This comment was a real eye-opener — or should I say an ear-opener — for me. Ever since, I have tried to listen at least twice as much as I talk in my meetings with students and I try to avoid thinking about anything other than the issue at hand.

are able to actively listen and then clearly and calmly make important and intelligent points in any conversation. Someone uncomfortable with speaking and who listens too much will not only fail to develop the ability to speak, but will be taken advantage of and treated as a doormat by people who choose to dominate a conversation.

On the other hand, Mark Twain was right when he quipped that "It is better to keep your mouth closed and let people think you are a fool than to open it and remove all doubt." People who do not listen are domineering, often jumping to conclusions or respond to someone's comments without listening to their entire point. You need to work your way to the Golden Mean of this important quasi-virtue. The virtue spectrum below demonstrates this point as it shows the two extremes of listening and places the Golden Mean in the middle. Make sure that you do not over-listen and never speak and make sure that you do not speak excessively. The secret is to actively listen before you speak for as long as it takes to get the complete picture and then respond intelligently.

EXTREME – too little listening	LISTENING (GOLDEN MEAN)	EXTREME – too much listening
DOMINEERING		DOORMAT

LAUGH (EVEN AT YOURSELF)

"Against the assault of laughter nothing can stand."
--- **MARK TWAIN**

"Time spent laughing is time spent with the gods."
--- **JAPANESE PROVERB**

"Laughter is the sun that drives winter from the human face."
--- **VICTOR HUGO**

"The most wasted of all days is one without laughter."
--- **E.E. CUMMINGS**

"A smile is the shortest distance between two people."
--- **VICTOR BORGE**

LAUGHTER IN GENERAL

Laugh. No, seriously, you need to laugh and do it far more often. In fact, a life without much laughter is not a life worth living. Laughing can make you healthier, comfort you through tough times and provide an antidote against an otherwise bad day. When you laugh or hear someone else laugh, you tend to forget about your troubles at least momentarily. This is also true when you muster the guts to laugh at yourself. There is something about laughter that generates a sincere contentment and happiness. We look forward to laughing in the presence of the people we care about the most and is one of the ways in which we express love.

The problem is that we don't laugh enough. We should, but we just don't. I notice this phenomenon in the workplace, in schools and generally out and about. People take themselves and their goings-on far more seriously than they should. A few years ago when I walked the halls of my law firm, I would continually notice people bustling about. They were apparently heading someplace terribly important judging by their pace and demeanor. They looked stone-faced, making it appear as if they had not even thought about laughing in a long while. Most importantly, very few of them actually seemed truly happy with their lives. A little laughter here and there would have been a good start. Today, I often encounter a student or a colleague with the same type of dour demeanor. These people really need to laugh but their attitude thwarts others from making an attempt.

How often do you laugh – truly and sincerely laugh – each and every day? We all tend to think that we laugh more often than we actually do. To find out for sure, I encourage you to carry around a piece of paper and mark each time you laugh each day. Make sure to distinguish between small giggles and mean-spirited laughter in one column and sincere, healthy moments of laughter in the other. The distinction will prove to be important when you analyze your current level of laughter. On an average day, anything less than five marks in the sincere laughter column means that you do not laugh enough and need to incorporate more humor into your life.

On the other hand, you can laugh too much. As we discussed much earlier, life is tough and not always a laughing matter. You need to incorporate more laughter into each of your days but only when it is sincere and not utilized to block out a problem or done in order to fit in with others. People who laugh too often or who laugh for appearance's sake appear to be phony. On this note, it is common for people to use laughter as a defense mechanism to avoid dealing with serious issues or to try and make others happy. We all know someone who laughs all of the time, but in a rather fake manner. They are always issuing little giggles and phony-sounding laughs but never a belly or snort-causing laugh. These people are never in the mood to really laugh and, instead, use fake laughter to make it appear that all is well. By "laughing" too much, these individuals are presented with a double-whammy problem – the fake laughter will lead to discontentment and their problems will remain unresolved.

Laughter, like the other three quasi-virtues discussed in this chapter – requires a delicate balance between its two extremes. The virtue spectrum below labels too little laughter as humorless and too much laughter as fake. It also allows you to mark down where you currently fall. As always, keep aiming for the Golden Mean. This is the spot where the perfect amount of laughter lies and, as you experiment and more closely approach it, you'll find that you are laughing your way closer to authentic success.

EXTREME – Failure to laugh	LAUGH (GOLDEN MEAN)	EXTREME – Laugh too much
HUMORLESS		FAKE

THE HEALTH BENEFITS OF LAUGHTER

> "A cheerful heart is a good medicine, but a crushed spirit dries up the bones."
> --- **PROVERBS 17:22**
>
> "The whole art of life is in knowing how to transform anxiety into laughter. . . ."
> --- **ALAN WATTS**

Laughter is gaining credibility within the medical community. Medical researchers are now crafting experiments designed to analyze laughter in an effort to understand and classify the potential healing benefits of humor.[48] To date, these projects have found that laughter produces various clinical health benefits. There is even an emerging area of treatment referred to as humor therapy which uses the positive feelings that come from laughter as part of a recovery regimen. With all this in mind, perhaps it's true that laughter is the best medicine. So

---

[48] For examples in the medical literature please see the following articles: Norman Cousins, *Anatomy of an Illness* (1979); Brian Seaward, PhD, *Humor's Healing Potential: Laughter Provides Emotional and Physiological Benefits to Patients and Care Givers Alike*, HEALTH PROGRESS, 73(3): 66-70 (April 1992) (hereinafter *Humor's Healing Potential*): *Humor. A Therapeutic Approach in Oncology Nursing*, CANCER NURSING 1989; *Seriously, Laughter Matters*, TODAY'S OR NURSE 1993. Laughter has many clinical benefits, promoting beneficial physiological changes and an overall sense of wellbeing. Humor even has long-term effects that strengthen the effectiveness of the immune system. In healthcare, humor therapy can help relieve stress associated with disease and illness...It also is a natural healing component for caregivers trying to cope with the stress and personal demands on their occupations" *Humor's Healing Potential*.

laugh a little and receive the following benefits to both your mental and physical health:

- Increased oxygen supply to muscles which provides more energy;
- Reduced hormones caused by stress such as cortisol, adrenaline and growth hormone;
- The release of health-enhancing hormones such as endorphins and neurotransmitters;
- The enhancement of your immune system through the strengthening of T-cells and an increase in the number of disease-destroying antibody cells;
- Reduced pain via the releasing of natural painkillers;
- Cardiac exercise that makes your heart stronger – laughing has even been referred to as internal jogging;[49]
- The stimulation of circulation;
- The relaxation of your muscles – during a belly laugh, the muscles not contributing to the laugh relax and, when the laugh ceases, the muscles involved in the laugh relax;
- The stabilizing of blood pressure;
- Easier digestion of food;
- The production of healthy tears – the tears caused by laughing release toxins from the body;
- Relief from certain allergies; and
- Easier respiration – laughter can empty your lungs of more air than your body takes in resulting in the cleansing of your lungs.[50]

---

[49] Paul E. McGhee, PhD, *Humor and Health* (hereinafter *Humor and Health*).

[50] This information was gleaned from Seaward, *Humor's Healing Potential*, McGhee, *Humor and Health* and William Fry and Waleed Salameh, *Handbook of Humor and Psychotherapy: Advances in the Clinical Use of Humor*, PROFESSIONAL RESOURCE EXCHANGE (1987).

THE BATTLE BETWEEN HEALTHY AND UNHEALTHY LAUGHTER

> Describe as many situations as possible from the past week in which you laughed so hard that you teared up, doubled over and/or snorted – or in other words, experienced a healthy kind of laughter. Reflect upon this past week and compare the number of times you experienced healthy laughter to the number of times you faked amusement or found humor in someone else's misfortunes – an unhealthy kind of laughter.

Do you remember this assignment from the beginning of the chapter where you were to list your episodes of daily laughter on a piece of paper? This experiment alludes to two very distinct types of laughter: (1) healthy laughter and (2) unhealthy laughter.

Healthy laughter occurs when you laugh sincerely at something genuinely worthy of such laughter. Laugh-worthy events include humorous predicaments, jokes, poems, songs, stories, television shows and movies and other randomly-funny occurrences. As demonstrated throughout this section, healthy laughter improves your emotional and physical health and is the perfect antidote for a bad day. Strive for a continual stream of healthy laughter in your life. Unhealthy laughter, on the other hand, occurs when you laugh at something unworthy of laughter. Things that produce unhealthy laughter are often another's misfortunes or emotional, mental and physical characteristics. Unhealthy laughter has no worthwhile health or emotional benefits, damages the feelings of others and is a complete waste of time. In addition to providing zero positive health benefits, unhealthy laughter also damages relationships and reputations.

Now that we have separated laughter into healthy and unhealthy varieties, you can see that there is a big difference between the two. Problematically, we tend to experience unhealthy laughter much more than healthy laughter. Reflect upon the list you made earlier and look at the total number of laughs you have marked down in each category. If your unhealthy laughter total exceeds your healthy laughter total, something needs to change. Make an effort to eliminate unhealthy laughter from your life completely. Every time you feel like laughing at someone else's expense, think back to your character and the Golden Rule discussed back in Chapter Three and reevaluate this reaction. You would not appreciate someone laughing at you, so try not to laugh at others. Instead, strive to incorporate a healthy dose of healthy laughter into each of your days.

LAUGH AT MYSELF ... ARE YOU CRAZY?

We have now reached the most serious part of this chapter and a topic that is not a laughing matter. We are about to discuss your ability to laugh at yourself. Let me start off by asking you if you ever laugh at yourself? When you make a trivial mistake that produces a funny outcome, say something silly or produce an audible bodily noise in front of others, are you able to laugh at the incident? Can you laugh at yourself in these situations even if others are laughing at you?

Most of us find that laughing at ourselves is an extremely difficult task to accomplish. Rather than laughing at ourselves when these things happen, we become embarrassed and angry or self-conscious and dispirited. A much better approach would be for us to just recognize the humor in the event and that the situation merits no reaction other than laughter. Always remember that living a humorless life will not cut it and that authentic success equals basic contentment with your life. Also remember that basic contentment requires laughter as a key ingredient. Therefore, make sure to incorporate a large helping of laughter (even at yourself) into each and every day.

* * * * *

FINAL THOUGHTS ON PART III

This third and final section of the book introduced crucial character traits and concepts which must be utilized every day in order to experience authentic success while living your life in real time. We discussed the importance of cultivating relationships instead of merely networking with as many people as possible. We analyzed the characteristics of an excellent decision and discussed the importance and difficulty of taking personal responsibility for your mistakes and failures. We walked through the causes of stress and drew a line in the sand of our lives that demonstrated which stressors should be eliminated from our consideration. We analyzed the concept of failure and I encouraged you to learn from your mistakes and adopt an attitude of fearless failure. Finally, we walked through four quasi-virtues required to live an authentically successful life. Add a little, hustle, fight, listening and laughter to your days and experience all that your life has to offer.

As you read through each chapter and practiced each of the principles described in this book, I hope you laughed at something you read, actively listened to most (or at least some) of the advice I offered and focused your efforts on the battle that lies ahead . . . the battle of living an authentically successful life in real-time. Below is a reproduction of Ralph Waldo Emerson's famous poem about success. I encourage you to read it thoroughly and then read it again and again for good measure. Analyze its words and implications and then use it to craft your own definition of what a successful life entails. While you are doing so, notice that, cloaked within the beautiful prose, the famous nineteenth-century author might have imagined hustling, fighting, listening and laughing as he encouraged us to play with enthusiasm and sing with exultation (hustle), earn respect and give of ourselves (fight), win people's respect and appreciate beauty (listen) and laugh often and love much (laugh).

∞∞

Success is this:
To laugh often and love much,
To win the respect of intelligent persons and the affection of children,
To earn the approbation of honest critics and endure the betrayal of friends,
To appreciate beauty, to find the best in everything,
To give of one's self, to leave the world a bit better, whether by a healthy child, a
garden patch, or a redeemed social condition,
To have played and laughed with enthusiasm and to have sung with exultation,
To know even one life has breathed easier because you have lived.

∞∞

CONCLUSION:
SHINE

"Shine
Make 'em wonder what you've got
Make 'em wish that they were not
On the outside looking bored
Shine"
--- **NEWSBOYS: SHINE**

"Staring at the blank page before you
Open up the dirty window
Let the sun illuminate the words you could not find

Reaching for something in the distance
So close you can almost taste it
Release you inhibitions
Feel the rain on your skin

No one else can feel it for you
Only you can let it in
No one else, no one else
Can speak the words on you lips
Drench yourself in words unspoken
Live your life with arms wide open
Today is where your book begins
The rest is still unwritten"
--- **NATASHA BEDINGFIELD: UNWRITTEN**

"My philosophy is that not only are you responsible for
your life, but doing the best at this moment puts you in the
best place for the next moment."
--- **OPRAH WINFREY**

"When it's all over, it's not who you were ... it's whether
you made a difference."
--- **BOB DOLE**

IN THE END . . . YOU WILL SHINE

Now that you are intimately familiar with what it means to be authentically successful, let me leave you with one final question. Have you ever met someone who was truly content with his or her life? The key words here are "truly" and "content." I am not talking about the guy you know who makes everybody laugh or your sister's friend who is good looking and happy, but completely superficial. I am also not referring to your buddy the genius or your dad's rich friend. Although each of these people may be popular and successful by worldly standards, they are not necessarily content. The type of person that I am talking about is someone who is genuinely at peace with where he or she is in life, someone with character and professionalism, someone who makes excellent decisions and takes personal responsibility, someone who consistently-persists and who hustles and fights and listens and laughs – someone who is authentically successful. Before you spend too much time looking, however, beware that authentically successful people are like the polar bear, the blue poison frog and the Chinese river dolphin – extremely rare and difficult to locate. In fact, authentically successful people as a group are beginning to resemble an endangered species.

The reason the number of authentically successful people is low directly correlates to the fact that the road leading towards such a goal is long and arduous. It is a journey that requires the serious dedication of will, time and intellect and it will be tough to find many role models to learn from along the way. You will find that the vast majority of people you encounter cannot muster the motivation to do what it takes to be truly happy and content or just don't care to do so. Instead, they sit uncomfortably in the same-old, same-old club and, at some point, they give up entirely.

Although I am unable to provide you with the motivation or the intelligence required for your trek, I have given you a set of detailed directions designed to get you safely to your destination. Think of this book as a roadmap, ever-present and ready to guide you on this important venture. Open it up whenever you need some reassurance, confidence or even just a smile. Do not be afraid to reread certain pieces of advice or entire sections when you are unsure of what you see in front of you or of the next step to take. Wear out its edges, write all over it and feel free to e-mail me with questions or comments.[51]

Please remember one more important piece of information: I am not an expert in this area. Just because I created the map does not mean that you will find me waiting for you at the destination. Although I am very content with my life, I still struggle from time to time with many of the areas described throughout this book. I find myself chasing a fake rabbit here and there and have to refocus my energy and attention on the real rabbits in my life. Therefore, even though we are about to part ways, we will still be headed in the direction of authentic success together.

SHINE AND THEN PAY IT FORWARD

With this in mind, the ball is now in your court and you have a great deal of work to do. Fortunately, you are now armed with all of the tools you will need to achieve authentic success. You can either choose to start your journey now or continue to wait for the perfect moment – a perfect moment that will never arrive. Whenever you do choose to venture out, however, make sure to

---

[51] No seriously, please e-mail me at corey.ciocchetti@alumni.duke.edu with any questions, comments or feedback (both positive and negative). My e-mail account is open twenty-four hours a day, seven days a week.

work through the steps in the order you find them here: (1) get on your mark and develop a solid foundation, (2) get set and prepare for the authentic success you are about to encounter and (3) go and begin to live your life successfully in real time.

Upon the completion of this journey, something special will happen to you. You will shine. You will be content and happy. Everything about you, from your outward appearance to your inner character will emanate success. This is not a one-time, nirvana moment. You will shine consistently – even on your worst days. Even better, your contentment will be contagious. People will notice something special about your life without you having to say a word. In time, you will begin to receive one of the biggest compliments a human being can receive as people begin to say: "You seem so content and happy with your life. Please tell me why?" Keep in mind that such wonderful compliments are not handed out like candy – you must earn them.

When you finally receive the opportunity to answer such a quandary, be sure to take the time to tell the story about Cash the greyhound, fake rabbits and the ramifications of chasing real rabbits in your life. Start by advising your inquirers that their character counts, that the Golden Rule really does matter and that acting virtuously can solve even the toughest moral dilemmas. Prod them to act like a professional regardless of their chosen career field. Encourage them to forget about luck and develop a strong work ethic in its place. Plead that they develop a big-picture perspective and set priorities they commit to stick with even in the toughest of times. Make sure they understand that learning how to think must precede genuine learning. Extol the virtues of consistent persistence, a recession-proof life and a time management system that issues an alert when key priorities are skipped or when too much mental or physical effort is dedicated to one day. Explain why networking stinks and why they should strive to cultivate relationships instead. Help them dig themselves out from under the influence of stress in their lives and to never fear failure. Finally, make sure they reserve some time each day to hustle, fight listen and laugh (even at themselves). Always remember that these are the types of actions that allowed you to shine. Now, it is your turn to pay it forward – it is your turn to help others shine as well.

THE FINAL COUNTDOWN OR JUST THE BEGINNING

There are two ways to think about your life at this very moment. The first is to consider yourself at the very end of an interesting book about success. Here, you feel that all of the effort you devoted to the previous fifteen chapters was time well spent and that you are glad you made it all of the way through a thought-provoking book on a tough topic. You find yourself at the end of something special. The second way to think about your current state is to consider yourself at the very beginning of your own book about success. Here, you are at the beginning of something special – in this case, a transformed and authentically successful life.

The sport of basketball provides an interesting analogy to describe both of these very different states of mind. At the end of every basketball game across the globe, a clock inevitably counts down until it reaches 00:00. The moment the last second ticks off, a loud buzzer sounds. This sound is the universal signal for, "time is up." At this point, the game is over and everyone stops focusing on the event and heads out – there is nothing else left to see or do. The buzzer represents the end of the line for this particular experience. What you may not realize, however, is that the same buzzer that officially ends a basketball game also sounds at the very beginning of each game. Upon its signal, the players come onto the court ready to play and the game officially begins. At this point, the players will need every bit of the practice and preparation undertaken to get them to this place. The starting buzzer serves to focus everyone's attention on the task at hand. Of the two buzzers, it is the starting buzzer that you need to focus on at this very crucial moment in your life. In fact, your newfound dedication to chasing real rabbits places you squarely at the beginning of something very special. You are about to create the life you have always imagined and you will strive to achieve authentic success the right way — you will earn it. Therefore, keep your ears open for the starting buzzer because, right now, the only thing that you are at the end of is the end of my book. Today is where your book begins. The rest is still unwritten.

ACKNOWLEDGMENTS

A significant project of this nature and on this subject must involve other people. I would be nowhere on my journey to authentic success without the efforts of everyone listed below.

Thanks first and foremost to Jillian Ciocchetti – my wonderful wife and best friend. I am truly blessed to have you in my life. You read every word of this book so many times that your head must have spun for weeks. Without your help, this project would be at square one. With you, 2 + 2 can equal 5.

A giant thank you is owed to Professor John Holcomb for being my mentor and friend for the past three years. I am not sure where I would be right now without all of your help. Someday I hope to know half as much as you do and to be as kind to others as you have been to me.

Special thanks to Jo Calhoun, Nathan Christensen, Margret Korzus, Justin Meineke, Jill Miller, Kevin O'Brien and John Polis for your thoughtful comments and encouragement throughout this process. Earning the respect of my peers is an honor and a privilege.

Thanks to Courtney Maynard and Bohemian Productions for taking all the photographs required to find one good one.

Thanks to Britini Adams, Tommy Bibliowicz, Lorinda Boothman, Lacey Broadland, Briana Cano, Ekta Dharia, Nami Ghebrheb, Grant Goerzen, Alyssa Hampton, Coley Holnback,

Halley Hu, Loren Kagan, Gregory Lau, Reanne Madsen, Grace Maxin, Angie McDermid (especially for the title to Chapter Seven), Julie Markham, Sabrina Merage, Josh Schaer, Kelesy Smetts, Chad and Debbie Storlie, Lindsay Thompson, Andrea Tilliss, Armando Vasquez (for your amazing copyediting assistance) and Greg Winter – my students and my friends. Each of you went above and beyond your duty to help me in this endeavor. You already shine in my eyes!

A final thanks to each and every one of my students at the University of Denver. I have only been at this wonderful place for three years, yet I feel like I have thousands of new friends. Thanks for listening so diligently to my "Professor C's Philosophy on Life" lecture at the end of each academic term and for your valuable comments and insights. Without your encouragement that this topic constituted a worthy subject to write about, I would never have been inspired to convert what was a thirty-minute lecture into a fifteen-chapter book. You are the reason why I love coming to work every day and why I have found my calling as a teacher. This book is for you.